The Killing of
JULIA WALLACE

The Killing of
JULIA WALLACE

JONATHAN GOODMAN

With a Foreword by
EDGAR LUSTGARTEN

GEORGE G. HARRAP & CO. LTD
London · Toronto · Wellington · Sydney

1969

ONCE AGAIN FOR SUSAN

First published in Great Britain 1969
by GEORGE G. HARRAP & CO. LTD
182 High Holborn, London, W.C.1

© *Jonathan Goodman* 1969
Copyright. All rights reserved

SBN 245 59217 2

Composed in Monotype Imprint type and printed by
C. Tinling & Co. Ltd., Liverpool, London and Prescot
Made in Great Britain

Foreword

You are *for* Wallace. Or *against* him. You are certain he was *innocent*. Or certain he was *guilty*.

That, I think, reflects ninety-nine per cent of views about the most contentious murder trial this century.

I belong, though, to the residual one per cent. The Public Opinion Polls would put me down as a Don't Know. For I have never been able to make up my mind.

Not from lack of thought. Not from lack of opportunity.

I was a young white-wigged junior on the Northern Circuit when Wallace entered the dock at Liverpool's St George's Hall. Subsequently I often heard counsel for the Crown proclaiming, in Bar Mess, his satisfaction with the verdict—his absolute belief that it was justified. I have since written about Wallace, and broadcast about Wallace, necessitating close examination of the evidence.

But I have never supposed my knowledge of the case to be exhaustive. And I have always hoped that someone—analytical, literate, really steeped in the facts (both central and peripheral)—would produce what could be deemed a scriptural Book of Wallace.

Here, I assert with confidence, it is.

Like the scriptures, it is open to interpretation. Like the scriptures, it is open to more than one interpreter.

Jonathan Goodman, to his credit, doesn't temporise. Not for him the easy get-out: On the one hand, On the other. He says, in the plainest terms, that there are a number of points "which prove *conclusively* that Wallace was innocent".

It is the word "conclusively" that I stumble over.

I have never doubted—not for a single moment—that Wallace should have been acquitted. Because his guilt was far from proved beyond reasonable doubt—the criterion properly applied by English law. But was his *innocence* proved *conclusively*? A very different thing.

Jonathan Goodman's arguments in support of his proposition

are plausible and fascinating and persuasive. He has done a fine piece of research. More difficult and notable, he has written a brilliant book. But is he right in saying that the Wallace debate should now be closed?

I doubt it. He *may* be right. He *may* be wrong. Either way the Wallace debate will go on for ever.

You may agree or disagree with Jonathan Goodman's inferences. But you will be absorbed. From the first line to the last.

EDGAR LUSTGARTEN

Preface

> *The Wallace case is unbeatable; it will always be unbeatable.* RAYMOND CHANDLER
>
> *This murder, I should imagine, must be almost unexampled in the annals of crime.*
> LORD WRIGHT OF DURLEY
>
> *Either the murderer was Wallace or it wasn't. If it wasn't, then here at last is the perfect murder.* JAMES AGATE

The Wallace case has provoked more conjecture, more argument, than any other murder case in living memory. There are people who believe that William Herbert Wallace was guilty of his wife's murder, and there are others who believe no such thing, who say that he was as much a victim of the crime as his wife. The non-believers are vastly outnumbered.

Many words have been spoken about the case; many words have been written about it. The odd thing, though, is that hardly any of the literary theorists have bothered to do the slightest bit of research before putting their hair-raising (and often hare-brained) theories to paper. Not one of them has obtained the official transcript of the trial; they have all of them, every single one, relied upon an abridged version that was published two years afterwards. This, it seems to me, is rather like setting oneself up as an expert on Shakespeare after reading Charles and Mary Lamb.

The literary theorists have made a great many mistakes, have drawn any number of false conclusions. To point out all their errors would take up far too much space. What I have done, therefore, is this—within the narrative I have drawn attention to a few of the errors in one of the books, *Two Studies in Crime*, by Yseult Bridges. I have chosen this particular work, not because it contains more errors than the rest, but, on the contrary, because it is by far the most accurate and valuable.

After more than three years of research I am convinced that

Wallace did not murder his wife. Although the main purpose of this book is to try to persuade others of his innocence, I believe that I have given a fair picture of the evidence presented by the prosecution. In writing about the people involved in the case I have tried to resist the temptation to draw conclusions from the facts, and have attempted to let the facts speak for themselves. I realize that I have not always succeeded, but I make no apologies for this; I believe the few conclusions that I have drawn to be irrefutable.

Unless otherwise stated, all conversations in this book are either taken from records or based on the recollections of the principals questioned by myself.

I should like to make it clear that my criticisms of the Liverpool City Police Force at the time of the Wallace case do not apply to the present-day force, which is one of the most efficient and enlightened in the country. If it is true that the public gets the police it deserves, then the people of Liverpool must be far more deserving now than they were back in 1931.

J. G.

Acknowledgments

In the writing of this book I am indebted to a great many people and organizations, but particularly to the following:

Richard Whittington-Egan, critic and criminologist, who has helped in a dozen different ways.

Sydney Scholefield Allen, Q.C., M.P.; Neville Laski, Q.C.

Professor Francis Camps; Dr Robert Coope; Professor James Henry Dible; Professor Donald Teare; Gavin Thurston; Molly Tibbs.

Harry V. Bailey; H. R. Balmer, O.B.E., Deputy Chief Constable of Liverpool and Bootle; William and Margery Bebbington; Herbert Gold; ex-Detective-Sergeant William Prendergast; ex-Detective-Inspector Jack Tilling.

Gerald Austin; P. J. Blades; The Chevalier Sir Frederick Bowman, K.C.E.; Fenton Bresler; George Burnett; P. F. Carter-Ruck; H. Golombek; Elwyn Jones; Edgar Lustgarten; Kingsley Martin; Mrs Pat Pitman; Paul Rotha; Ronald Settle; Eric Tyler; Mrs Anne Wallace; B. H. Wood, Editor of *Chess*; W. F. Wyndham-Brown.

J. A. Blackwood, J.P., H.M. Coroner, City of Liverpool; Henry Harris, ex-Clerk of the Liverpool City Magistrates' Court; M. J. Hayward, Assistant Secretary of the Magistrates' Association; Ian Macauley, C.B.E., Clerk of Assize, Northern Circuit; H. Spanner, Chief Clerk and Sergeant-at-Mace of the Liverpool Court of Passage.

Thomas Alker, C.B.E., Town Clerk of Liverpool; Dr N. V. Hepple, Medical Officer of Health for the West Riding of Yorkshire (Division 7); H. Linfoot, Superintendent and Registrar of Cemeteries, Harrogate; K. H. Moon, Liverpool City Estates Surveyor; W. J. Taunton, Air Historical Branch (RAF).

M. A. R. George, Senior Solicitor of the Prudential Assurance Co., Ltd.

Thomas Scrafton, General Secretary of the Prudential Staff Union.

J. Dixey, Assistant General Manager, *Liverpool Daily Post and Echo*.

J. H. H. Gaute.

The Law Society.

The British Broadcasting Corporation.

The Liberal Party Organization.

The Peninsular and Oriental Steam Navigation Co.

The Meteorological Office.

Peter Weston, Ltd.

The Chief Librarians and the staffs of the Ealing, Liverpool, and Wandsworth Public Libraries; of the British Museum and the British Museum Newspaper Library; of the *Daily Express*, the *Daily Mail*, the *Daily Mirror*, and the *Liverpool Daily Post and Echo*.

The staff of the Liverpool Prosecuting Solicitor's Office, St George's Hall, Liverpool.

The staff of the GPO Telephone Manager's Office, Liverpool, and of the Liverpool Corporation Passenger Transport.

I am especially indebted to Hector Munro, without whose help this book could not have been written.

J. G.

Contents

Illustrations

The Year

1931 was given the usual quota of three hundred and sixty-odd days, but it could have done with a few more, if only to allow breathing space between one event and another. To use the title of a hit show of a few seasons before, the year was jam-packed with "One Dam' Thing After Another".

Some of the things that happened were good things, but mostly they were bad.

While children played with hoops and spinning tops, and ate sugar butties, and chortled at the antics of Pip, Squeak, and Wilfred, the year was shaken half a dozen times by earthquakes. Few people in Britain paid much attention to the reports from the far-away disaster regions: certainly not the people of the Rhondda, or those living in the Lancashire cotton towns, or on Tyneside, or in Paisley. They had other things to worry about.

How long's the depression going to last? . . . How much longer am I going to be out of work? . . . How will I manage if there's a strike—a close-down—a lock-out?

Then, in June, an earth tremor was felt over a wide area of England and Scotland. Many parents told their children that it was simply the earth sighing in its sleep. But other people had other ideas. Some of them said that God had whispered a warning of Armageddon. For a long time afterwards, until it became clear that the warning had been either misheard or premature, sign-writers did a roaring trade in posters that exhorted the unrepentant to change their ways while there was still time.

It was a hectic year. Everyone seemed to be in a hurry. Perhaps most people were simply in a hurry to get the year over as quickly as possible, to start on 1932.

Hardly a week went by without a record of some sort being broken by someone somewhere. Captain Malcolm Campbell, in his car *Blue Bird*, broke the world land-speed record; a couple of weeks later he was knighted. The millionaire sportsman Lieutenant Glen Kidston broke the air-speed record from London to Cape Town; the following month he was killed in a crash. C. W. A. Scott flew from England to Australia in 9 days 3 hours 40 minutes, and Jim Mollison took eight hours or so less to make the journey in the opposite direction. The *Cheltenham Flier* set up a record of 78 m.p.h. as the world's fastest train; by flying at an average speed of 408 m.p.h. Lieutenant J. H. Stainforth became the world's fastest man; the French athlete Ladoumegue ran a mile in the fantastic time of 4 minutes 9.2 seconds. Messrs Post and Gatty went round the world in nine days, and an Austrian schoolmaster named Karl Nanmestik crossed the English Channel on a pair of water-skis.

At least the mortality rate was average in this far-from-average year. Among the people who did not live to see 1932 were Anna Pavlova, the fragile flower of the ballet; Arnold Bennett, author; Dame Nellie Melba, the Australian songstress who gave her name to a dish of ice-cream; Thomas Edison, inventor of many things; Alfred Arthur Rouse, murderer; and Julia Wallace, murder victim.

The Night before the Killing

MONDAY, January 19th, 1931

*"Begin at the beginning," the King said,
very gravely, "and go on till you come to
the end: then stop."*[1]

It had been a most unpleasant day. The strong winds that had blown around Liverpool during the morning had died away, but only to allow the clouds to interweave and slowly descend beneath their own weight. By midday a grey, damp blanket had been tucked in around the city. Mist had manufactured an early twilight. Then, just before tea-time, the rain had started—an insidious drizzle, that fine sort of rain that you hardly notice before you realize that you are drenched.

Twenty minutes past seven.

And outside Cottle's City Café in North John Street the pavements were still damp from the rain. The dozen or so stone steps that led down to the café were covered with a thin film of slush.

Samuel Beattie, captain of the Liverpool Central Chess Club, had been at the café since six o'clock. As usual on Mondays and Thursdays during the autumn, winter, and early spring, he had come straight from work to the café where the chess club meetings were held. Most of the members would not arrive until between half-past seven and eight, but Beattie liked to give himself plenty of time to make sure that everything was ready for the evening's play.

Beattie had left his office near Exchange Station and walked the short distance to North John Street. At the foot of the steps that led down to the City Café there was a tobacconist's kiosk. He had bought a packet of twenty cigarettes and pocketed fourpence change from his shilling before pushing open the door and entering the café.

[1] The quotations at the beginning of chapters are taken from the works of Lewis Carroll.

B

It was a large place, split up into four sections by an arrangement of square arches, and decorated in Tudor-bethan style, with strips of oak scrawled across the plastered walls, brass brazier-type light sconces, a few brightly coloured Dutch tiles patching the plaster. Just inside, in a prominent position on the wall between the door and a public-telephone box, was a baize-covered board used for displaying chess club notices.

The penultimate round in the Second Class Championship was due to be played that evening, and Beattie glanced at the notice giving details of the tournament as he was taking off his hat and coat. The quarto sheet of paper had been pinned to the board since the end of October, and it was a trifle dog-eared and dusty by now.

```
              2nd Class Championship
         1st Prize 10/-   2nd Prize 5/-

       Mondays           NOV       DEC       JAN     FEB
                        10  24    8   15    5   19    21
    1. Chandler F. C.    X   2    3    4    5    6     7
    2. Ellis T.          7   1    X    3    4    5     6
    3. Lampitt E.        6   7    1    2    X    4     5
    4. McCartney         5   6    7    1    2    3     X
    5. Moore T.          4   X    6    7    1    2     3
    6. Wallace W. H.     3   4    5    X    7    1     2
    7. Walsh J.          2   3    4    5    6    X     1
```

Beattie walked through to the section of the café reserved for the chess club, and made sure that the placing of the tables was correct before setting the chess boards and pieces upon them. Then he ordered some tea from Gladys Harley, the middle-aged waitress who was normally on duty on chess club evenings.

Shortly before seven Mr Baruch, a member of the club and a personal friend of Beattie, arrived. They chatted together for a few minutes and then settled down to a game of chess.

Twenty minutes past seven.

The telephone started to ring.

Gladys Harley hurried across to answer it. She pulled open the door of the call-box and lifted the receiver.

" Hello."

A woman operator's voice: "Bank 3581?"

"Yes."

"Anfield calling you. Hold the line."

Gladys Harley waited for the call to be connected. She did not know it, of course, but she was waiting to speak to a man who, the following night, would commit murder.

She waited, the receiver pressed to her ear. Several seconds passed, and all that she heard was a far-away mumbling of voices on the line.

"Do you require this number?" she asked impatiently.

She heard the operator saying something about two pennies.

Then a man's voice. It was not one that she recognized; a cultured voice, perhaps belonging to someone fairly elderly, she thought. "Is that the Central Chess Club?"

"Yes."

"Is Mr Wallace there?"

Gladys Harley knew only a few members of the chess club by name. Wallace was not one of them. "Hold on," she said, "and I'll find out for you."

She placed the receiver on the ledge and walked across to the table where Beattie was playing.

"Mr Beattie . . ."

He looked up from the chess board. "Yes?"

"There's someone on the telephone wanting to speak to Mr Wallace."

"Well . . ." Beattie glanced at the other tables, just to make sure. ". . . he's not here yet. He's down to play a match, so he might be along later."

"So what shall I tell this gentleman who wants him?"

"I suppose I'd better speak to him," Beattie said. He got up and walked to the telephone-box.

Beattie had been friendly with Wallace for eight years—for nearly as long as Wallace had been a member of the chess club, in fact. He liked the man, as did all the other members who knew him. Once you had broken through his slight shyness, his reserve, you discovered that he was a very pleasant fellow indeed. He was by no means a regular attender at the club. Looking back, Beattie supposed that he came along about once every fortnight. He had not been at the club since before Christmas. Wallace had once explained, excused, his infrequent appearances by saying that he did not like leaving his wife alone at night. This seemed a reasonable explanation because, although he was a poor chess-player, he obviously derived much enjoyment from the game.

Beattie knew that Wallace was a Prudential Assurance agent, and he guessed before he picked up the receiver that this telephone call might have something to do with his work.

He spoke into the receiver, saying who he was.

"Is Mr Wallace there?"

"No, I'm afraid not," Beattie said.

"But he will be there?"

"I can't say. He may or may not. If he's coming he'll be here shortly. I suggest you ring up later."

"Oh, no, I can't. I'm too busy. I have my girl's twenty-first birthday on, and I want to do something for her in the way of his business. I want to see him particularly. Will you ask him to call round to my place tomorrow evening at 7.30?"

"I will if I see him," Beattie said, "but he may not be here tonight. However, there's a friend of his, Mr Caird, who's fairly certain to be here tonight, and I'll try to get the message delivered through him. I can't promise that Mr Wallace will get the message, but you'd better give me your name and address, so that I can pass it on."

"The name's R. M. Qualtrough," the caller said.

Beattie fumbled a used envelope from his pocket. "Would you mind spelling that?"

The caller spelt the name, and Beattie wrote it down on the back of the envelope. Then an address in Mossley Hill, Liverpool. Beattie read the address back, and the caller rang off.

William Herbert Wallace alighted from a No. 14 tram at the corner of Lord Street and North John Street.

Even in the gaslight-dappled darkness he was easily recognizable. He was six foot two inches tall, and his slim build gave an impression of additional height, as did the old-fashioned clothes that he wore—the high-crowned bowler hat; the starched, white "choker" collar; the Raglan-style, slate-grey mackintosh. His clothes were also partly responsible for the fact that he looked a good deal older than his fifty-two years.

He walked quickly towards the City Café, his head jutting forward, his shoulders slightly hunched. He was in a hurry, for it was a rule of the Central Chess Club that tournament matches had to be started by quarter to eight. A member arriving later than that could be penalized.

Descending the steps, he pushed open the door of the café. The sudden transition from darkness to light caused him to blink a few times. He took off his hat and mackintosh, and turned towards the section of the café reserved for the chess club, his brows still puckered, shielding his eyes from the light. They were grey eyes, slightly protruding, that peered from behind steel-rimmed spectacles. He had a sallow complexion, perhaps to some degree a legacy from the years he had spent in India and China, but mainly caused by the kidney complaint that had troubled him since his early twenties. His grey hair, parted on the left and combed straight across, accentuated a high, rounded forehead. His moustache was dark, and still showed remnants of the ginger colour of his youth.

Wallace hesitated in the archway to the left of the public-telephone box. As far as he could see, there was no sign of Mr Chandler, whom he was due to play in the Second Class Championship this evening. As he searched the faces of the men sitting at the tables, and the group of three or four standing, quietly chatting together, in a far corner, Wallace's lips pursed, emitting a series of breaths that, with a little more effort, might have turned into a whistled tune. It was a habit of his, this almost-whistling—an accompaniment to uncertainty, nervousness, or cerebration. Looking for a mislaid Prudential document, sitting in Dr Curwen's waiting-room, pondering over a move in chess, his lips would form an O, produce the sound that never quite became a melody.

"Feel like a game?"

Wallace turned his head to see that James Caird had sidled up to him.

Caird was a grocer by trade, and some of his shopkeeping manner rubbed off on his private life. He was a great believer in goodwill; eager to please, anxious to be liked. With Caird, it was not only the customer that was always right, but almost anyone that he happened to know or meet. A near neighbour and friend of Wallace for about fifteen years, Caird had often visited Wallace's house and played chess with him there. Also, in the last couple of years since Wallace had started to learn the violin, Caird had several times been invited along to musical evenings, audience to duets played by Herbert on the violin and his wife, Julia, at the piano. Not wishing to offend, Caird had always accepted these invitations, had sat wearing an appropriately rapt expression as Wallace struggled, most of the time not too successfully, to stroke notes from his violin that were at least roughly approximate to what the composer had in mind. Perhaps, hiding behind the rapt expression, Caird forced his ears to ignore that part of the duet supplied by Wallace, and concentrated on the playing of his wife, who was a very good pianist indeed.

Wallace told Caird that he had come along to get a tournament game wiped off, as he was in arrears. He explained that Julia was suffering from a cold and he himself had only just recovered from influenza, and if this had not been a match night he would have stayed at home. The influenza had attacked him on the previous Thursday; the following day, as was usual on Fridays, he had not done any insurance collecting, but had worked at home on his accounts; on the Saturday he had still felt unwell, and, instead of doing his normal round of collections from about ten o'clock till midday, he had spent the morning with his feet in a mustard bath, taking occasional sips of whisky and water. He assured Caird that he now felt completely fit again, but Caird detected a slight huskiness to his voice.

Having asked Caird if he had seen anything of Mr Chandler and received a definite no in reply, Wallace noticed that Mr McCartney —whose match with Wallace in the Second Class Championship had been scheduled for November 24th but had not taken place— was standing by one of the tables, watching a game in progress. Wallace approached him and suggested that they should play the overdue match. McCartney was agreeable, so the two men found a vacant table and began to play.

Caird watched the opening moves, then wandered around, examining the positions on the other boards. Eventually his wandering took him to the table where Beattie was playing.

It was several minutes before Beattie looked up and saw Caird standing beside him. He greeted him: "Hello, Mr Caird."

Beattie's eyes drifted back to the board, then jerked up again as he remembered the telephone message. "You know Mr Wallace's address, don't you?"

Caird nodded. "Yes, but if you want him he's over there"—he pointed—"playing with McCartney."

Beattie got up and, followed by Caird, walked across to Wallace's table. "I've got a telephone message for you, Mr Wallace."

Wallace was still gazing at the chess board as he said, "Oh, who from?"

"A man named Qualtrough."

"Qualtrough . . ." Wallace murmured. He looked up, a small frown untidying his forehead. "Qualtrough?"

Beattie nodded.

"But I don't know anybody named Qualtrough. Who is he?"

"Well, if you don't know him, I certainly don't," Beattie said.

"But he left this message for you. He wants you to call on him tomorrow evening at 7.30, at 25 Menlove Gardens East, Mossley Hill. He says it's something in the nature of your business. He can't phone you later tonight because he's too busy with his girl's twenty-first birthday party."

Wallace shook his head in a bemused fashion. "I don't know the chap," he said. "Where is Menlove Gardens East? Is it Menlove Avenue?"

"No, Menlove Gardens East." Beattie placed the envelope on the table, message side up. "Here's the address."

Wallace felt in his pockets and produced a silver propelling pencil from one, a small Prudential give-away diary from another. It was a week-a-page type of diary, and he wrote the details on the right-hand page, covering the spaces for January the 26th and 27th, opposite the 19th and 20th. He copied the details exactly as Beattie had written them, apart from writing "East" in capital letters and giving it a line to itself.

Handing the envelope back to Beattie, Wallace said, "I don't know where the place is, but I suppose I'll find it."

Although Beattie lived in Mossley Hill, little more than half a mile from Menlove Avenue, he was not at all sure where Menlove Gardens East was. It was a rapidly growing district: new houses, whole new streets of houses, were appearing, turning the semi-rural area of a few years before into a dormitory suburb.

" I know that one of the Gardens comes into Menlove Avenue, and another, I think, goes into Queen's Drive," Beattie murmured. "Wait a minute. Deyes lives in that neighbourhood. I'll ask him if he knows where this place is."

But Mr E. B. Deyes, apart from agreeing that Menlove Gardens East must be somewhere off Menlove Avenue, was no help at all in fixing its exact location.

Beattie returned to Wallace's table. "I'm sorry, but I can't help you any further," he said. "You'd better look it up, as it's an awkward place to be knocking about in the dark to look for. You might be there all night."

"Oh, I belong to Liverpool," Wallace replied. "Anyway, I've got a Scotch tongue in my head. I can enquire."

Beattie suggested that the best thing to do was to take a tram to Penny Lane, then ask the way.

That was the end of the conversation. Wallace resumed the match with McCartney; Beattie returned to his table to be soundly beaten in the game with Baruch; Caird continued his peregrinations, and, at long last, found someone who was willing to play with him.

In company with Caird and another club member named Bethurn, Wallace left the City Café at about twenty past ten and walked to the tram-stop.

He appeared to be in an extremely happy frame of mind, delighted at having beaten McCartney, who was considered quite a good player.

Waiting at the tram-stop, he talked about the match, describing the moves and counter-moves. Not for long, because a West Derby Road tram arrived and the three men boarded it. Bethurn had farthest to travel, so he sat next to a window, with Caird beside him, Wallace on the seat in front of them.

The tram moved off towards Anfield.

Alighting at the stop by St Margaret's Church, Anfield, Wallace and Caird started to walk home. Wallace was still chattering happily about his success at the chess club, Caird still dutifully listening and making appropriate comments. It was not until they were passing the Belmont Road Hospital that the subject changed.

To Qualtrough.

"It's a funny name," Wallace said. "I've never heard a name like that before, have you?"

"I've only heard of one person of the name of Qualtrough," Caird replied.

They discussed the best way of getting to Menlove Gardens East. Caird suggested that Wallace should go on the bus from Queen's Drive, but Wallace said no, he would take the most direct route, travelling towards town and then getting a tram to Menlove Avenue. That was if he went at all, Wallace added; but he was not at all sure that he would bother.

Again the subject changed.

This time to Wallace's kidney complaint. Caird wanted to know if it was troubling him these days, and if he was still taking some German medicine that had been prescribed for its relief. Wallace said that he was not taking any medicine at present. "If my complaint doesn't trouble *me*," he said, "I won't trouble *it*."

Wallace walked as far as the front door of Caird's house in Letchworth Street, and there the two men stood chatting for a few minutes before saying good night.

Wallace crossed the road that was incongruously named

Richmond Park, and walked into the entry leading to Wolverton Street.

These "entries" were a feature of the Richmond Park area of Anfield. They turned the area into a maze, confusing to strangers and even to people who had lived there for only a few years, but used by most of the older inhabitants, in preference to the streets, as the shortest distance between two points. Sparsely lit, covered either with cobblestones or earth that had been trodden to rock-hardness, they ran between the back yards of one street and the back yards of another, with branches running through to the streets themselves.

The entry that Wallace used tonight—and, for that matter, almost invariably when he was returning home from the direction of Belmont Road—ran from opposite the Church Institute in Richmond Park and cut through to between 19 and 21 Wolverton Street.

In previous writings Wolverton Street has been described as a cul-de-sac, but, in fact, it was blind only to vehicles. One of the ubiquitous entries ran along the top of it, like the horizontal stroke of a T. It was a street of thirty-four small, red-brick houses; and on this night when Wallace came home from the meeting of the chess club it was already a street of sadness, of tragedy. Some of the residents even went so far as to say that the street was jinxed. It had certainly received an unfair share of death. In the last year or so three people had committed suicide in Wolverton Street. There were five widows living there whose husbands had died in tragic circumstances: one man, a fan of the near-by Liverpool Football Club, had dropped dead while watching a match; another, holidaying at Llandudno, had fallen from the top of the Great Orme.

The epidemic of sudden death was not the only thing that was causing concern among the residents. In common with other people in the neighbourhood, they were worried about the activities of "the elusive Anfield housebreaker". Between twenty and thirty cases had been reported of houses being entered during the temporary absence of the occupants, and in every case a duplicate or skeleton key had been used. Two houses in Wolverton Street had been visited, the last visit being just before Christmas at No. 19.

Turning left out of the entry, Wallace walked to 29 Wolverton Street and, unlocking the door with his key, entered the house, which he rented for 14s. 3d. a week.

As usual, Julia was waiting up for him, on this, her last night alive.

Probably the best way of summing up Julia Wallace is to say that she was an anachronism. Everything about her contributed to the feeling that she was fifteen, twenty, years behind the times. Like one of those delicate porcelain figures enclosed beneath glass domes that can be seen in so many contemporary homes dependent upon *Good Housekeeping* for their style of decor, Julia Wallace looked out of place, as well as out of date. Out of place because the grimy streets of Anfield were a far, a very far, cry from the stately parades and crescents of the spa town of Harrogate, where she had been born and brought up. Imagine a character created by Pinero being transplanted into a kitchen-sink drama, and this will give some idea of the impression made by Julia Wallace. Her clothes were old-fashioned, often home-made; her dark hair, once flecked with auburn but now starting to grey, was coaxed into a chignon with the aid of a pad at the nape of her neck. She possessed many of the attributes of an Edwardian governess—the ability to speak text-book French; a genteel taste in literature; a knowledge of music, both practical and theoretical; a certain artistry in water-colours (evidence of which could be seen on the walls of the parlour).

She was in the kitchen when Wallace returned, putting the finishing touches to a table laid for a light supper. The gaslight, touching her with a patina of amber, aided and abetted the impression of someone from another time, another place.

Wallace began to tell her about his success at the chess club, but Julia was not her usual attentive self this evening. Her black cat had disappeared. The cat had originally belonged to a neighbour, and Julia had looked after it while the neighbour was away on holiday. She had become so attached to the cat, and the cat to her, that the neighbour, when she returned, had agreed that Julia should keep it.

Superstition, as well as fondness for the cat, subscribed to her distress at its disappearance. She wondered if she would ever see her lucky black cat alive again. It never occurred to her that she might not live long enough for the cat to see her.

The Day of the Killing

TUESDAY, January 20th

> *"The horror of that moment," the King went
> on, "I shall never, never forget!"*
>   *"You will, though," the Queen said, "if you
> don't make a memorandum of it."*

It looked like being another nasty day. Rain accompanied the dawn,
and drizzled steadily throughout the morning.

It was not the best sort of weather for trudging around collecting
insurance payments, especially for a man only recently recovered
from the effects of influenza, but Wallace left home at his usual
time of half-past ten and took a tram to Clubmoor, the district
allotted to him by the Prudential. It was a fairly considerable area
that he had to cover, with 560 calls to make, and, because of
staying at home the previous Saturday, he was behind with his
collections.

Clubmoor, only a penny tram-fare away, was an even less desirable neighbourhood than Anfield, but Wallace had collected here
for nearly sixteen years, and seemed content to remain in the
district until he died or retired, whichever came first. Liked and
respected by his clients, he was assured of more offers of cups of
tea and biscuits than his stomach could contend with. His salary
from the Prudential was £260 a year, and he was entitled to commission on any motor or life business which he introduced, so his
earnings were more than sufficient for the needs of his household.

He continued his calls until just before two o'clock, by which
time the rain had stopped and the breeze had stiffened, blowing
the clouds away and revealing a blue sky for the first time in
several days. He boarded a tram, and was home within fifteen
minutes and sitting down to his lunch.

Afterwards, while Julia cleared the kitchen table and did the
washing-up, Wallace retired upstairs. But not for an after-lunch

nap. His interest in chess and, more recently, the violin was small compared with his interest in matters of science, and he had converted the small back bedroom into a rough laboratory and workshop. He spent much of his spare time in this room, conducting experiments in chemistry, electricity, and biology. A few years before he had started to make a microscope, but had given up the idea, deciding that it would take too long, the result might not justify the effort—and, in any case, he could afford to buy one. The microscope he had bought was his most prized possession. It had cost nearly £80, but he was always telling friends who accused him of extravagance that it was money well spent.

of ammonium Sulphate.
To 10cc. of Sodium Hydrate add an excess of dilute Hcl . evaporate to small volume to form crystals.
of Sodium chloride.
To 10cc. of Sodium Hydrate add an excess of dilute H₂SO₄ . evaporate to small volume to form crystals.
of Sodium Sulphate

Record of a chemical experiment made by one of Wallace's students at the Liverpool Technical College, signed by Wallace.
Richard Whittington-Egan Collection

Although Wallace had something of a grasshopper mind, his interest in science was real and abiding. It could be traced back to his early twenties, when he had attended technical schools and gained certificates in electricity and chemistry. Some ten years before he had resumed his chemical studies at the Liverpool Technical College in Byrom Street, and had eventually been appointed a part-time assistant lecturer on the subject, a position he had held for five years.

Wallace could not spend much time in his laboratory today. He had to get back to work. The weather was still fine, and he decided to wear his light fawn-coloured coat instead of the mackintosh he had worn during the morning. He said goodbye to Julia and left the house again soon after three.

26 Pennsylvania Road, Clubmoor, was where the Wallaces

lived when they first came to Liverpool in March 1915. They stayed there for four months before moving to Wolverton Street.

Although Wallace can have retained few memories, happy or otherwise, from the short stay in Pennsylvania Road, he no doubt looked forward to his three-weekly return visits: some of his favourite clients lived in the road.

One of them was Mrs Louisa Harrison, a young housewife, who lived at No. 11. Wallace had been collecting from her for three years. She thought him a complete gentleman. He always spoke very highly of his wife, and gave the impression of being devoted to her. On this Tuesday afternoon he called on Mrs Harrison at about twenty past three. While she paid him the insurance money and he entered the amount in the book, they laughed and joked together. Then he raised his hat and, still smiling, said goodbye.

Half-past three.

P.C. James Rothwell was cycling along Maiden Lane on his way to Anfield Police Station. He noticed the tall man walking towards him, and recognized him at once as Mr Wallace, the insurance agent who had been calling at his house for about two years. Wallace was dabbing his eyes with his sleeve.

Some days later Rothwell was to say that Wallace looked as if he had been crying, and that he was "haggard and drawn . . . very distressed—unusually distressed".

At about half-past three Mrs Jane Harbord opened the door of her house in Worcester Drive. Recognizing Mr Wallace's knock, she had brought the insurance money with her. She knew him as a pleasant, jolly man, and this afternoon he was his usual self. He joked with her, and spoke about the welcome change in the weather, saying that it was almost like spring.

"Let's hope it's going to stay this way," he said.

He moved on to the house of Mrs Caroline Keill. If P.C. Rothwell, now almost arrived at the police station, had known this lady, and had asked if she could confirm his suspicion that Wallace had been crying in the street, she would have told him that she had passed Wallace in Maiden Lane on several occasions, and had often seen him put his handkerchief to his eyes and wipe them, then blow his nose. To her it was quite a normal sight. She had mentioned it to her daughter, saying:

"That man never seems to get rid of his cold."

* * *

Four o'clock.

And Amy Wallace, the wife of Wallace's elder brother Joseph, knocked at the door of 29 Wolverton Street. She had come to find out if Julia's cold was any better—but not because she was worried about the state of Julia's health (on the contrary, she was inclined to pooh-pooh the various but apparently petty illnesses that afflicted her sister-in-law; in her opinion these illnesses were simply signs of weakness, and weakness was something she abhorred). The reason for her visit was that she wanted to know if Julia would feel fit enough to accompany her to the Empire Theatre on Friday, to see Dorothy Ward and Shaun Glenville in *Mother Goose*. She had bought the tickets and did not want to waste them. (. . . Because waste was something else she hated. She had seen too much of it in the years she had spent in Malaya. The waste, the appalling smells, the disgusting habits of some of the natives, the intolerable heat that proved the lie to what her dear mother had told her about only horses sweating, and—oh, so many other things had influenced her decision to return to England in 1929, leaving her husband behind to continue working as a printer for the Malayan Government.)

Would Julia never answer the door? she thought tetchily. Only last Sunday she and her nineteen-year-old son, Edwin, had spent the evening in the parlour of 29 Wolverton Street, and she remembered distinctly, just before leaving, saying that she would call round this afternoon.

Hearing Julia's footsteps in the hall, Amy—a very fashion-conscious lady—made sure that her hat was straight, tugged at the back of her Bon Marché coat, patted the ends of her permanently permanently-waved hair, and, as soon as the door was open wide enough to allow smooth passage, cruised into the house. Julia closed the door after her and paddled along in her wake.

It would have been difficult to find two women as unlike as Amy and Julia Wallace: one—Amy, of course—domineering, definite, up to the minute in the clothes she wore and the hair styles she assumed, worldly-wise, and not caring a damn for anyone or anything; and the other—Julia—gentle, uncertain, a trifle eccentric, old-fashioned in almost every respect, shy, and caring very much whether people liked her or not. Their married name seems to have been the only thing they had in common.

It was probably not quite such an ordeal for Julia when Amy visited the house and Wallace was there, too, but she must have dreaded occasions like this, when she was left alone with her

sister-in-law. Not just because of Amy's overbearing manner—
although, goodness knows, that alone must have been bad enough
for anyone as timid and nervous as Julia—but because of the
remarks that were passed and the complaints that were made.
According to Amy, nothing that Julia ever did was right. Last
summer, for instance, when Wallace had been in hospital, Julia
had helped with his insurance round. Amy still talked in shocked
tones of this breach of womanhood. She had also found out that
when Julia went shopping in Anfield she often walked from one
shop to another with her handbag wide open. A lecture had
followed: a lecture in several parts, one part per visit, on the perils
of absent-mindedness.

The two women went into the kitchen. Julia already had the
kettle on to make tea, but Amy said no, not for her, as she was in
a hurry. Asked about the pantomime, Julia said that she did not
know if she would feel well enough by Friday, and, in any case,
she was not particular about going.

They talked for another ten minutes or so, Amy punching her
remarks through the twitteringly-quick chatter from Julia. Amy
asked after Wallace, and was told that he seemed much better.
Julia said that he had been at the chess club the previous night,
and she expected him to be out again this evening, as he had
received a telephone call from someone in Calderstones who
wanted to discuss some insurance business with him.

Saying goodbye, and adding that she would call again before
Friday to find out if the trip to the pantomime was on or off, Amy
walked out of the house, leaving Julia to recover from the visit.

Mrs Blanche Richards, standing in the doorway of 17 Worcester Drive, Clubmoor, received her insurance book back from
Wallace, and agreed with him when he said that the flowers in
her parlour window were very beautiful.

"I'll see you again in three weeks' time," he said.

It was only one of many appointments that he would not be
allowed to keep.

At half-past four, when Mrs Wallace opened the door to Neil
Norbury, a baker's boy, she had "a kind of scarf, a bit of sort of
material", wrapped round her neck. The boy thought that she did
not look very well; he told her so. She smiled and said that she had
a slight touch of bronchitis, that was all. Thanking him for
delivering the bread, she closed the door.

The following day Neil Norbury's photograph would appear on the front page of the *Liverpool Evening Express*, and he would be referred to as the last-but-one person to have seen Julia Wallace alive.

In fact, he was the last-but-two . . . or three.

Only a couple more insurance calls to make.

Penultimately, at the home of Miss Ann Miller, who afterwards had this to say about the man, the call, the time:

"I have never really met a nicer man than Mr Wallace. He came into the house and passed some jovial remarks. He asked me the time. I looked at the clock and it was a quarter to six. It was a constant habit of his to ask the time, and he would always look down at his own watch after he asked the time. He was perfectly normal and quite his usual self."

And lastly, a special call to arrange the surrender of a policy held by Mrs Margaret Martin in Eastman Road. The time of the call is of far greater importance than any details about the call itself, but Mrs Martin was rather vague about this.

"Did Mr Wallace call on you on Tuesday, the day of this murder, the 20th January?" she was to be asked by defence counsel at the trial.

"Yes."

"At about what time?"

"I can't give the correct time."

"About, approximately?"

"About half-past five; it might be anything up to ten minutes."

"Up to ten to six?"

"No, not up to ten to six; between half-past five and ten to."

Defence counsel gave up.

If, however, the definite statement of Miss Miller is accepted— that Wallace was at her house at a quarter to six, it is reasonable to assume that he was with Mrs Martin, helping her to complete a surrender claim form, until between 5.50 and 5.55. It is also reasonable to assume that, after leaving her, he boarded a tram at the junction of Queen's Drive and Townsend Avenue, and arrived back at Wolverton Street no earlier than five minutes past six.

For the next hour and a minute, until six minutes past seven, no-one saw—or, at least, afterwards remembered seeing—Wallace;

and only one person—apart from Wallace himself, of course—
admitted to having seen his wife.

What definitely happened during these crucial sixty-one
minutes, and also what probably happened, are two questions
that will be answered later. But, for now, let us move on to six
minutes past seven.

[2]

At the Royal Court Theatre, in the centre of Liverpool, the
audience was arriving to see "A Play Enacted Entirely by WOMEN,
WITHOUT MEN, with Mannequins Displaying the Latest Parisian
Lingerie". Having watched the play the night before, the drama
critic of the *Liverpool Weekly Post* commented:

"Now I know what kind of girl wears the pea-green vests and
panties with broad red stripes that have been advertised as such
bargains in the recent sales."

The play was called *Nine Till Six*.

In a few days' time people would be remarking on the fact that
the title seemed to have a sort of back-to-front appropriateness to
the mystery surrounding the killing of Julia Wallace.

By six minutes past seven Wallace was over two miles from his
home at Wolverton Street, and waiting for a tram at the junction
of Smithdown Road and Lodge Lane.

The first tram that came along was a No. 4, and Wallace asked
the conductor, Thomas Phillips, if it would take him to Menlove
Gardens East.

Phillips said no, and told him the numbers of four trams that
went up Menlove Avenue. Then, as Wallace was stepping back to
the pavement, Phillips changed his mind. "Stay on the car," he
said, "and I'll give you a penny ticket for a transfer at Penny
Lane."

Before sitting down in the corner seat by the conductor's platform, Wallace explained to Phillips that he was a complete stranger
in the district, adding that he had an important call to make in
Menlove Gardens East.

Phillips started to collect the fares. "You won't forget, will
you, that I want Menlove Gardens East?" Wallace reminded him.

A ticket inspector named Edward Angus boarded the tram.
Phillips must have spoken to him, because Angus went up to
Wallace and said, "You'll find Menlove Gardens East, sir, if you
get off this car at Penny Lane and get a 5a."

C

Phillips collected the fares from the passengers upstairs and returned to the platform. Wallace leaned round the partition, and for the fourth time mentioned that he wanted to get to Menlove Gardens East.

When the tram arrived at Penny Lane, Phillips shouted, "Menlove Gardens, change here."

A No. 7 tram was already in the loop[1] heading towards Calderstones, via Menlove Avenue; and another tram, a No. 5a, was pulling up at the stop.

Phillips pointed them out to Wallace, shouting after him as he hurried away, "Either that one coming along or the one in the loop."

Wallace boarded the No. 5a tram, and was sitting on the left, beside the platform, when it left Penny Lane at quarter-past seven. He asked the conductor, Arthur Thompson, to put him off at Menlove Gardens East.

It was a short journey—about 650 yards—to the first tram-stop in Menlove Avenue.

Thompson beckoned Wallace on to the platform and pointed to where Menlove Gardens West entered the Avenue. "You'll probably find that Menlove Gardens East is in that direction."

"Thank you. I'm a complete stranger round here," Wallace said as he alighted from the tram.

As Wallace wandered around, searching for the home of Mr R. M. Qualtrough, he asked several people for their assistance in finding Menlove Gardens East. Afterwards he stated that he spoke to seven people; but only four came forward or were traced by the police.

The first of these[2] was Sydney Green, a young, fair-haired clerk, who was walking down Menlove Gardens West in the direction of Menlove Avenue when Wallace approached him. He told Wallace that, as far as he knew, there was no such place as

[1] On the single-line system, short "loop" lines were fitted for stationary trams, so that other trams could pass.

[2] In his Proof of Evidence, Wallace said: "After alighting from the tram-car I walked up Menlove Gardens West, turned into Menlove Gardens North, and, being uncertain as to where Menlove Gardens East was, I decided to ask the first person I met. This was a woman who came out of one of the houses in Menlove Gardens North ... She ... suggested it might be along the road in continuation of Menlove Gardens West. I went back to the corner, and walked along the West Road ... until I met a man walking towards me." (This man was Sydney Green.)

Menlove Gardens East. Wallace said he would ask at 25 Menlove Gardens West, in case a mistake had been made in the message he had been given.

An elderly lady named Mrs Katie Mather lived at this address. She answered the door to Wallace, who asked if anyone named Qualtrough lived in the house. No, she said. He told her that he was looking for 25 Menlove Gardens East, and asked, "This isn't it, is it?" Mrs Mather shook her head. She could give no help at all. She had lived in the area for only a short time; her house, like most of the others, was new, and all around were fresh streets with names she did not know.

The next person to see Wallace was P.C. James Sargent.[1] He had just left the Allerton Police Station to commence a duty round, and had reached the corner of Green Lane and Allerton Road when Wallace came up to him and asked:

"Do you know of Menlove Gardens East?"

"There's no such place," Sargent replied, "but there's a Menlove Gardens North, South, and West."

"I've been to Menlove Gardens West," Wallace said. "The person I'm looking for doesn't live there, and the numbers in Menlove Gardens North and South are all even." He went on to explain that he was an insurance agent, and that a Mr Quallthorpe (this was how he spelt the name to Sargent) had rung up his club and left a message, asking him to call at 25 Menlove Gardens East.

Sargent said that he knew of no-one of that name in the district, but suggested that Wallace try 25 Menlove Avenue.

Wallace thanked him and started to walk away; then turned back to ask, "Is there anywhere where I can see a directory?"

Sargent told him to try the post-office in Allerton Road. "If you don't see one down there, you may be allowed to look at the directory at the police station." He pointed out both these places to Wallace.

[1] Wallace's Proof of Evidence: "After calling at 25 Menlove Gardens West, I then walked back to Menlove Gardens South with the idea of enquiring at No. 25 there, but they all turned out to be even numbers, and I went towards Menlove Gardens North, and there again the numbers were even. I hesitated for a few moments, and then went to Menlove Avenue, and I walked across to a man waiting at a tram shelter, and asked him. He informed me he was a stranger and did not know. I then went to Green Lane, which is quite near, and called at the house of my Superintendent, thinking he might know the address. I could not get an answer . . . I walked down Green Lane until I came to the road in which the Plaza Picture House is situated, and just before turning out of Green Lane I saw a policeman [P.C. Sargent]. . . ."

"It's not eight o'clock yet, is it?" Wallace asked, pulling out his watch. "No, it's just a quarter to."

Sargent consulted his own watch. "Yes, a quarter to eight," he agreed.

Saying good night to the policeman, Wallace walked off down Allerton Road.

The next person[1] to see him was Miss Lily Pinches, the middle-aged manageress of Allday's newsagent's shop, opposite the post-office. Here he was given a street directory. After searching through the pages for a few minutes he asked Miss Pinches if she knew what he was looking for. As might be expected, Miss Pinches said no, she had no idea.

"25 Menlove Gardens East," Wallace told her.

"There's no such place as Menlove Gardens East," Miss Pinches said. "There's only South and West."

She looked in her newspaper account book and told Wallace that the people who lived at 25 Menlove Gardens West were not customers of hers. Wallace said that he had already called at that address, but the person he wanted did not live there.

That was the end of the conversation between Wallace and Lily Pinches. It was also the end of Wallace's search for a man unborn, a house unbuilt, a street that did not exist.

He started on the journey home.

John Sharpe (and therefore nicknamed "Toffee") Johnston worked as an engineer in the mammoth shipyards of Cammell Laird, "over the water" on the Birkenhead side of the Mersey. He and his wife Florence had lived at 31 Wolverton Street for ten years, but now they were looking forward to moving to their married daughter's house in West Derby, a couple of miles away. The move was planned for early February, and Mrs Johnston had already started packing their twenty-five-year-old wedding presents of unused dinner services and tea-sets.

Mr and Mrs Johnston were on friendly terms with their next-door neighbours, the Wallaces. Mrs Johnston thought of them as a devoted couple. Not once had she seen or heard a quarrel between

[1] Wallace's Proof of Evidence: "I went to the post-office and asked if they had a directory, and they had not. I enquired as to whether they knew the name or the address, but they did not. Whilst there, I glanced at the clock, and remember it was six or seven minutes to eight. The post-office official suggested I might get a directory at a paper shop on the other side of the road." (The Allerton Road Post Office was housed in a sweet shop. The post-office closed at 7 P.M., but the sweet shop stayed open till 8 P.M.)

them. True, they were not the sort of people to quarrel in public, but the dividing wall between the two houses was thin, and Mrs Johnston was sure that she would have heard the smallest argument, the slightest tiff. When Amy Wallace was visiting, Mrs Johnston was well aware of the fact. And she knew the Wallaces' musical repertoire almost by heart.

Tonight the Johnstons were going out.

As Mrs Johnston tidied her hair in front of the kitchen mirror, she heard knocking at the back door of No. 29. She was in a hurry, so she did not take much notice of it. Her husband—ready, as usual, before her—stood at the door leading to the back kitchen and told her to "For goodness' sake, look at the time."

It was nearly quarter to nine.

Ready at last, Mrs Johnston accompanied her husband through the back kitchen and into the yard. As they opened the yard door and walked through to the entry Wallace hurried past them towards his own yard door, which was standing open.

Mrs Johnston said, "Good evening, Mr Wallace."

He looked worried, she thought. There was no return of her greeting; but a question: "Have you heard anything unusual tonight?"

"Why, what's happened?"

"I've been out this evening since a quarter to seven," Wallace explained, "and when I returned just now I found the front door locked against me. I've been to the front and the back."

"You've tried the back kitchen door?" Johnston asked.

"Yes, but I couldn't open it."

"That's funny," Johnston said. "Try it again, and we'll wait. If you can't manage to get it open I'll see if my key fits it."

As Wallace walked across the yard he looked over his shoulder to say, "She won't be out. She has such a bad cold."

He twisted the door handle and, almost at once, turned back to them, a slight frown of surprise or puzzlement on his face. "It opens now," he murmured.

"We'll stop here while you have a look round," Johnston said.

Wallace entered the house.

Mrs Johnston noticed that the light was on, but turned low, in the middle bedroom; also in the bathroom. A heavy green blind and plush curtains covered the kitchen window, preventing her from seeing if the light was burning there.

Twice she heard Wallace calling his wife's name before the light in the middle bedroom was turned up. Then she saw a match being struck in the small room that Wallace used as a laboratory.

The seconds spread out into what seemed like a small eternity of waiting; but afterwards the Johnstons estimated that it was no more than a couple of minutes from the time Wallace entered the house to when he came rushing out again.

He looked distressed, agitated.

"Come and see," he cried. "She has been killed."

A moment of stillness, of silence; then the Johnstons ran into the yard and followed Wallace through the lighted kitchen . . .

(Mrs Johnston noticed a spent match on the floor, just inside the door)

. . . into the hall . . .

("What is it?" Johnston shouted. "Has she fallen downstairs?")

. . . to the parlour. A room measuring only thirteen feet by eleven, and made to look smaller by the amount of furniture it contained. Against the wall to the left of the door was a sideboard, its top littered with ornaments and framed photographs. Behind the door was, first, an occasional chair, then Julia's piano—the lid open, music on the rest. There were two round tables: the larger of them supported an aspidistra in the bay of the window (over which the blinds were drawn); the other stood between the window and the piano. Opposite and slightly to the right of the door was the fireplace, fitted with a Sunbeam gas-fire. On either side of the fireplace was an easy chair. Wallace's violin-case lay across the arms of the chair to the right. Also on either side of the fireplace was a gas bracket; the one on the right was alight. Other items: a few pictures on the walls, including some examples of Julia's ability with water-colours; Wallace's music-stand, which was near the piano, on the window side of the room; and, on the floor in front of the fireplace, a black rug.

It was across this rug that the body of Julia Wallace was lying face downwards, her feet not quite touching the right side of the fender, her battered head, haloed by a great oval of blood, by the corner of the rug nearest the door. She was staring at the pedals of her piano. Her left arm was extended; her right arm was by her side. Bone and brain substance protruded from a three-inch wound above and in front of her left ear. At the back of her head, also on the left side, there was a great depression of the skull, caused by many blows. Her matted hair obscured the details of the wounds. The chignon pad had been pulled away from the nape of her neck, and was lying, confused with torn strands of hair, at the edge of the encircling blood clot, nine inches from her head.

As well as the blood around her head, there were two large overlapping clots on the side of the rug nearest the sideboard. The room was stippled with splashes of blood. The majority of the splashes on the walls were no more than four feet high, but a few had reached a height of seven feet.

None of the furniture in the room appeared to have been disturbed; even the rug on which the body lay was uncreased and set exactly parallel to the fireplace.

Johnston remained in the doorway while his wife accompanied Wallace into the room. Wallace's face, sallow at any time, was now the colour of bleached parchment. He stopped beside the body.

"They've finished her," he kept saying. "They've finished her."

"Oh, you poor darling," was Mrs Johnston's first remark. It sounds the sort of thing one might say to a child with a grazed knee, a troublesome tooth—a kiss-it-better sort of remark; but to Mrs Johnston, a lady who underplayed most things and understated just about all of them, it was an expression of strong emotion.

Wallace and Mrs Johnston knelt beside the body and felt Julia's left hand.

"Is she cold?" Johnston asked.

His wife shook her head.

Johnston had no stomach for the sight of so much violence. He turned back to the door. "Don't disturb anything. I'm going for the police."

"Yes, and a doctor," Wallace said. "But I don't think it's much use. They've finished her."

"Any particular doctor?"

"The nearest one."

The three of them left the parlour and went into the kitchen.

Wallace appeared to be suffering from shock. He wandered about the room as if uncertain of where he was, or of what he was doing there. His lips formed words, but no sound came from them.

On the few occasions when Mrs Johnston had been invited into the house by Julia she had always been entertained in the parlour. So tonight she was seeing the kitchen for the first time. When she had run through the room—was it only a minute or so ago?—all that she had noticed was a spent matchstick on the floor.

Now she took stock.

The table, situated beneath the gas-pendant in the centre of the ceiling, was covered with a white cloth: on it was a sugar-basin and a small crumb-specked plate; a needlework basket; a copy of that evening's *Liverpool Echo*, lying open at the centre pages. An upright chair was tucked in beneath the table, and Mrs Johnston could just see Julia's handbag on the seat, which was almost hidden behind the fall of the cloth. There was an armchair on either side of the kitchen range; the one on the left, the smaller of the two, was obviously Julia's. Beside this armchair, in the recess to the left of the range, shelves rose to a height of over seven feet. All but one of the shelves were eleven inches deep, and held books and small box files, pieces of bric-a-brac. But the bottom shelf, which was supported by a cupboard, was seventeen inches deep. This shelf held—from the left—Wallace's microscope, a box of chessmen, a few books, and a home-made cabinet containing photographic equipment. The door of the cabinet had been wrenched off, and was lying in two pieces on the floor.

Wallace pointed to it. "See, they've broken that off," he said. His voice was little more than a whisper.

Johnston looked down and noticed three coins—a half-crown and two separate shillings—lying close to the foot of the shelves. "What have they taken?" he asked.

Wallace reached up to a cash-box on the top shelf. He opened it and pulled out the tray. There was nothing in the box, apart from a crumpled American one-dollar note and four penny stamps. "I can't tell for certain until I've examined my books," he said, "but I think it's about four pounds."

"You'd better see if everything's all right upstairs before I go for the police and the doctor," Johnston said.

Wallace nodded uncertainly.

He was gone from the kitchen only a couple of minutes. When he came back, he said, "Everything's all right up there. There's five pounds in a jar they haven't taken."

"Was the light on in here when you got back?" Johnston asked.

Wallace shook his head. "I put it on. And the one in the parlour."

As Johnston was leaving the house by the back door, Wallace indicated the crockery and cutlery on the draining-board in the back kitchen. "She hasn't even had time to wash up the tea-things," he murmured.

Soon after Johnston had left (to go, first of all, to the house of Dr Dunlop, in Lower Breck Road—where he was told that this was a job for the police surgeon—and then on to Anfield Police Station), Wallace and Mrs Johnston returned to the parlour.

Mrs Johnston felt Julia's hand, and noticed that the flesh was much colder now.

"They've finished her," Wallace said. "Look at the brains."

Mrs Johnston had no desire to do any such thing.

"Whatever have they used?" Wallace said.

Glancing round the room, Mrs Johnston could see no sign of a weapon; but on the floor between Julia's left shoulder and the sideboard she spotted two spent matchsticks, and, on the table in the window, a Bryant and May matchbox. She asked Wallace if the box was Julia's, and he said that it was.

Treading carefully to avoid the splashes of blood on the floor and the rug, Wallace walked round the body to the side nearest the fire.

He stopped. "Whatever was she doing with a mackintosh . . . and *my* mackintosh?" he murmured, fingering a shapeless and bloody mass of material that protruded from beneath Julia's right shoulder.

Mrs Johnston had not noticed the mackintosh before. As she looked at it now the thought flashed through her mind that perhaps Julia, suffering from a cold, had thrown it over her shoulders before answering the door to a caller.

"Is it your mackintosh?" she asked.

Wallace smoothed out a few of the folds. "Yes, it's mine," he said.

They went back to the kitchen, and Wallace slumped in Julia's armchair, his hands covering his face. Mrs Johnston could hear him sobbing. It was the only sound to break the silence, the dead silence, of the house.

The minutes crept by.

How much longer before the police arrive? Mrs Johnston wondered. If only there were something she could do: something —anything—that might occupy her mind, stop her thoughts from wandering back to the parlour.

The fire in the range had burned very low.

"Well, we'll have a fire," Mrs Johnston said. And her voice sounded unnaturally—shockingly—loud.

But Wallace gave no sign of having heard her. He still sat with his face hidden, his body rocking slightly, forward and back, forward and back, the small sobbing sounds escaping from him.

Mrs Johnston found a bundle of wood in the oven in the back kitchen. She knelt in front of the range and stirred the embers of the fire together. After a few moments Wallace dropped his hands away from his face. He watched Mrs Johnston's movements as if fascinated by them, as if seeing something being done for the first time. Then he leaned forward in the chair and helped to get the fire burning.

Mrs Johnston asked if there was anything she could get him . . . Some tea, perhaps? But he said he did not want anything. For a while he sat staring at the fire, occasionally muttering to himself and shaking his head. Then he covered his face with his hands and started to sob again.

At about ten past nine there was a knock at the front door. The first member of the Liverpool City Police Force had arrived.

The Liverpool City Police Force, which was known to a good many local people as "The Jiggery-Pokery Brigade", was in very poor shape indeed.

The reason could be traced back to the police strike of 1919, which was precipitated by the progress of the Police Bill through Parliament. Under the terms of this Bill, the Police Union, organized and controlled by the police themselves, was to be abolished, and a new union, the Police Federation, formed, with officials appointed by the Chief Commissioner. The Police Union called for a nation-wide strike of its members in protest against "this perversion of democratic principles". Throughout most of the country the call went unheeded; only two cities, London and Liverpool, were affected to any great extent.

In Liverpool more than half the members of the police force went on strike.

In the climate of post-war hopelessness and despair, the Liverpool police strike created a situation that was conducive to anarchy. Men who had been unemployed since demobilization were soon prowling the streets, forming themselves into gangs, breaking into shops and private houses, and looting anything they could lay their hands on. At night candles lit street corners where men gambled with the loot of the day. The Lord Mayor appealed for law and order, for volunteers, for special constables to report for duty; troops were called in to patrol the worst-hit areas of Scotland Road and Byrom Street; a battleship and two destroyers steamed into the Mersey to protect the docks.

The Watch Committee issued a statement saying that all strikers would be dismissed from the force, and none would be reinstated. This caused a few of the strikers to return to duty; but 951 members of a force of 1874 remained on strike and were dismissed.

Recruitment began. Advertisements appeared in the local papers

*offering commencing wages of seventy shillings a week, uniform,
pension, good opportunities for advancement. There was no shortage of
applicants; there was no time for the recruiting officers to take up
references. Within a fortnight over 500 men were sworn into the
Liverpool City Police Force. Some of these new constables were of
excellent character; others were not. More than a few of them found
themselves in the distinctly odd position of having to patrol the streets
where, a few days before, they had engaged in looting and gambling.*

*There had been a certain amount of corruption within the police
force before the strike; but now it increased: a few nasty sores became
a rash. The force became overstocked with dishonest policemen—
"bent Jacks"—some of them only slightly bent, but a lot of them bent
almost double. In at least one division a Chicago-style protection
racket was organized. Some members of the force took up housebreaking, either as a spare-time occupation or to ease the monotony of
long spells of duty. This often led to situations wherein the criminals
investigated their own crimes. Needless to say, they never solved them.*

*Forty-eight of the dismissed strikers were sergeants; many others
had passed examinations and were waiting for their promotions to be
authorized. So the strike created a shortage of officer material, and
men were promoted to positions they were unqualified to fill.*

*Some members of the force, trying to justify their ranks by large
numbers of arrests, used decidedly unconventional methods in the
investigation of crime. Results were what counted. On the few occasions
when an officer was reprimanded for overzealous conduct he generally
pleaded that he was fighting fire with fire. A lot of innocent people were
burned by these counter-arson activities. The overzealous conduct was
ascribed to a genuine but misplaced desire to combat crime; in fact,
crime was simply being used as an excuse for making arrests, and the
kudos attached to these arrests was being used as an aid to the retention
and pursuit of power.*

*By 1931 much of the Liverpool City Police Force was hardly up to
the task of dealing with parking offences, let alone a full-scale murder
investigation.*

Wallace followed, a few steps behind, as Mrs Johnston ran to the
front door to answer the knock. She tried to open it, but, after a few
moments of frantic fumbling with the handle, stood aside to let
Wallace get to the door. He soon had it open.

(The reason, Wallace said afterwards, why Mrs Johnston could
not open the door was because it was bolted. Whether this was true
or not is a matter of argument. The policeman standing outside

did not hear a bolt being drawn. Mrs Johnston stated: "I cannot say how he opened the door, and whether or not he had to un-bolt it.")

Fred Williams was the name of the first policeman to arrive at the scene of the crime. Red-haired and freckle-faced, P.C. Williams was, by all accounts, a "good Jack". He had passed his promotion examination some time before, and was waiting to be made up to the rank of sergeant.

"Come inside, officer," Wallace said. "Something terrible has happened."

P.C. Williams went into the parlour and knelt beside the body. He felt Julia's right wrist, but could detect no movement of the pulse. The flesh, he noticed, was slightly warm. He walked back to the hall, where Wallace and Mrs Johnston were standing.

"How did this happen?" he asked.

It was the cue for the first of Wallace's many statements. Unfortunately, and somewhat inexplicably, P.C. Williams did not make a note of this statement at the time. An hour and a half later he recorded it as follows:

"At 6.45 P.M. I left the house in order to go to Menlove Gardens, and my wife accompanied me to the back-yard door. She walked a little way down the alley with me, then she returned and bolted the back-yard door. She would then be alone in the house. I went to Menlove Gardens to find the address which had been given me was wrong. Becoming suspicious, I returned home and went to the front door. I inserted my key to find I could not open it. I went round to the back-yard door; it was closed, but not bolted. I went up the back yard and tried the back door, but it would not open. I again went to the front door, but this time found the door to be bolted. I hurried round to the back and up the back yard, and tried the back door, and this time found it would open. I entered the house, and this is what I found."

Wallace had just completed this statement when two more policemen arrived with an ambulance. While P.C. Williams stood on the doorstep talking to them, Julia's black cat returned home. As Mrs Johnston saw it slithering between the policeman's legs and into the hall she shouted, "Don't let it go into the front room." But the cat ran straight through to the kitchen.

After telling the other two policemen that an ambulance "was the wrong sort of vehicle for this job", P.C. Williams closed the front door and asked Wallace to accompany him while he searched the house. They went upstairs.

The first room they entered was the middle bedroom. Situated above the kitchen, and therefore the warmest of the upstairs rooms, it was where the Wallaces slept. The light was burning, and P.C. Williams asked Wallace if it had been on when he returned.

"I changed myself in this room before I left the house," Wallace replied, "so I probably left the light on myself."

He walked across to the mantelpiece and partly extracted some one-pound notes from a small ornamental jar. "Here's some money which hasn't been touched."

Hastily P.C. Williams told him to replace the notes and the jar in their original positions. The damage had been done, but at least P.C. Williams acknowledged the rule of "don't disturb", which is fundamental to the investigation of crime. Later he himself was to be slightly neglectful of this rule. Only slightly. But the superior officers who took over from him seem to have waived the rule altogether.

Wallace pointed to a curtained recess to the right of the fireplace. "My wife's clothes are kept there. They haven't been touched." As P.C. Williams lifted the curtain to make sure Wallace moved back to the door. "There appears to have been no-one here," he said.

They crossed the diminutive landing to the doorway of Wallace's laboratory, and P.C. Williams flashed his torch over the bench and shelves.

"Everything's all right here," Wallace told him.

Asked if the light in the bathroom had been on when he entered the house, Wallace nodded and said, "We usually have a low light here."

They moved on to the front bedroom, which was in darkness. The bed, situated left of the door, was in a state of disorder. The two pillows were on the floor at the foot of it, one on top of the other, and the sheets and blankets were pushed over the fireplace, exposing part of the mattress. There were two handbags and three of Julia's hats on the bed. The door of the wardrobe and the drawers in the dressing-table were closed.

The two men went downstairs. While P.C. Williams was standing in the doorway of the parlour Wallace walked between his wife's body and the sideboard, and lit the gas-bracket to the left of the fireplace. Watching him, P.C. Williams detected not the slightest flicker of emotion on his face; asked afterwards to describe Wallace's demeanour, he said that Wallace was "cool and calm— well, I thought he was extraordinarily cool and calm". They left the room, P.C. Williams closing the door after them, and walked down the hall to the kitchen.

They were alone in the house now; Mrs Johnston had gone next door to send her daughter to inform Amy Wallace of the tragedy.

Picking up the handbag from the chair beneath the kitchen table, Wallace opened it and took out a one-pound note and some silver. He murmured something about the money, but his voice was so low that P.C. Williams did not catch what he said.

"Was the light on in here when you entered?" P.C. Williams asked. Wallace shook his head. "Except for the two lights upstairs, the house was in darkness."

P.C. Williams parted the heavy curtains over the kitchen window. "When you first came up the yard, did you notice any light escaping through these curtains?"

"The curtains would prevent any light from escaping."

"I'll try them." P.C. Williams started towards the back door.

But Wallace murmured, "It's no use now—you've disturbed them."

Williams turned away from the door and continued his investigation of the room. But not for long. Police Sergeant Joe Breslin— one of the many Irish members of the Liverpool City Police Force, and Williams's immediate superior in G Division—arrived at the house. The two policemen entered the parlour.

Although Williams had been in the room twice before, it was not until now that he noticed the mackintosh lying, rumpled up, beneath and beside the body. He pointed to it. "This looks like a mackintosh," he said.

Without hesitation Wallace, who was standing by the door, said, "It's an old one of mine." He looked in the direction of the hallstand and added, "It usually hangs here."

Any further talk about the mackintosh—which was to become probably the most controversial article of clothing in the annals of crime—was cut short by the sound of a car drawing up outside the house.

The time was ten minutes to ten.

Professor John Edward Whitley MacFall had arrived to conduct the medical examination.

MacFall was a big man, over six foot three inches tall and with the build of a heavy-weight boxer. An all-round athlete in his youth, whose Combined Universities record for putting the shot stood for thirty years, he was proud of the fact that, at fifty-seven, he was as fit as most men half his age. During the First World War he served as an officer in the R.A.M.C.; posted to France, he was gassed and twice wounded in the fighting around Arras. The gassing left him with his only apparent sign of weakness—an asthmatic condition that husked his voice and gave a slight wheeze to his breathing.

After the War he resumed medical practice in the Liverpool suburb of Stoneycroft; but he had no intention of spending the rest of his life as a run-of-the-mill G.P. The 1920s were notable for courtroom clashes between counsel and medico-legal experts, and MacFall coveted the prestige and fame of men like Spilsbury, Smith, and Glaister. Although, in the field of forensic medicine, his abilities did not measure up to his own high opinion of them, he was an impressive exponent of the art of self-advertisement. Later to be described as "more of a placard than a person", he bulldozed his way towards eminence.

Always an egotist, it would seem that the sudden and unnatural death of his younger son (who suffocated in his pillow at the age of fifteen) tilted MacFall's mind towards megalomania. He deluded himself—and, unfortunately, a great many other people—with the idea that he was a sort of real-life Dr Thorndyke. He stated his opinions, often based on scanty evidence, as facts; he refused to accept the arguments of others.

By 1931 MacFall was a well-known figure, not only in the courts of Liverpool, but on the whole Northern Circuit. He had amassed an impressive list of credits. As well as being the Liverpool Bridewell Surgeon and Honorary Adviser to the Liverpool and Birkenhead Criminal Investigation Departments, he occupied the Chair of Forensic Medicine at the University of Liverpool, and was an Examiner in Medical Jurisprudence at four other universities.

He was disliked by the other members of the Medical Faculty in the University of Liverpool, who considered he was using his appointment as a means to an end—as a stepping-stone to further glory, as a qualification to impress juries. They also felt that he was a careless diagnostician. Another reason for their dislike of him was his language, which was decidedly unprofessorial.

Within the police force MacFall was as renowned for his oddities of behaviour as for his work as a medical examiner. He was an opium smoker, and some of the police attributed certain of his eccentricities to this fact.

* * *

Arriving at 29 Wolverton Street at ten minutes to ten, MacFall at once set about the task of attempting to ascertain the time which had elapsed since Julia Wallace's death.

It is worth mentioning at this point that MacFall's predecessor at the university, Dr Buchanan, was the author of *A Text-book of Forensic Medicine and Toxicology*, and MacFall revised and enlarged the 1925 edition of this book, in which the following statement appears:

"The time of death can scarcely be determined with precision, as so much depends upon the conditions under which the body may have been placed. . . . Its elucidation will require the greatest care on the part of the medical expert."

In the light of this statement—which, if not written by MacFall, must surely have been approved by him—it is hard to explain the laxity of his observations in the case of Julia Wallace, and even harder to explain his conviction that the conclusion he drew from these observations was absolutely correct.

In order to assess the value of his evidence, it is necessary to consider not only the observations that he made, but also the observations that he might—and *should*—have made.

The temperature of a body is said to drop one degree Centigrade for each hour after death until, within six to eight hours, it approaches the temperature of the surroundings. It is possible, then, to estimate the approximate time of death by measuring the fall in temperature with a thermometer inserted in the rectum. Although the rectal temperature is dependent upon several factors, it is thought to be the most reliable and constant guide to the number of hours that have elapsed since death.

But MacFall did not even bother to measure the temperature of the parlour, let alone that of the body.

Another guide is post-mortem lividity, which is caused by the blood sinking to the lowest level of the body. Usually occurring three to four hours after death, it will happen earlier in the case of a person killed instantaneously.

MacFall did not observe post-mortem lividity in the body of Julia Wallace. It certainly *ought* to have been present if he was correct in his estimate of the time of her death. . . .

Because MacFall's conclusion, which he arrived at within a matter of minutes and never altered, was that Julia Wallace had been dead for at least four hours. In other words, since before six o'clock. If he was correct, then her husband's story was a pack of lies. It was as simple as that. If she was dead before six o'clock she

Anfield 1627

The call-box which encompassed the short existence of R. M. Qualtrough.

11 St Mary's Avenue, Harrogate

The solid stone villa where, in 1914, the Wallaces began their married life.

Photo Bertram Unné

William Herbert Wallace
'The Man from the Pru'.

Julia Wallace
"She fluttered around like
a rather drab butterfly".
*Photo Liverpool Daily Post
and Echo*

could hardly have said goodbye to her husband at quarter to seven, the time he said he left the house to commence his fruitless search for R. M. Qualtrough.

The observations upon which MacFall based his conclusion were (*a*) the presence of rigor mortis in the neck and upper part of the left arm and (*b*) the condition of the effused blood around the head.

Rigor mortis, the stiffening of the muscles after death, begins from the head and gradually spreads down over the whole body, taking between eight and twenty hours before it is complete. The time of its onset is extremely variable, and is a notoriously unsafe and inexact guide to the time of death. The small degree of rigor noted by MacFall at ten minutes to ten could have developed as early as two hours or as late as eight hours after death, depending upon many factors which affect the time of onset of rigor and the speed of its progress.

But MacFall took none of these factors into account.

Factor No. 1: *The temperature of the room.* The progress of rigor mortis is retarded by warmth, accelerated by cold. MacFall didn't bother to measure the temperature of the surroundings. An important omission, this, as it was later established that the gas-fire in the parlour must have been alight at some time during the evening. According to MacFall, the temperature of the room was "ordinary, not very cold"; but he had come straight in from the street, and his impression may have been blunted by comparison with the outdoor temperature of 5·1° Centigrade.

Factor No. 2: *The muscularity of the body.* Rigor appears earlier, but is less pronounced, in persons of slight build than in the muscular. MacFall noted that Mrs Wallace was "frail and feeble", but he did not take this fact into consideration when estimating the time of her death.

Factor No. 3: *The medical history of the victim.* In the Buchanan text-book the following statement appears:

"It is a general rule that whatever exhausts the muscular irritability before death causes the early appearance and the more rapid disappearance of rigor mortis."

MacFall did not know, and had no desire to find out, about the state of Mrs Wallace's health. But she had undergone a long series of illnesses, and it is possible that the "cold" from which she was suffering at the time of her death was, in fact, an acute exacerbation of a chronic lung disease. One night, only a short time before her death, she had started spitting blood; suspecting pneumonia, Wallace had telephoned Dr Curwen, who had told

D

him not to be alarmed, but to put a linseed poultice on her chest and give her a hot-water bottle. It is an axiom in medicine that, unless and until some other cause is found, spitting of blood should be regarded as due to tuberculosis of the lungs. Whether Mrs Wallace's condition was as severe as this is not known, but there seems little doubt that she was suffering from a lung or chest complaint of some sort, which would have accelerated the onset of rigor.

Factor No. 4: *The time of completion of rigor mortis.* This is important in estimating the time of death, as the speed of its progress is proportionate to the speed of onset; the more rapid the onset, the sooner is the stiffening universal in the body. In the case of Julia Wallace, MacFall made no notes of the progress of rigor. By one o'clock the following morning, before the body was removed to the mortuary, the rigor was apparently practically complete, only being absent from the left leg. Such rapid spread is evidence in favour of an equally rapid onset after death.

Factor No. 5: *The time of disappearance of rigor,* which is an important indication of the speed of onset, since the more rapid its development, the shorter is its duration. MacFall made no observation upon this point.

To corroborate his theory that Julia Wallace had been dead for at least four hours, he cited the condition of the blood around the head. But, in fact, far from supporting his theory, it indicated a much later time of death.

"This clot," MacFall stated, "had the dark appearance seen in a blood clot that has been shed two or three hours. It was getting a darker red."

In other words, his estimate of the age of the blood clot put the time of death between seven and eight o'clock, contradicting his estimate based on the extent of rigor mortis by over an hour.

"There was a small amount of blood serum," he went on, "but that is very little to go upon, because the liquid portion of the blood, the serum, runs out very soon."

What could MacFall have meant by "very soon"? Blood sets, after effusion, into a jelly-like mass; the threads of fibrin in the blood begin to contract, squeezing out the yellowish, watery substance which is known as serum. In clean conditions the serum is usually apparent to the naked eye within two or three hours after the blood has been shed—but in Julia Wallace's case the processes of clotting would have been greatly accelerated (*a*) by the presence of foreign materials (the dirty hearthrug and her hair, for example);

(*b*) by the blood being mixed with bone and brain tissue, both of which contain a good supply of one of the essential clotting ingredients; and (*c*) by the large amount of blood which, because of its weight, would have helped greatly in the squeezing out of serum. It would seem that the "small amount of blood serum" noted by MacFall was a sign that Julia Wallace had died some time later than six o'clock—as much as an hour or two hours later, in fact.

As soon as the murder was reported the desk sergeant at Anfield Police Station telephoned a message to Police Headquarters in Dale Street. But it was nearly ten o'clock before Detective-Superintendent Hubert ("Rory") Moore, the Head of the Liverpool C.I.D., was informed of the murder. The reason for the delay was that nobody at Police Headquarters knew his exact whereabouts: he was probably in a pub or a club, imbibing his favourite drink of Jameson's whiskey, but Liverpool was well stocked with licensed premises, and Moore might be in any one of them, or in transit between one and another.

It goes without saying that the earlier an investigation begins, the more chance there is of its proving successful, but apparently it did not occur to anyone at Police Headquarters to send another C.I.D. officer to Wolverton Street ahead of, or instead of, Moore; for some reason which is hard to fathom it was decided that the investigation could not begin without him. So a search was started for the lost leader, and he was eventually traced to the Press Club in Lime Street.

Born in Ireland, and retaining a strong brogue in his speech, Moore was a devout Roman Catholic (or a "rat catcher", as Liverpool Protestants prefer to call a believer in the Catholic faith). A member of the police force for over thirty years, he looked less like a policeman than a prosperous butcher. A heavily-built man, with dark red hair brushed away from a centre parting, he sported a large moustache—which, according to one of his compatriots, "was waxed almost lyrical". Lacking in imagination and humour (it was said that if you wanted to make a joke with him you had to arrange an appointment first), Moore was an able and hard-working policeman, but by no means a brilliant detective.

Over the previous ten years the effects of two very different forms of rebellion had assisted him in his rise to the high rank of superintendent.

The police strike of 1919 had resulted in the dismissal of many, if not most, of Moore's competitors for promotion. It had provided him with a golden opportunity for advancement—all that he needed was an equally golden chance to impress the men at the top. He did not have to wait long. Soon after the strike he was appointed as an inspector in the Special Branch, a position which, at that time, fitted his talents like a glove. He was in the right job at the right time.

During the 1920s Liverpool was the main centre of Sinn Fein disturbance in this country. Fighting for full Irish independence, the Sinn Feiners used arson, sabotage, and armed violence as the means of publicizing their cause and forcing the British Government to accede to their demands. It was the duty of the Special Branch to combat the terrorists, and Moore was ideally suited to the task. Himself an Irish Catholic, he understood and agreed with the motives of the Sinn Feiners, but hated them for the methods they used. These methods, he felt, could only defer the freedom they demanded. He fought them with the passion and ruthlessness of an extreme patriot—an Irish patriot—and, before long, he was as much admired by the people of Liverpool as he was hated by the Sinn Feiners.

At the beginning of 1930 he was promoted to the rank of superintendent; at the end of the year he was placed in charge of the C.I.D. He had reached the top. Now the only direction in which he could travel was down. If he fell he would fall a very long way, and nobody would bother to help him up again.

Occurring so soon after his appointment as Head of the C.I.D., the murder of Julia Wallace provided a personal test for Moore—probably the greatest challenge of his career. The thud-and-blunder methods he had used so successfully in the fight against Sinn Fein were of no use in dealing with a murder case, and his detractors said that these were the only methods he knew. He had to prove his detractors wrong. If he did not, then his position would be very insecure indeed. It was not just his reputation, but possibly his whole future, that was now at stake.

When Moore arrived at 29 Wolverton Street the time was five past ten. P.C. Williams opened the door to him, and at once showed him into the parlour, where Professor MacFall was sitting on the arm of one of the fireside chairs, making sketches of the position and shape of the bloodstains.

Moore and MacFall had worked together on several previous occasions, but there was no love lost between them. While Moore made it plain that he had little respect for the value of medical evidence, and even less respect for MacFall's judgment as a forensic expert, MacFall openly stated his opinion that Moore was "a jumped-up Jack . . . good at breaking down doors, nothing else".

MacFall glanced up from his papers and noted, either from Moore's appearance or from the smell of alcohol, that the super-intendent had been drinking. At the time he made no comment. But later, in private conversation, he said that Moore was in no fit state to take charge of a murder investigation.

After having a quick look at the body and observing the state of the parlour Moore went back into the hall, where P.C. Williams told him about the search he had made of the house, and repeated from memory the statement Wallace had given him.

Moore walked through to the kitchen. Mr and Mrs Johnston had returned from their separate errands and were sitting with Wallace in front of the fire.

"Did you see anybody hanging about the house, or in the house, when you returned?" Moore asked.

"No," Wallace said, shaking his head.

And neither, said the Johnstons, had they.

For the time being Moore had no further questions to ask. He left the house and was driven to Anfield Police Station, whence he telephoned the eight Liverpool Divisional Inspectors, ordering a search of lodging-houses, all-night cafés, railway-station waiting-rooms, and the homes of known criminals for a man with blood-stains on his body or clothing. He also telephoned the Fire Brigade, asking for a couple of high-powered floodlamps to be dispatched to Wolverton Street.

Having answered—to his own satisfaction, at least—the question of *when* Julia Wallace was murdered, Professor MacFall set about answering the less difficult question of *how* she had met her death.

It appeared that the most severe blow (which had caused the lacerated wound measuring two inches by three in front of the left ear, and severed the meningeal artery) had been the first blow struck by her assailant. The reason for this deduction was simple: there was no trace of brain substance or pieces of bone beneath Julia Wallace's head. MacFall explained: "The other blows on the back of the head must have been produced afterwards [while she was lying on the floor], because the striking had produced great pressure upon the inside and had squeezed out the blood, the brain substance, and the small pieces of bone which lay around."

MacFall examined the bloodstains on the walls and furniture, and discovered several with characteristics indicating the direction of their flight through the air: "soda-water bottle marks", as he called them. (When the first part of a drop of projected blood touches a surface the remaining part tumbles over the top, forming a shape similar to an exclamation mark. The top of the exclamation mark points the direction from which the blood has flown.) All the "soda-water bottle marks" found in the parlour pointed to a position in front of the easy chair to the right of the fireplace, indicating that this was where Mrs Wallace was situated when the first blow was struck. The majority of these marks were no more than four feet from the ground, and MacFall took this to mean that Mrs Wallace had not been standing, but probably sitting on the edge of the chair, the violin-case across the arms behind her.

This assumption, though strengthened by the fact that there were only a few small bloodstains on the seat of the chair, was based on rather dubious reasoning. "Characteristic" seems to have been one of MacFall's two most favourite words—the other being "typical"—but no bloodstain is so characteristic that it can have originated in only one way; great experience is needed in order to draw anything like correct conclusions, and MacFall's experience was certainly not as great as he imagined and stated it to be.

Many of the "soda-water bottle marks" he found may have been caused by blood flying from the murder weapon, after the first blow was struck. Mrs Wallace was lying across the hearthrug, and her murderer must have stooped or knelt beside the body to deliver the subsequent blows: blood from the murder weapon would have described a similar trajectory to the one deduced by MacFall, and would have formed "characteristic" marks on the walls and furniture. Another point is that Mrs Wallace was almost certainly falling while the blood gushed from her head—this could have caused some of the drops to swerve, to alter their direction slightly, and to form misleadingly-shaped stains. A third point: MacFall found the largest proportion of "soda-water bottle marks" in the area round the sideboard, several feet from the fireplace. Blood spurting from a long distance will quickly gravitate towards the ground, and, even if the spurt was originally travelling horizontally, the stain it produces may show the exclamation mark pointing in the opposite direction to the actual movement.

The fact that MacFall found most of the "soda-water bottle marks" less than four feet from the ground was insufficient evidence to support his theory that Mrs Wallace was sitting in the easy chair when the first blow was struck.

But he went further than this, suggesting that Mrs Wallace "had been sitting on that chair, with the head a little forward, slightly to the left, as if talking to somebody".

Perhaps he was right. Unfortunately his theory was never tested. The rough sketches he made, showing the shape and position of the bloodstains, were not seen by other medical experts until MacFall was actually giving his evidence at the trial. By that time it was too late. In any case, the sketches were so rough as to be almost useless.

Within three-quarters of an hour of his arrival at 29 Wolverton Street, MacFall had made all the observations he thought necessary in the parlour.

He had also observed the demeanour of the dead woman's husband, and been "very much struck" with it.

"It was abnormal," he later stated. "He was too quiet, too collected. . . . Whilst I was in the room examining the body and the blood, he came in smoking a cigarette, and he leant over in front of the sideboard and flicked the ash into a bowl upon the sideboard. It struck me at the time as being unnatural."

Odd behaviour, indeed. A wonder that MacFall did not refer to it as being "characteristic"—characteristic of a murderer rather than a bereaved husband. But was Wallace's behaviour as odd as all that? Does the sudden and violent death of a wife provoke the same reaction from all husbands? Can grief—or any other emotion, come to that—be judged from its outward signs?

There are two ways of looking at the question of Wallace's behaviour. If he was innocent of the murder of his wife, then his behaviour was unusual; his grief must have been either deadened by shock or disguised behind a mask of stoicism. But if he was guilty, then his behaviour was more unusual still. Almost certainly, his paramount emotion was that of fear—fear of being found out, arrested, hanged. In most men, surely, such fear would have provided a powerful incentive to deception. Although Wallace was not the consummate actor that people afterwards made him out to be, he could easily have counterfeited an appropriate distress, mimicked the outward signs of a grief that he did not feel. In this situation and setting, both of which were worthy of the highest excesses of Grand Guignol, he could hardly have overplayed his performance.

Returning to the house, Detective-Superintendent Moore found two Anfield C.I.D. officers waiting for him. (Moore's delay in arriving at the scene of the crime has been explained, but no explanation can be offered for the gap of an hour and a half between the time the murder was reported and the time the first members of the local C.I.D. showed up.)

The senior of the two officers was Detective-Inspector Herbert Gold, an ex-Guardsman, dark-haired and prominently jaw-boned, who, at the age of forty-seven, was already looking forward to his retirement from the police force. He was insured by the Prudential, and Wallace had been calling at his house for about ten years to collect the premiums. The other officer was Detective-Sergeant Harry Bailey, a large, jovial, farmer-faced man, who could drink beer until the cows came home, and who—although considered to be a first-class detective—was too easy-going ever to achieve a rank higher than that of sergeant.

The three men—all of them wearing bowlers, the traditional headgear of the C.I.D.—stood in the hall for a few minutes, discussing the case in general and the behaviour of the dead woman's husband in particular. Gold said that he had seen Wallace sitting in the kitchen: "He had the cat on his knee and was stroking the cat. . . . I didn't see any sign of emotion in him at all at the death of his wife."

Bailey agreed with Gold's comments. "Wallace," he said, "impressed me as a very cool, collected man—cool under the circumstances."

Moore, a great believer in the saying that a still tongue makes a wise head, listened to the other two officers, but said very little himself. He was thinking of the last murder case he had been connected with—the brutal slaying of an Irish Catholic in the Scotland Road area of Liverpool. On that occasion the dead man's wife had gone almost berserk, tearing her hair, throwing pieces of furniture about, and screaming imprecations to the Almighty and a large number of her favourite saints. Her behaviour had gone a long way towards satisfying Moore of her innocence, an innocence that was eventually proved. Using his own simple brand of logic, Moore decided that if the Irish woman's behaviour had been that of an innocent wife, then Wallace's behaviour, the exact opposite, was almost certainly that of a guilty husband. His suspicion of Wallace, based on a comparison between an Irish Catholic woman and an English agnostic man, was strengthened by the knowledge that, in the majority of cases, the killing of a wife was proved to be the husband's doing.

The discussion broke up. Gold and Bailey searched the house, starting in the parlour and continuing upstairs, while Moore went into the kitchen to have another word with Wallace.

"Where did you find the cash-box when you returned?" he asked.

"Where it is now," Wallace said.

Moore lifted the cash-box down, looked inside, replaced it on the top shelf. He was looking straight at Wallace as he said, "I can't understand why a thief would go to all that trouble, putting the lid on the box and placing it back where he had found it."

Wallace made no reply, but simply shook his head and shrugged slightly to show that he was equally baffled by the criminal's tidiness.

Moore asked Wallace to accompany him on a tour of the upstairs part of the house, and the first room they visited was Wallace's laboratory.

"There was a number of tools," Moore later stated, "and I asked him to have a good look round to see if there was a tool missing. There was a couple of hammers there and other weapons, and he had a good look round and said, 'I cannot see anything missing.'

"Then we went into the bathroom, and there was nothing in the bathroom, with the jet burning. In the bedroom, which we next visited, there was a light burning, and nothing appeared to be disturbed in this room whatever. . . . On the mantelpiece I saw a little pot, which I looked in and could see there were some Treasury notes there.

"There was no light in the front room, and the blinds were not drawn. The bedding was disturbed on the left inside the door. It appeared to me as though a person had just come in and taken the two pillows and flung them across the bed to the window side of the fireplace. It did not give the impression of a thief looking for valuables."

"Was this bedroom like this earlier today?" Moore asked.

"I cannot say," Wallace replied. "I cannot say I have been in this room for a fortnight."

Returning downstairs, Moore asked Wallace for his front-door key; and while Wallace stood in the hall with Inspector Gold, Moore tried the key in the lock. "I worked it for a couple of seconds," he later stated, "and I found out what was the matter. I went outside and pulled the door to me and locked it, and I opened it at the first attempt."

Pocketing the key, Moore said, "I could open the door all right—but the lock is defective."

"It wasn't like that this morning," Wallace said. He did not tell

Moore what he had earlier told P.C. Williams—that the front door was bolted when he returned home. If this was true, then obviously the door could not have been opened, no matter what state the lock was in.

After sending Wallace back to the kitchen Moore went into the parlour to complete his search of the house. Whether by accident or by design, his entrance coincided with Professor MacFall's exit from the murder room; for all the notice they took of one another, they might have been working on different cases rather than inter-locking aspects of the same case.

But if there was a lack of communication between Moore and MacFall, there was also a less obvious but equally damaging lack of communication between Moore and the other police officers. With no specific duties assigned to them, the detectives hurried about the house in a haphazard search for possible clues, each man conducting a separate investigation, without reference to the activities of his colleagues. A murder investigation was turned into a sort of undisciplined scavenger hunt, a free-for-all, a contest to see who could find the most clues in the shortest possible time. Many items that were later to be used as exhibits were re-discovered three or four times over, picked up, examined, and replaced in *roughly* the same position. The cash-box, for example: when eventually examined for fingerprints it was found to be covered with them, inside and out; apart from those identified as the Wallaces', the box was abundantly petalled with the prints of at least three members of the police—official handiwork had obliter-ated and smeared prints that might have provided a vital clue to the identity of the murderer.

Wallace had hardly returned to the kitchen before Moore called him back to the doorway of the parlour to ask, "How did you find the blinds in the parlour when you returned home?"

"The blinds were drawn and the gas was not lit," Wallace said. "I lit a match."

"Did you not scream or shout?"

"No. I lit the gas. I thought she might be in a fit and I could go to her assistance."

Before calling Wallace, Moore had taken a quick look at the mackintosh and noticed that it was lying "round the shoulder and tucked in by the side, as though the body was a living person and you were trying to make it comfortable; no portion was resting under the body."

Sergeant Bailey, who had been in the parlour for some time, had made a more thorough examination of the mackintosh, and had discovered two spent matchsticks in the folds. (The matchsticks which Mrs Johnston had noticed earlier in the evening, lying on the floor beside the body, had now completely disappeared, so it seems certain that those discovered by Bailey were the same ones; either the mackintosh had been moved and had covered the matchsticks, or, less likely, they had been kicked into the folds.) Bailey had also found that the mackintosh was quite severely burnt on the right side, near the hem. Noticing, too, a large number of fragments of burnt material on the hearthrug, he had assumed that the damage to the mackintosh had been caused by contact with the gas-fire. He had communicated his findings, and his assumption, to Moore, who now pointed to the mackintosh and asked Wallace if it belonged to him.

Stooping slightly, Wallace put his left hand to his chin, but made no reply.

After waiting "for probably half a minute or so" Moore asked, "Had Mrs Wallace a mackintosh like this?"

Still no reply.

From Wallace's silence Moore drew the inference that "he was beginning to think the mackintosh was dangerous, and that the police had formed a certain idea". No doubt Moore was right about this. But he was wrong in using the inference as an indication of Wallace's guilt. He did not know that Wallace had already admitted ownership of the mackintosh to Mrs Johnston; to P.C. Williams and Police Sergeant Breslin; and to an unidentified, "tall" officer —probably Gold—who had come into the kitchen while Wallace was sitting there with the Johnstons, and said, "There's a mackintosh here, Mr Wallace. What about it?"

Whether innocent or guilty, any man in Wallace's position, taking for granted a liaison between the members of the police force, might well have hesitated before admitting *for the fourth time* that the mackintosh was his.

Moore turned to Bailey, who was standing in front of the sideboard. "Take it up and let's have a look at it."

Although Bailey may have questioned the wisdom of moving the mackintosh before photographs had been taken of the murder room, he did as he was told, lifting the mackintosh by the collar and holding it up for inspection.

"It's a gent's mackintosh," Moore observed, pulling out the sleeves.

Wallace fingered the material. "If there are two patches on the inside it is mine." Finding the patches, he nodded to Moore. "It is mine. I wore it this morning, but, the day turning out fine, I wore my fawn coat this afternoon." He pointed down to the right side of the mackintosh, and added, "Of course, it wasn't burnt like that when I wore it."

"Where did you leave it?"

"Hanging in the hall."

Moore had no other questions to ask. He allowed Wallace to return to the kitchen, while he and Bailey re-positioned the mackintosh beside the body for the benefit of the police photographer, and then went their separate ways, continued their separate investigations.

By now it was nearly eleven o'clock, and the tiny house was becoming overcrowded with plain-clothes and uniformed policemen—"about a dozen or so, more or less", according to Moore's estimate.

"When the police were, as I call it, rooting around everywhere," Mrs Johnston said, "I heard Mr Wallace say, 'Julia would have gone mad if she had seen all this.'"

At eleven o'clock Professor MacFall made an interesting discovery in the bathroom.

On the rim of the lavatory-pan—at the front and slightly to the right—was a blood clot measuring three-sixteenths of an inch in diameter and one-eighth of an inch in height; there was a slight streak of blood away from the clot and in the direction of the centre of the pan.

How had the blood got on to the lavatory-pan? There seemed to be only two possible answers.

It could have been picked up accidentally in the parlour and dropped in the bathroom by one of the investigating officers. (Or, for that matter, by MacFall himself, who had been moving about in the bathroom for five minutes before he discovered the blood clot.) The possibility that the blood had been deposited by one of the detectives, or by MacFall, was strengthened by the fact that it was not noticed until eleven o'clock, nearly two hours after the arrival of P.C. Williams, during which time several policemen had searched the bathroom. If it was there all the time, how had it escaped the notice of these supposedly trained observers?

MacFall had an answer for this. "The gas is to the right of the window," he said, "and it throws a shadow over the pan . . . and it is quite in the shade, quite dark." But this did not sound very convincing: it takes a good deal of shadow to hide a blood clot on a background of white porcelain, and, in any case, the police were using torches.

MacFall preferred to think that the blood had been dropped by the murderer. Positive that the crime could not have been committed without the murderer getting bloodstains on his body,[1] MacFall decided that the blood clot on the lavatory-pan was an indication that the murderer had washed himself in the bathroom before leaving the house. Why else, he reasoned, should the murderer have gone into the bathroom if not to rid himself of the tell-tale stains? If MacFall was right, then the blood clot was a strong, if rather oblique, pointer to Wallace's guilt, since it seemed unlikely that an unknown assailant would have taken the risk of remaining in the house to wash himself after the murder; he would surely have wanted to get as far away as fast as possible, hoping that the bloodstains on his body would not be visible in the darkness outside. On the other hand, supposing that he had decided to take the risk of being discovered in the house, it was hard to explain why he should have washed himself in the bathroom rather than the back kitchen, where there was a supply of hot and cold water, as well as a convenient door for a hasty exit.

MacFall made a very thorough examination of the bathroom, but found no evidence to support his theory. A rather grubby white towel which hung over the side of the bath was completely dry, as was the bath itself. "There was no sign of any colouring, blood or otherwise," on a large nail-brush, the bristles of which were moist and the wooden handle partly dry.

After informing the police of his discovery MacFall continued his search for bloodstains in the other parts of the house, paying special attention to the hall and the stairs. His search went unrewarded.

At ten minutes to midnight Dr Hugh Pierce, the Police Medical Officer, arrived to assist MacFall. Pierce—a rather absent-minded and unworldly little man, who preferred the company of dogs to human beings—went into the parlour to examine the body. MacFall accompanied him.

It will be remembered that, when MacFall examined the body at 9.50, he observed the presence of rigor mortis in the neck and the upper part of the left arm; from this he concluded that death had occurred four hours before.

---

[1] In his preliminary report to the police MacFall said that "the effect of the blows was like hitting and bursting a bag with a wet sponge in it".

Now, at 11.50, Pierce also observed the presence of rigor mortis in the neck and the upper part of the left arm—but he concluded that death had occurred *six hours before*.

In other words, Pierce's conclusion contradicted MacFall's, but only in order to confirm MacFall's opinion that Julia Wallace had died at about six o'clock. Instead of agreeing to differ, Pierce differed to agree. Unanimity was achieved at the expense of integrity.

With the aid of one of the floodlamps provided by the Fire Brigade, Superintendent Moore inspected the doors and ground-floor windows at the front and back of the house, but found no sign of forcible entry. He went back into the house, which was now crowded with about twenty people, including the dozen or so policemen, the two medical examiners, Wallace, the Johnstons, and Amy Wallace and her son Edwin.

Now, at long last, Moore decided to relieve the congestion. After sending a few of the policemen away he went into the kitchen and asked Wallace to accompany Gold and Bailey to Anfield Police Station to make a full statement. Wallace agreed to do this; but he did not agree so readily to the suggestion that he should spend the remainder of the night at his sister-in-law's flat in Sefton Park. "I don't want to put anybody out," he kept saying. But his small protests were quickly pushed aside by Moore, who insisted that it was out of the question for him to sleep at home that night.

The news of the murder had spread rapidly through the neighbourhood, and a large crowd was gathered in Wolverton Street when Wallace, flanked by the two Anfield C.I.D. men, emerged from the house. The crowd shuffled forward, their voices rising for a moment, then dying to a whisper-flecked silence as Wallace was hustled into a waiting police car.

The silence was short-lived. Before the car had turned the corner into Richmond Park the crowd was buzzing with the rumour that Wallace had been arrested. The rumour grew in strength and size, and when James Caird arrived in the street a few minutes later he was told by several people that Wallace had broken down and confessed to the murder of his wife. One person, more imaginative than the rest, swore that he had seen a pair of handcuffs glinting on Wallace's wrists.

At the police station Wallace's hands and clothing were examined, but no trace of blood was found upon them. He made his first recorded statement[1], and then answered a series of questions put by Gold, who later stated in evidence:

"I asked him if he heard anybody moving about in the house when he got back, and he said, 'I think someone was in the house when I went to the front door, because I could not open it, and I could not open the back door.' I asked him if his wife would be likely to let anyone in the house during his absence . . . and he said, 'No, she would not admit anyone unless she knew them personally; if anyone did call she would show them to the parlour.'

"I asked him if his wife had any money, and he said, 'I think she had some, but I do not know where she keeps it.'

"I asked him if he knew anyone who knew he was going to the chess club . . . and he said, 'No, I have told no-one I was going, and I cannot think of anyone who knew I was going.' "

While Wallace was being questioned Harry Bailey returned to Wolverton Street to supervise the removal of the body to the mortuary. As the body was turned over and lifted into a wooden shell the detective noticed three severe horizontal burns on the front of the dead woman's blood-stained skirt, "directly opposite her private parts". The burns, like those on the mackintosh, appeared to have been caused by contact with the hot fire-clays of the gas-fire.

Here, then, was a strong indication that, after the first blow was struck, Mrs Wallace had fallen against the fire and been dragged away to the position in which she was found; and it could also be deduced, but with a lesser degree of authority, that the murderer had seized Mrs Wallace by the neck of her jumper (which was badly torn on the left-hand side), and by her hair (thus pulling off the hair-pad, which was lying on the hearthrug, some inches from her head).

At Prince's Dock Mortuary the clothing was stripped from the body, and Mrs Wallace's undergarments were found to be not only old and shabby, but also, to use Bailey's words, "rather unconventional".

The underskirt, which was obviously home-made, was fashioned from a length of woollen material only slightly lighter in weight than the skirt itself. (Although the front of the skirt was burnt right through, there was no sign of scorching on the underskirt.) The corsets were frayed and loose-fitting, and it seemed to Bailey that they had been worn, not for support, but simply as a means of

[1] See Appendix.

suspending the stockings. What at first sight appeared to be a small patch on the side of the corsets turned out to be a pocket containing a one-pound note and a ten-shilling note. The oddest of all Mrs Wallace's odd undergarments was the last to be taken from the body—an unhemmed square of white flannel, folded into a triangle and pinned in the position of a diaper.

It was after 2 A.M. when Bailey returned to Wolverton Street, and he spent the next hour or so assisting Moore in yet another—and, once again, unfruitful—search for traces of blood outside the parlour. Then, deciding that it was time to clear up and clear out, he took possession of Mrs Wallace's handbag; the three coins found near the base of the shelves on the kitchen floor; and, from the mantelpiece in the middle bedroom, the ornamental pot containing four one-pound notes (which he placed, still folded together, in an envelope), a postal order for 2s. 4d., and a half-crown.

He drove to police headquarters, where, immediately upon arrival, he removed the one-pound notes from the envelope—for no other reason, apparently, than to count them before handing them, together with the rest of the items collected from the house and the body, to a station officer for safe-keeping.

There was no need for Bailey to unfold the notes: placed on a table, they unfolded automatically. And he saw that the top note—the note, that is, which had been in the centre as they were folded—was smeared with blood on the extreme left-hand side. The smear was heaviest at the bottom of the note, gradually narrowing as it went up.

There seemed little doubt that the smear had been caused by a bloodstained finger or thumb being drawn across the surface of the note. But *whose* finger or thumb? There were five possible answers to this question, but the police—for obvious reasons—only considered four of them.

1. Supposing that Mrs Wallace was murdered by an intruder, or by someone she admitted to the house after her husband had left for his appointment with the mythical R. M. Qualtrough. After committing the murder this person went upstairs to the middle bedroom and handled the notes in the pot. But this was unlikely, the police decided. The broken cabinet and cash-box, the money which Wallace said had been stolen, indicated a motive of financial gain; therefore why should the notes have been touched but not taken?

2. Supposing that Mrs Wallace was murdered by her husband. If so, then the material evidence of theft was fabricated by Wallace

Wolverton Street

"Thirty-four small, red-brick houses
...already a street of sadness,
of tragedy".

No. 29

Photo Stanley Walton

Left: Detective-Sergeant Harry Bailey in the entry behind 29 Wolverton Street

Right: The back yard of 29 Wolverton Street

"As Wallace walked across the yard, he looked over his shoulder to say: 'She won't be out. She has such a bad cold.'"

as a means of diverting suspicion from himself. It was he who had broken the cabinet and the cash box: had he also thought of removing the notes from the pot and then, with the notes actually in his hand, decided against the idea?

3. The explanation put forward by the defence at the trial was (in the words of the brief) "that the smear was made by Wallace himself when he went upstairs with P. C. Williams and handled the notes, after having previously held his wife's hand, and also handled the bloodstained mackintosh".

4. The smear of blood may have had no connection with the crime; in other words, the blood may have been deposited on the note *before* the night of the murder. An unlikely coincidence? Perhaps so. But, as a high-ranking C.I.D. officer remarked recently to the present writer, "In most murder cases there are as many coincidences as clues."

At the committal proceedings William Roberts, the City Analyst, stated:

"I stained other notes and left them varying dates, folded up as these others were, and that is why I say the stained note was consistent with its having been stained on the 20th January."

After reading Roberts' deposition, James Henry Dible, Professor of Pathology at the University of Liverpool, observed, "It is not clear how the witness arrives at his conclusion upon this point. . . . He could not make a comparison unless he already had in his possession a series of bloodstained notes of different ages. Change of colour is an inexact guide and depends upon many factors—*e.g.*, exposure to air and light, acidity of the atmosphere, condition of the paper, etc. I know of no reliable estimate of the age of stains upon paper, and this is also the opinion of Lucas (*Forensic Chemistry*, p. 23), who says, 'there is at present no reliable test for the age of bloodstains'."

5. The blood may have been deposited upon the note during the investigation. According to Roberts, "the smear was distinct . . . it extended right the way up to the top"; the notes were not folded tightly so as to obscure the surface of the top note: yet *seven hours* elapsed between the start of the investigation and the discovery of the smear of blood. Considering how the other articles of an evidential nature in the house were examined and re-examined, over and over again, it is difficult to explain how the bloodstained note escaped attention. Moore stated that, in the early stages of the investigation, he and Inspector Gold "looked at" the notes; neither of these trained observers saw the smear of blood—perhaps for the

E

simple reason that, *at that time*, there was no smear of blood to be seen.

Not long after Bailey had left for police headquarters Hubert Moore decided to call it a night. Leaving two uniformed constables on duty at the house, he and the other officers drove to Anfield Police Station, where Wallace was still waiting, some three hours after completing his statement to Gold.

As soon as Moore appeared Wallace stood up, resting his hands on a table in front of him. The table was bare, except for an ashtray containing the evidence of the large number of cigarettes he had smoked. Several minutes passed before Moore acknowledged Wallace's presence; he spoke in low tones to Gold and then walked across to Wallace and dropped a copy of the statement on the table.

"Is there nothing more you'd like to tell us, Mr Wallace?"

Wallace shook his head.

"You're sure?" Moore persisted.

" What about?" Wallace's voice was little more than a whisper.

Moore did not reply. The two men stood in silence, one on either side of the table.

The scene was recently recalled by a retired police officer in these words: "They were both tall men. Wallace especially. But Hubert Moore was big, thickset. I don't know which of them was more exhausted. Wallace was blinking a lot, but I don't think this was due to nervousness—not altogether, anyway; it was just that he could hardly keep his eyes open. They just stood there, the two of them. If anyone had waved a bus ticket I think both of them would have toppled over."

Still looking at Wallace, Moore picked up the copy of the statement and, without bothering to fold the foolscap pages, stuffed it into his pocket. Then he turned and walked away.

Accompanied by Inspector Gold, Wallace was driven to his sister-in-law's first-floor flat at 83 Ullet Road, where a bed had been made up for him on the couch in the living-room. Gold did not go along just for the ride: he followed Wallace into the house and took statements from Amy Wallace and her son Edwin.

Edwin, a first-year medical student at Liverpool University, stated: "Except for periods of absence at boarding school I have been in close touch with my uncle and his wife. I never saw any quarrels between them, or anything other than an atmosphere of mutual trust and happiness. Up in the upstairs back room my uncle has a laboratory. My aunt rather objected to his being up in the back room, as she said it was too cold and damp for him, as he was not strong. There was no hint of ill-feeling about this."

Amy Wallace had this to say: "I visited the Wallaces frequently, and very often they would play music to us for an hour or so. Everything about the household was perfectly normal, and seemed very happy. Mr Wallace relied on his wife a great deal to look after him. She did it without his bothering, and, for example, she would change his wet clothes when he had been out collecting. On the evening of Sunday 18th January last I was at Wolverton Street with my son, and everything passed off in the usual way. As usual, the Wallaces were very comfortable and happy, except that Mrs Wallace had a cold. Mrs Wallace was telling us about a burglary about two doors down the road."

One of the main reasons for the police's suspecting Wallace of his wife's murder was his "cool and collected" demeanour. But, like the Johnstons, neither Amy Wallace nor her son thought that he had behaved in a manner inappropriate to a bereaved husband.

Amy Wallace stated: "I and my son were taken into the house by the back way, having been directed to do so by the police. Mr Wallace was sitting by the fire in the kitchen, almost heart-broken, very much cut up, and crying. Usually he is rather a calm man, but tonight he was very much upset indeed, as was to be expected."

According to Edwin: "He was awfully upset, and had his handkerchief to his eyes, as he was crying profusely. I told my uncle I was terribly sorry, and he said, 'Yes, I realize that, and nothing said at this time can help.' He continued to be terribly upset all the time we were there."

At about 5 A.M., with the statements completed and signed, Gold left the flat and drove back to the station. As soon as he was gone Wallace lay down on the couch.

"Aren't you going to undress?" Amy asked him.

He shook his head wearily. His eyes were filled with tears as he murmured, "I shall miss her terribly."

Amy turned off the living-room light and walked to the door.

"Yes, naturally," she said, "because she's looked after you so well."

All through the night, all over Liverpool, the search went on for a man with bloodstains on his clothing or body. A small army of policemen patrolled the Pier Head, examining the passengers boarding the ferries to the Wirral side of the river; other policemen stood at the platform barriers in the three main railway stations. The police visited lodging houses, all-night cafés, shebeens, brothels, and the homes of known criminals. At the Salvation Army hostel in Norton Street the night was made restless by police activity—so restless, in fact, that, the following morning, the superintendent of the hostel received a deputation of men demanding a refund of their "bed money".

Although the full-scale search produced no results as far as the murder was concerned, it was not an entire waste of time and effort. A man in Everton, known to the police as a petty thief, was asked to explain why he was wearing a large bandage on one of his hands. Told the reason for the inquiry, he at once confessed that he had cut his hand on some broken glass while breaking into a shop—a shop, he added fearfully, that was nowhere near Anfield. He was arrested and charged, and appeared in court the next day.

Wolverton Street was quiet for a few hours.

At No. 29 the two policemen who had been left on duty made themselves comfortable in the kitchen. While one of them dozed in Wallace's armchair, the other searched the shelves beside the range for a book to help pass the time until they were relieved at seven. He did not think much of Wallace's literary tastes: nearly all the books were scientific works, and the rest were mostly classics. *The Hunting of the Snark* was sandwiched between *The Mentality of Apes* and *The Quantum Theory*, and these in turn were flanked by well-thumbed copies of *The Life of Gordon* and *The Meditations of Marcus Aurelius*.

At the end of one of the shelves, lying one on top of the other, were four large page-a-day diaries for the years 1928 to 1931. The policeman slid them from the shelf and settled down at the table for a quiet read.

Inside the front cover of each diary Wallace had meticulously filled in the details of his height and weight and age, his hat, collar, and glove sizes. He was a conscientious diarist: few of the pages were left blank. As well as recording the events of his not very eventful life, he had set down his thoughts on a wide range of subjects.

On January 7th, 1928, he had written that he had "fallen out" with Julia because she was buying too many newspapers. This was the only instance recorded in the diaries of a quarrel between them. If the diaries presented a true picture of their life together during the previous three years, then Wallace, it seemed, far from having any motive for murdering his wife, had every reason to hope that she would live to a ripe old age.[1]

The Wallaces' compatability was not so complete as to exclude differences of opinion between them. On March 20th, 1929, they had listened to a radio broadcast of Ibsen's *The Master Builder*. Wallace had thought it "a fine thing", but Julia was unimpressed. "Curious that Julia did not appreciate this play! I feel sure she did not grasp the inner significance and real meaning of the play."

Their views on religion were diametrically opposed. Most Sundays Julia attended the morning service at Holy Trinity Church, but Wallace was "indifferent to the dogmas and ritual of the Churches and Chapels ... if there is a hereafter the man without any so-called religious beliefs, and a non-church attender, but who lives a decent life, and who abstains from telling lies, or cheating, or acts of meanness, and who honestly tries to do good, has as much chance of getting there as the professed Christian who attends his place of worship regularly".

Less than a fortnight before the murder—on January 7th, 1931 —Wallace had written:

"A night of keen frost. The heavy fog gives a wonderful appearance to all plants and trees. Every twig and leaf was most beautifully bordered and outlined with a white rim of frost. Holly leaves, owing to their wavy edges, presented a most charming appearance, and I cannot recollect an occasion on which the hoar had produced such wonderfully beautiful effects.

"After dinner I persuaded Julia to go into Stanley Park. She was equally charmed. A gradual thaw seems to be settling in now."

---

[1] Some writers on the case, working on the heads-I-win, tails-you-lose principle, have suggested that Wallace killed his wife because they were *too* happy together—because he became bored to death with the sheer monotony of contentment.

The Day After

WEDNESDAY, January 21st

This was a puzzler.

Wednesday was a busy day for the telephone operator at police headquarters. Long before the news of the murder appeared in the early editions of the two Liverpool evening papers (the crime received no mention in the morning paper, the *Daily Post*), the switchboard was a mess of wires, the operator's ears buzzed with voices, many of them female, most of them anonymous. As the day wore on, the volume of calls increased.

In the main the calls came from cranks or from people who were simply curious to know more about the murder and naïve enough to think that the police might provide them with a few inside details. One person telephoned to offer astrological assistance in discovering the identity of the murderer; another, claiming power as a faith healer, offered to lay hands on the body of Julia Wallace as a means of reviving her. Neither of these offers was accepted.

The call which produced the most spectacular results—although not at all in the way anticipated—came from a man who said that, until recently, the Wallaces had employed a maid, and that Wallace and the maid were lovers. The caller (who, needless to say, preferred to remain anonymous) suggested that the police should put two and two together: Wasn't it obvious, he asked rhetorically, that Julia had found out about the illicit relationship and got rid of the maid; and that Wallace, tit for tat, had got rid of his wife in order to continue the relationship, which he hoped would eventually, after a decent period of mourning, be sanctified by marriage?

Anonymous or not, the man sounded so definite in what he said, his triangle-motive theory was so geometrically tidy, that the police decided to check up. If there was no maid there was no motive. The obvious person to ask about the Wallaces' domestic help was Wallace himself, who had arrived at police headquarters at 10 A.M. and spent most of the morning giving fuller details of his movements, and of the people he had encountered, while searching for Menlove Gardens East.

Wallace said that he and his wife had never employed a maid. The only assistance his wife had needed in running the tiny house was from a charwoman who came in on Wednesday mornings. He could not remember her name, but he believed she lived somewhere in the West Derby district.

Inspector Gold was given the task of tracing the woman—a simple task, as it turned out, since she had called at 29 Wolverton Street earlier on this Wednesday morning with the intention of carrying out her normal cleaning duties. Before being turned away she had left her name and address with one of the policemen at the house: Mrs Sarah Draper, 38 Tollerton Street, West Derby.

She told Inspector Gold that she had worked for the Wallaces for nine months. "I think it was Mr Wallace's idea for me to do the cleaning. Mrs Wallace was never very well, and she was not strong enough to do any rough work about the house. I used to clean the house right through, and I was paid 2s. 6d. for the half-day. Mrs Wallace used to help me. I have not been for two weeks because I lost my husband. The last time I was at the house was on January 7."

Driven back to Wolverton Street by Gold, Mrs Draper was asked to "take a good look round to see if anything is missing". Having done so, she informed the inspector that there was no sign of a thin poker, about nine inches long, which normally rested beside the kitchen range.

And something else was missing:

"A large piece of iron, about a foot long and about as thick as a candle, and it always stood in the fireplace in the parlour."

The piece of iron was used, Mrs Draper said, for raking cigarette-ends and spent matches from beneath the gas-fire. She particularly remembered seeing it on her last visit to the house, because she had used it to retrieve a screw that had fallen from one of the gas-brackets and rolled under the fire.

Gold telephoned this information to police headquarters, and it was arranged that Wallace should go to the house to make a similar search.

But Wallace noticed nothing missing from its accustomed place, except for a wooden chopper—which was promptly found by Gold in the cupboard under the stairs. Told of what Mrs Draper had said, Wallace replied, "Perhaps she has thrown the poker away with the ashes. I don't know anything about a bar of iron in the parlour."

While Wallace was searching the house Mrs Draper was taken to the mortuary, where she described the missing piece of iron to Professor MacFall. Could it have been used as the murder weapon? he was asked.

MacFall deliberated for a moment, then gave his opinion: Taking into account the estimated weight of the piece of iron, its size and shape, it could quite conceivably have been used in the commission of the crime. (What MacFall did not take into account, apparently, was the *condition* of the piece of iron, which Mrs Draper said was "heavily rusted". Great force had been used to inflict the blows on Julia Wallace's head, yet no traces of rust were found in the wounds. Negative evidence? . . . Of course; but in the field of forensic medicine negative evidence is often the most conclusive evidence of all. In many instances it is the *absence*, rather than the *presence*, of evidence which leads the forensic expert to the solution to a problem: a classic example of this is found in the Buck Ruxton case.)

At police headquarters Superintendent Moore called a conference of C.I.D. officers, at which it was unanimously agreed that the only reason for the iron bar being missing was that it had been used as the murder weapon and afterwards removed from the house by the murderer. "It may take some time to find—but we'll find it," Moore said confidently.

The police belief in Wallace's guilt was demonstrated by the fact that the search for the iron bar was confined to two areas— Richmond Park and Menlove Gardens—and to the vicinity of the tram-stop at Smithdown Road. If Wallace was the murderer, then he could have disposed of the weapon only (*a*) before boarding the first of the three trams that took him to Menlove Gardens; (*b*) between the time he alighted from the first tram and boarded the second; or (*c*) during the time he spent looking for the non-existent address. Obviously the likeliest place was Richmond Park. Although Wallace could have carried the weapon with him on his journey—concealed, perhaps, beneath his coat—he would surely have considered the possibility that, wherever he hid it and however well contrived the hiding-place, it might later be found; if it was found anywhere along the tram route or in the area of Menlove Gardens it would provide damaging evidence against him.

As well as bringing in dozens of extra policemen from other divisions, Moore called on the assistance of the Sanitation Department to search the drains and even the main sewers, and to examine the contents of dust-bins. While one detachment of policemen combed the patch of waste land at the bottom end of Wolverton Street, another much larger detachment traversed the grounds of the near-by Belmont Road Hospital and Institution. Other policemen scoured the entries in Richmond Park. The triangular stretch of ground in the centre of Menlove Gardens received similar attention, as did the front gardens of the houses in the neighbourhood.

The search went on for several days, but neither the iron bar nor any other possible murder weapon was discovered.

At midday, after Amy Wallace had made the formal identification, Professor MacFall conducted the post-mortem examination on the body of Julia Wallace.

In his report he stated:

"The body was that of a lightly-built woman of about 55 years of age. The height was about 5 ft 2.

"There was a small recent bruise mark on the inside of the left upper arm. There were no other external marks of violence on the trunk or limbs.

"I removed the matted hair. 2 inches above the zygoma was a large lacerated wound measuring 2 inches by 3 inches from which brain and bone was protruding. On the back of the head, towards the left side, were ten diagonal, apparently incised wounds. . . . The appearance was as if a terrific force with a large surface had driven in the scalp, bursting it in parallel lines. . . .

"The body was healthy. Death was due to fracture of the skull by someone striking the deceased eleven times upon the head with terrific force. My opinion is that one blow was harder and more severe than the rest. That is the blow which produced the front, open wound, and caused death. Death took place in less than one minute."

MacFall did not think of examining the condition of the dead woman's stomach—or, if he did, he must have decided that it was not worth the bother. Either way, forgetfulness or indolence, this was a most important error of omission, since such an examination could have provided vital evidence as to the time of death.

In MacFall's opinion death had occurred not later than six o'clock on the Tuesday evening; yet Wallace said that he had arrived home at about five past six and that he and his wife had then eaten a meal together. Police inquiries roughly confirmed the time of arrival—but, although the dirty dishes found in the back kitchen indicated that the second part of Wallace's statement was also true, they were evidence only of the fact that a meal had been prepared and cleared away, not that it had actually been eaten.

An examination of the stomach would have established whether or not Julia Wallace had eaten this meal. If the stomach had been found to be virtually empty,[1] then MacFall's estimate of the time of death would have been strengthened, perhaps even confirmed—and, more important still, Wallace would have been proved a liar. If, on the other hand, the examination had shown that the meal *had* been eaten, then certain conclusions could have been drawn from the extent of digestion. When death occurs within a few hours after a meal the post-mortem digestion—which normally continues for about twenty-four hours—is very slight. In Julia Wallace's case, therefore, a large stomach content (large in the comparative sense, measured against the size of the last meal) would have indicated that she died soon after eating the meal, possibly before her husband left the house at quarter to seven; if, however, the stomach content had been at all diminished by the digestive process it would have indicated that the murder was probably committed while Wallace was away from the house.

After completing the post-mortem examination MacFall was driven to the University by his chauffeuse-cum-secretary, Miss Florence Brook. There he shut himself away in his laboratory to perform certain chemical tests upon the small clot of blood which, the previous night, after it was photographed, he had scooped from the lavatory-pan on to a piece of glazed paper and placed inside his silver spectacles case.

First of all, he used three tests—Kastle-Meyer's, Teichmann's, and the guaiacum test—to establish that it was definitely blood; he then used the precipitin test to determine whether the blood was of animal or human origin.

He emerged from the laboratory at about five o'clock to give the police his verdict that the clot of blood "had typical human red cells and white corpuscles. No epithelial cells were found in it. This was looked for in view of the fact that the woman was wearing a peculiar piece of cloth, pinned in the position of a diaper, for

---

[1] The stomach of a living person empties in two to six hours, so there might have been a few remains of the meal Julia Wallace had eaten with her husband in the early afternoon.

which I found no reason on post-mortem examination. The blood was not menstrual blood."

Although these conclusions of MacFall's were never questioned, there is some doubt as to whether he did, in fact, perform all the tests he claimed. A few months later, when he was working on a case in which a suspicious stain was found on a piece of clothing, he had to ask another member of the Medical Faculty in the University of Liverpool to perform the precipitin test for him, explaining that he "never could get the hang of it".

Harry Bailey—who, during the whole of the investigation, appears to have been landed with the foot-slogging, errand-running jobs that nobody else wanted to do—spent most of Wednesday checking on the people named Qualtrough living in the Liverpool area.[1] There were fourteen families of that name, and Bailey contacted all of them; but, as he must have anticipated, none of them could throw any light upon the mysterious telephone-call.

Bailey's hope of finding the caller was a forlorn one—but no more forlorn, it seemed, than Moore's hope of tracing the call. By the early afternoon the superintendent's desk was littered with reports and statements: one of the reports was from a detective who had visited the General Post Office in Victoria Street, a stone's throw from police headquarters, and had been told that it was impossible to trace the call; one of the statements was from Gladys Harley, who said that, just before the call was put through, the operator had said, "Anfield calling you. Hold the line."

On the strength of the waitress's statement Moore telephoned the supervisor at the Anfield exchange and asked if any of the operators remembered connecting a call to Bank 3581, the number at the City Café, on Monday evening. The supervisor said she would ring him back.

Within a few minutes she was speaking to Moore again, telling him that none of the operators had any recollection of the call—and adding that this was hardly surprising, considering the large number of calls that were dealt with each day. (Anfield was a "manual" exchange: the operators were responsible for connecting

[1] Qualtrough is a common Manx name. Early in the sixteenth century the prefix Mac was almost universal in the Isle of Man, but it gradually disappeared, the final consonant coalescing with the first consonant of the following personal name and producing the characteristic Manx surnames beginning with C, K, or Q—Costain (MacAustin); Quilliam (MacWilliam); Qualter, Qualters, Qualtrough (MacWalter).

all calls made in the area.) She said that two girls who were on duty on Monday evening had not yet arrived at the exchange, and she would speak to them as soon as they came in.

Moore spent the next hour or so at Wolverton Street, conducting the Chief Constable, Lionel Everett, and his Deputy, Colonel Winstanley, around the house and explaining to them the difficulties of the case.

While he was there Moore received some depressing news from William Roberts, the City Analyst. Earlier in the day the sink in the back kitchen and the basin and lavatory in the bathroom had been removed and taken, with their waste pipes, to Roberts's laboratory. But a microscopical examination of these fittings had failed to reveal any traces of blood. As a postscript to his report, Roberts said that the bath, which he had come to the house to examine, had not been used since it was last cleaned.

Moore drove back to police headquarters. He was not feeling at all happy. His first major case as Head of the C.I.D. was proving to be something of a nightmare.

He had been back in his office only a few minutes when his telephone rang. He lifted the receiver, barked his name, listened.

It took him a second or two to recognize the voice on the line as that of the supervisor at the Anfield exchange. Her voice, previously so clipped, official, unemotional, was now blurred with excitement —so much so, in fact, that Moore had to interrupt to ask her to start again, speaking more slowly this time. She did her best, but still the apparent fantasy of what she had to say prevented complete coherence.

The thousand-to-one chance of tracing the Qualtrough telephone-call had paid off—not just once, not twice, *but three times*.

Moore could hardly believe his ears. The worried look dwindled from his face, was replaced by an expression that combined astonishment with happiness: "Moore looked as if the Pope had just handed him the winning ticket in the Irish Sweep" was how one of the C.I.D. officers put it.

The supervisor explained that the two operators who had been off-duty when Moore first telephoned had now arrived at the exchange—and both of them remembered the call to Bank 3581 on Monday evening. This was staggering news indeed; but there was more to come. The night supervisor also remembered the call. She had a note of the number of the telephone which the caller had used, and of the exact time the call was connected.

Moore wasted no time in having the three girls brought to the central G.P.O. building, where he himself interviewed them.

The name of the first operator was Louisa Alfreds.

"At 7.15 P.M. last Monday," she stated, "I received a call from a public box, Anfield 1627. It was a male voice. I made the connection right away and heard someone from Bank 3581 on the line. About two minutes later Miss Lilian Kelly, another operator, made a communication to me and I saw her endeavouring to get Bank 3581 and I heard the same voice asking, 'Is that the City Café?' I remember the voice particularly by reason of the way he pronounced the 'e' in 'Café'. I remarked to Miss Kelly at the time, 'What a funny thing to say—"City Caf-ay".' "

Lilian Kelly continued the story.

"At about 7.17 P.M. I received a call from Anfield 1627. A man said, 'Operator, I have pressed button A, but have not had my correspondent yet.' I replied to him, and also said something to Miss Alfreds. A light on the board showed that he had pressed button B and received his money back. I tried to get Bank 3581, but failed."

The call had then been referred to the supervisor, Annie Robertson, who stated:

"I spoke to the subscriber, and he explained to me his difficulties and asked me to try Bank 3581. This I did. The trouble was there was no reply from this number. Later, at 7.20, the caller was put through to this number."

Miss Robertson showed Moore the note of the call that she had made at the time, and explained: "It is the usual thing to do when an inquiry is made like that. We just keep it for reference."

The statements of the three girls dovetailed remarkably neatly—but, apart from the last sentence in the supervisor's statement, they bore no relation to the statement made by Gladys Harley, in which she said, "The telephone at the café is in full view, and the bell is audible, and I am absolutely positive that our line had not been used by anyone for the previous half-hour before the call came through."

Louisa Alfreds's statement, then—that she "made the connection right away at 7.15 and heard someone from Bank 3581 on the line" —could not be reconciled with Gladys Harley's.

If the waitress's statement was correct and the telephone at the City Café had not rung before 7.20, it was hardly surprising that Lilian Kelly and Annie Robertson had received no reply. Possibly some mechanical defect prevented the telephone from ringing;

but it must have been a very slight defect, since it was cured when Miss Robertson tried the number a second time.

The three girls from the exchange were unanimous in stating that the caller's voice was "quite ordinary". And Gladys Harley remembered "nothing strange about the voice"—but added that "it seemed like the voice of an elderly gentleman". Samuel Beattie, however, described the voice as "strong and gruff, ready of utterance, confident, definite in knowing what to say, peremptory". The disparity between Beattie's description and the others was taken by the police as an indication that the caller disguised his voice when speaking to the captain of the chess club. Of all the assumptions made by the police, this was one of the most tenuous. The telephone girls' description of the voice was not really a description at all: "quite ordinary" meant simply that, apart from the odd pronunciation of the word 'Café', the voice possessed no marked peculiarities—no impediment, no unusual dialect.

Moore's main concern, of course, was to establish the location of the telephone-box from which the call had emanated. He received the information he needed on this point from Leslie Heaton, a G.P.O. engineer, who stated, "This telephone-box, Anfield 1627, is situated at the northern corner of a triangular-shaped small park at the junction of Breck Road and Rochester Road, Anfield."

Moore marked the position on a map of the district. His gaze descended, but only an inch or so, to where Wolverton Street was shown. He estimated that the distance from the Wallaces' house to the telephone-box by the shortest route was no more than a quarter of a mile. (Which was a good guess: the exact distance—measured a day or two later by William Harrison, Surveyor to the Liverpool Corporation—was 400 yards.)

From the start of the investigation it had been clear that whoever made the telephone-call was the same person who, the following night, murdered Mrs Wallace. But was this person someone who had conceived the idea of the bogus message as a means of luring Wallace away, thus leaving his wife alone and unprotected in the house? . . . Or was it Wallace himself who made the call as a necessary prelude to a cunningly contrived alibi? After taking the statements of the telephone girls and the G.P.O. engineer Moore had no doubt as to the answer: his belief in Wallace's guilt was strengthened to stone-cold certainty. As he later told a *Daily Express* reporter: "Without the telephone evidence, we would never have arrested Mr Wallace."

Wallace's story was that he had left home at about 7.15 on the

Monday evening and walked to the junction of Breck Road and Belmont Road, where he had boarded a tram to North John Street. But there was no-one to substantiate this statement. Moore pointed out that Wallace could just as easily have left home three or four minutes earlier than the time he stated and made his way to the telephone-box; after making the call to the City Café, he could have boarded a tram at a stop only twenty-five yards away.

It is worth noting that, although the police made great efforts to trace the conductors of the trams which Wallace used on his journey to Menlove Gardens, they made no attempt whatever to trace the conductor of the tram that took him to the vicinity of the City Café. There seems to be only one explanation for this. Moore realized that if the conductor were traced his evidence—as to the time of the tram's departure from Breck Road—would either partially confirm or completely demolish the theory that Wallace made the telephone-call. If the theory were demolished, then the whole case against Wallace would be demolished, too. The possible reward for the police for tracing the conductor was small compared with the equally possible penalty. Moore decided to play it safe: an unconfirmed theory was better than no theory at all, no case.

Wednesday evening.

Everyone in Anfield was talking about the murder. It was the main topic of conversation in pubs and clubs and cafés; it brought people together—many of them complete strangers to one another—on street corners, in the lighted doorways of houses and shops. Anyone who had known Mrs Wallace, even if only by sight, inherited a brief celebrity, became a centre of attraction.

In the pubs, especially, quite a few people who had never heard of Mrs Wallace until her death now fabricated first-name friendships with her and concocted memories of her; these fake friends were plied with almost as many free drinks as questions, until, by closing-time, their tipsy imaginations were producing disclosures about Julia Wallace's life that were far more sensational and dramatic than any of the facts surrounding her death.

There were more visitors at the Belmont Road Hospital than on a normal Wednesday evening; they came, most of them, not to comfort the sick, but in the hope of finding out why the police had been searching the hospital grounds that day.

Outside the Church Hall in Richmond Park four children—three fourteen-year-old boys and a girl of thirteen—stood talking about the murder.

One of the boys was Kenneth Caird, the son of Wallace's chess-playing friend, James Caird.

Also there was Harold Jones, who delivered newspapers in the district for Mr Yates, the owner of a stationery shop in Breck Road.

The third boy's name was Douglas Metcalf. Whereas both Caird and Jones were rather timid and shy—Jones, especially—Metcalf possessed a self-assurance far in excess of his years. He too was employed by Mr Yates, and it was his newspaper round that had brought him into contact with the Wallaces:

"Every Tuesday morning at about 7.45 I used to deliver the *Financial Times* to Mr Wallace's house, and the Wallaces were not usually up at that time. Mrs Wallace used to come into our shop a deal, and she used to speak very quickly, and seemed nervous to me. Whenever they came into the shop together they seemed very friendly, and they were nicknamed in the neighbourhood 'Darby and Joan'. I have heard Mr and Mrs Yates call them this."

The girl's name was Elsie Wright. In the mornings and evenings, before and after school, she worked at a dairy in Sedley Street, sharing the job of delivering milk in the Richmond Park area with Alan Close, the son of the people who kept the shop.

"I've just been to 29 Wolverton Street with Alan," she told the three boys. "A policeman answered the door, and he said that we weren't to leave any more milk until further notice."

"Did you deliver the milk there last night?" Douglas Metcalf asked.

"No," Elsie Wright replied. "Wolverton Street is part of Alan's round, not mine. When I saw him first thing this evening in the dairy we talked about the murder. I asked him what time he delivered the milk to Mrs Wallace, and he said, 'Oh, about a quarter to seven.'"

Douglas Metcalf fumbled in his newspaper satchel and produced a copy of the *Liverpool Echo*. He pointed to the account of the murder. "The paper says it was the bread boy[1] who saw her last. Alan ought to go and tell the police it was him, if he saw her at a quarter to seven."

Elsie Wright said that Alan Close would be along any minute. She explained that, as she was "a bit scared of the dark", she had arranged to wait for him outside the Church Hall, so that they could walk together through the unlit entry to Sedley Street.

She had hardly finished speaking before fourteen-year-old Alan Close appeared from the direction of Wolverton Street.

[1] Neil Norbury.

Douglas Metcalf called out to him:

"Hey, Alan, what time did you see Mrs Wallace last night?"

The reply came without hesitation:

"Well, when I took the milk it was a quarter to seven."

"What did she say to you?"

"She told me I had a bad cough and I'd better hurry up home, and she said she had a cough, too."

"Well, the police ought to know that," Douglas Metcalf said, "because in the papers it says that Mr Wallace went out at a quarter past six,[1] and if you saw her at a quarter to seven, people couldn't think Mr Wallace had done it."

Alan Close laughed. "Why should I want to go to the police?"

"Because it would help them out a lot," Douglas Metcalf replied.

Kenneth Caird said, "You'd be a fool not to go, Alan. The police might give you a reward for your information."

But Alan Close seemed to take it all as a huge joke. He jabbed his thumbs under the lapels of his coat and wiggled his fingers. "I'm the missing link," he chortled.

"If you'll go back to the house we'll come with you," Douglas Metcalf offered.

Alan Close was still grinning. "All right, then, come on," he said. He sauntered back towards Wolverton Street, with the other children following. He was so pleased with his remark about the missing link that he kept repeating it. But by the time they reached the house the grin had gone from his face; he was silent.

Elsie Wright knocked on the door.

"You'll stay here, won't you?" Alan Close said nervously.

"Yes, we'll wait," Douglas Metcalf assured him.

A policeman answered the door. He looked first at Elsie Wright, then at Alan Close. "What, you back again?" he said.

"I've come to tell you that I saw Mrs Wallace at quarter to seven last night," Alan Close said.

The policeman contemplated the statement for a moment or so before taking the boy's arm and ushering him into the hall. The door closed behind them.

Alan Close was in the house for less than ten minutes. When he came out the other children clustered round him, expecting to hear a full account of what had happened. But all he would say was: "The police told me that I'm not to mention it to anyone." He

[1] The report in the *Liverpool Echo* (21.1.31) said that "Mr Wallace left home at 6.15 and got back at 7.45".

refused even to explain whether "it" referred to his evidence or to the interview.

"My parents will be wondering where I've got to," he said as he hurried away, with Elsie Wright scampering after him, frightened that he was leaving her to walk through the dark entry alone.

Superintendent Moore was discussing the case with other C.I.D. officers when the message about Alan Close's evidence was telephoned to police headquarters.

Herbert Gold pointed out that there was no doubt that the milk was delivered *some time* during the early evening. "There was a jug of fresh milk in the back kitchen. It's still there."

"It isn't," Harry Bailey murmured. "When I was at the house today I poured the milk into three bowls for the cat."[1]

Gold left the office to ask Wallace if he remembered the milk being delivered the night before. Wallace thought for a moment, then he shook his head. "I can't say that I can remember the milk boy calling," he said. "He may possibly have called while I was upstairs, getting ready to leave the house—if so, I might not have heard his knock."

While Gold was questioning Wallace, Moore telephoned Professor MacFall to tell him about the milk boy's evidence. MacFall's reaction to the news was not entirely unexpected.

"I don't believe it," he wheezed. "I still say that death occurred not later than six o'clock."

Moore slammed down the receiver. "We're stuck between the devil and the deep blue sea," he muttered. His meaning was clear: if MacFall's estimate of the time of death was accurate, then Wallace could not have murdered his wife, since he had not arrived home from work until about five minutes past six; if, on the other hand, Alan Close's evidence was true—and if Wallace did, in fact, leave the house at the time he stated—then the murder must have been committed after Wallace had commenced his journey to Menlove Gardens.

"We'd better start looking for another suspect," one of the younger detectives suggested.

For a few moments there was complete silence in the office. Then Moore spoke. His voice was very quiet.

"No," he said. "The milk boy must be mistaken."

[1] Years later Harry Bailey told a friend: "The Wallace case was different from other murder cases in several respects. It's certainly the only case on record in which material evidence was lapped up by a cat."

* * *

At 10 P.M., twelve hours after his arrival at police headquarters, Wallace was allowed to leave.

Because Amy Dennis, Julia's unmarried sister and only living blood-relation, had arrived in Liverpool and was staying at Amy Wallace's flat, Wallace received permission from the police to spend the night at Wolverton Street.

Amy Dennis did not stay long in Liverpool. The following morning she returned to her home in Brighton, leaving behind a brief statement to the police and an even briefer note to Wallace—not a message of condolence, but a request.

DEAR MR WALLACE,

I would ask for nothing that belonged to my late sister apart from her fur coat as a keep-sake in memory of her. When this trouble is over I would be grateful if you could despatch the coat to me by registered post.

Yours,
AMY DENNIS

Investigation, Rumour, Arrest

THURSDAY, January 22nd–MONDAY, February 2nd

"Contrariwise," continued Tweedledee, "if it was so, it might be; and if it were so, it would be; but as it isn't, it ain't. That's logic."

On Thursday Dr C. G. Mort, the Liverpool City Coroner, formally opened the inquest on Mrs Wallace. The only evidence taken was that of Amy Wallace, who was called to establish identity.

After concluding her evidence Amy Wallace created a stir in the court by complaining that, the previous day, some newspaper reporters had gained admittance to her flat by posing as members of the C.I.D. "When I found out who they were I asked them to leave, but they refused to go unless I answered their questions."

Dr Mort pointed out that it was no part of his duty to take notice of the complaint—"but rather than that you should bottle up your wrath, I will allow you to state your objection."

This Amy Wallace did—at some length and in no uncertain terms. She objected most strongly, she said, not only to the methods employed by the reporters to obtain the interview, but also to the fact that the newspaper had printed an account of the interview without first asking her permission. "They might at least have said, 'Do you mind if we use this in the paper?' "

"Is any part of the account inaccurate?"

"I don't know. I was so annoyed that I have not read it."

"Naturally you are annoyed that you are connected with any case like this—but that is not your fault, is it?" Dr Mort asked, rather obliquely.

Without giving Amy a chance to reply, he hastily adjourned the inquest until February 5th, "by which time we might know what the position is".

Amy Wallace would have been better advised to restrain her anger, or to vent it in some less public place. The account of the interview—innocuous and hardly noticed within the context of matters directly relating to the murder—had appeared in only one paper; but her objection to the interview received a far wider coverage.

Some people, reading the verbatim report of her exchange with Dr Mort—or, at least, reading between the lines of it—decided that she had protested too much. If she so disliked publicity, they asked themselves, why had she caused so much fuss in the inappropriate surroundings of a coroner's court? Was it really anger that had provoked her outburst—or fear that the Press might ferret out information connecting her with the crime?

In the next few days and weeks the ripples of conjecture about Amy Wallace widened to oceanic proportions. As Sir Edward Carson said in the Archer-Shee case, "When suspicion gets into the mind, it is extraordinary what small things seem to confirm it."

One of the small things that seemed to confirm the suspicion about Amy Wallace was the fact that Wallace was staying at her flat. Out of this grew a rumour so strong, so logical in its progression, that it is still accepted by some people in Liverpool as being true. Wallace, it was said, was not *staying* with his sister-in-law: he was *living* with her. If the truth were known, the two had been lovers for years. Julia—a bit slow on the uptake, poor woman—had only recently discovered what was going on. Ergo: Wallace, egged on by Amy, had murdered his wife to prevent the scandal she threatened.

Another rumour had it that Joseph—Amy's husband and Wallace's brother—had not been seen for some time. What had happened to him? . . . Oh, he was dead, of course—murdered, but less obviously than Julia. How he had met his death would soon be found out, because the police were making arrangements to exhume the body. But *why* had he been murdered? The answer to that was simple: his death had left the way clear for Amy to marry Wallace, once Wallace had disposed of Julia. The widow and the widower—both states self-imposed—did not intend to stay single for long. (While the "exhumation rumour" was scuttling around Liverpool, Joseph Wallace was on his way from Malaya to England, to assist in his brother's defence.)

In the main, the rumours about Amy Wallace suggested only that she had provided the motivation for the murder of Julia—or, at most, the instigation of it. But there was one rumour that went further than the rest, suggesting that she had played an active and important part in the crime itself.

Long before Alan Close gave evidence at the committal proceedings there were few people who had not heard that a milk boy had seen Mrs Wallace alive at a time which seemed to preclude the possibility that her husband had killed her. This choice titbit of information was still hot from the grapevine when along came the rumour that the police were working on the theory that the person the milk boy had seen—and conversed with—was not Julia, but Amy Wallace, dressed in her already late sister-in-law's clothes.

There was a variation on this rumour which suggested that the person who answered the door to the milk boy was none other than Wallace himself, whose daring as a criminal was only matched by his brilliance as a female impersonator. After murdering his wife, it was suggested, Wallace had donned some of her clothes (which must have been an extremely tight fit, since he was a foot taller than Julia) and mimicked her voice so successfully that the milk boy, who had been calling at the house for nearly three years, was completely taken in by the deception. The double-barrelled rumour that Mrs Wallace was already lying dead in the parlour when the milk boy called was accepted as the truth by a large number of people—including at least one person who was selected to serve on the jury at Wallace's trial.[1]

Poor Amy Wallace was invested with a false notoriety as a *femme fatale*—as the woman whose charms had proved so fatal to Wallace as to induce the far more drastic fatality to his wife. By her outburst in the coroner's court she sparked off a chain-reaction of rumours connecting her with the crime—and the force of these rumours was strengthened by the fact that she was not called to give evidence at the committal proceedings or the trial. At the beginning she said too much—so, in the opinion of the pioneer rumour-mongers, she was frightened of what might be discovered by the Press; later she said nothing—which was interpreted to mean that she was hiding a guilty secret. No matter what she did, or did not do, Amy Wallace was an unwitting, unwilling contributor to the rumours about herself.

During Thursday morning an identification parade was held at police headquarters. Wallace stood in line with some men of

[1] The "Charley's Aunt Theory" is still put forward by certain students of the case—most recently by John Nance in an article, "A Theory about the Wallace Case" (*Criminology*, May 1964).

similar height and build to himself, and seven persons who had encountered him on the night of the murder were asked to identify him.

These witnesses, in the chronological order of their encounters with Wallace, were:

Thomas Phillips, the conductor of the tram which Wallace boarded at the junction of Smithdown Road and Lodge Lane.

Edward Angus, the ticket inspector who, after boarding the same tram and being told by Phillips that a passenger was uncertain of the location of Menlove Gardens East, gave Wallace instructions on how to get to his imaginary destination.

Arthur Thompson, the conductor of the tram which Wallace boarded at Penny Lane.

Sydney Green, the young clerk who met Wallace in Menlove Gardens West.

Katie Mather, the elderly resident of 25 Menlove Gardens West.[1]

James Sargent, the police constable who met Wallace at the corner of Green Lane and Allerton Road.

Lily Pinches, the manageress of the newsagent's shop in Allerton Road, where Wallace consulted a street directory and at last came to the conclusion that there was no such place as Menlove Gardens East.

After the identification parade, and after statements had been taken from the seven witnesses, the theory that Wallace made the journey to Menlove Gardens with the object of establishing a pre-arranged alibi was strengthened—in the minds of the police, at any rate—by three assumptions:

1. Wallace's repeated reminders to Arthur Phillips that he wanted to get to Menlove Gardens East were intended to impress this fact upon the conductor's memory.

2. Wallace was unnaturally persistent in his inquiries in the Menlove Gardens area—a strong indication that he was anxious that his presence there should be noted by as many people as possible.

3. Before leaving P.C. Sargent and walking away in the direction of the post-office Wallace said, "It is not eight o'clock yet"; he then consulted his watch and said, "It is just a quarter to." The assumption here was that Wallace was not concerned that the post-

[1] Neither Sydney Green nor Katie Mather was able to identify Wallace; but he obliged the police by reversing the normal procedure and identifying *them*.

office might be closed before he arrived there, but that he wanted to impress upon Sargent the exact time of the encounter.

The three assumptions—plus the assumption that because the call to the City Café was made from a telephone-box close to Wallace's home, it must have been Wallace who made it—were enough to convince Moore that the alibi theory was correct. He had to admit, though, that the theory was somewhat undermined by the failure of the police to locate anyone who remembered seeing Wallace before he boarded the tram at Smithdown Road. No-one remembered seeing him as he walked to the tram-stop opposite St Margaret's Church. And no-one remembered seeing him on the tram to Smithdown Road. This was distinctly odd, since it surely must have occurred to Wallace that the most important part of the alibi was the beginning of it—that the time of his departure from the house was the most material time to establish.

Of course, if Wallace was innocent there was no earthly reason why he should have drawn attention to himself during the early part of his journey: he knew how to get to Smithdown Road—it was only from there on that he needed to ask the way.

But why, if he was guilty, did he not invent some excuse for talking to the conductor of the first tram, thus impressing himself upon the man's memory? There appeared to be only two possible answers to this question: perhaps—after murdering his wife, cleaning himself up, fabricating the evidence of robbery, getting rid of the weapon, and hurrying to the tram-stop—he was too breathless to say more to the conductor than "Smithdown Road, please"; either that, or he was in such a state of nerves that he could not trust himself to speak.

Thomas Phillips told the police that, on the Tuesday night, his tram left the junction of Smithdown Road and Lodge Lane at six minutes past seven. Considering this time in relation to Alan Close's statement that Mrs Wallace was still alive at about a quarter to seven, Moore decided to investigate the possibility that Wallace could have murdered his wife directly after she was seen by Close and still have managed to get to Smithdown Road in time to board Phillips's tram.

Seven detectives—Inspector Herbert Gold; Sergeants Harry Bailey, Adolphus ("Dolly") Fothergill,[1] and James Hill; and Constables William Prendergast,[2] Walter Oliver, and William

---

[1] Fothergill was later to become the Deputy Chief Constable of Liverpool.

[2] William Prendergast is now Police Adviser to the BBC television series *Z Cars*.

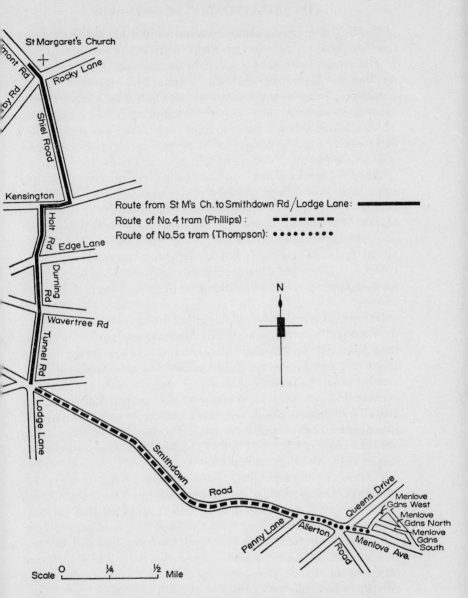

Route from St M's Ch. to Smithdown Rd / Lodge Lane: ━━━━━

Route of No. 4 tram (Phillips) : ▬ ▬ ▬ ▬ ▬

Route of No. 5a tram (Thompson): ● ● ● ● ● ● ● ● ●

Scale 0 ¼ ½ Mile

Gilroy—were given the job of timing the journey. Working singly and in pairs, the detectives walked from 29 Wolverton Street to St Margaret's Church—a distance of 605 yards—and then travelled by tram to Smithdown Road—an additional distance of 1·7 miles.

These "tram tests", as they came to be called, provided an incomplete—and, therefore, unfair—comparison with the duration

of Wallace's journey, in that the detectives timed only the journey
from the house to Smithdown Road, whereas Wallace was timed
from the house to when he boarded the second tram. The tram tests,
in other words, did not take into account the almost inevitable
period of waiting at the Smithdown Road stop for a tram going
towards Menlove Avenue—a period of waiting which could have
added as much as five minutes to some of the times recorded by the
detectives, since the tram service along this route was of 5-6
minutes frequency.

When the results of the tram tests were given in evidence at the
committal proceedings Sydney Scholefield Allen, Wallace's
counsel, grouped the seven detectives together under the collective
title of "The Anfield Harriers". And outside the court the detectives, already known as "Jacks", were referred to as "Spring-
heeled Jacks". Certainly it would seem that at least four of the
detectives were more concerned with establishing a speed record
for the course than with establishing the likely duration of Wallace's
journey.

On one occasion, for example, Harry Bailey managed to cover
the distance from the house to St Margaret's Church in exactly
three minutes. To achieve this time he must have 'walked' at a
speed of 7 m.p.h.—an astonishingly fast rate compared with the
average walking speed of between $3\frac{1}{2}$ and 4 m.p.h. On another
occasion Bailey—this time in company with Sergeant Fothergill—
arrived in Belmont Road to see a tram moving away from a request
stop about fifty yards down the road. The two detectives sprinted
after the tram and boarded it, thus cutting the walking distance by
almost half. Although Bailey and Fothergill left the house two
minutes after Gold and Gilroy, who were also timing the journey,
all four detectives travelled on the same tram to Smithdown Road.

Somewhere in the region of twenty-four tram tests were carried
out by the detectives. Apart from a time of fifteen minutes which
was recorded by Bailey and Fothergill, the times recorded for the
journey varied between a minimum of seventeen minutes and a
maximum of twenty. So—even supposing that Wallace was lucky
enough to have alighted from the first tram at Smithdown Road
and straight away boarded the second—he could not possibly have
left the house any later than 6.49. Far from disproving the time of
departure given in his statement, the tram tests more than adequa-
tely confirmed it.

The police could not complain of lack of public support in trying to solve the crime. Reams of foolscap, reels of typewriter ribbon, and pints of ink were used in taking down statements from people who came forward with information.

One of the statements was from Miss Lily Hall, a young typist employed by Littlewood's, the bookmaking firm, who lived with her parents in Letchworth Street, a few doors away from James Caird.

"I knew Mrs Wallace," she said, "because my mother and I sometimes spoke to her after attending service at Holy Trinity Church. I have never actually spoken to Mr Wallace, but I have known him by sight for three or four years.

"I saw him at 8.35 P.M. on January 20th. He was talking to another man at the bottom of the entry by the Parish Hall. I was walking from Breck Road along Richmond Park, and I was about thirty or forty yards away when I first saw him. I was on the pavement on the opposite side, and I crossed over to reach Letchworth Street. I passed Mr Wallace before I crossed over. I then saw the two men part company. One went down the entry by the Parish Hall, and the other along Richmond Park, walking in the direction of Breck Road.

"I am able to fix the time definitely as 8.35 P.M., because I was on my way to the pictures, and I looked at Holy Trinity Church clock."

If Lily Hall was telling the truth, then her statement was of twofold importance to the police case against Wallace: not only did it show that Wallace was lying when he said that he had not spoken to anyone on his way home from Menlove Gardens, but it also went a long way towards disproving his statement that, after deciding that there was no such place as Menlove Gardens East, he "became suspicious" and *hurried* back home.

There were, however, at least four good reasons for believing that Lily Hall was mistaken.

1. Despite repeated police appeals, the man she claimed to have seen talking with Wallace never came forward. There was little doubt that if Wallace murdered his wife he committed the crime without the aid of an accomplice; even supposing that Wallace did employ an accomplice, it was hardly likely that he would have stopped to chat with him in full view of anyone who happened to be passing. It was virtually certain, then, that if the man existed he had no reason to fear police questioning—and, therefore, no reason (apart, perhaps, from extreme shyness) to ignore the appeals.

2. Why should Wallace have told such a deliberate and un-necessary lie? In so doing he must have recognized the possibility that the man (and Lily Hall—since if she saw Wallace it was reasonable to suppose that he must have seen her) would come forward with an account of the meeting, and so expose him as a liar. No-one was able to explain why Wallace should have lied so recklessly—or, indeed, why he should have lied at all. He could have admitted the encounter and still stuck to his statement that he was in a hurry to get home—all he would have needed to say was that he was not in so great a hurry as to ignore anyone who approached him in the street.

3. Lily Hall said that she was "able to fix the time definitely as 8.35 P.M., because I was on my way to the pictures and I looked at Holy Trinity Church clock". But this statement was contradictory. If she was on her way to the pictures, why was she walking in the direction of her own home, and away from the locality of the cinemas in the Anfield district?

4. Although she could not have been more than ten yards away from the two men when they parted (compared with a distance of thirty or forty yards at which, she said, she first saw Wallace), and although she was interested enough to be looking over her shoulder at them, she was unable to identify one man from the other. She was sure, though, that "one went down the entry by the Parish Hall, and the other along Richmond Park, walking in the direction of Breck Road". In order to accept her testimony, it was necessary to believe the almost unbelievable—that Wallace had walked from the tram-stop at St Margaret's Church *to within a hundred yards of his house*, and then, instead of simply crossing the road to the entry leading to Wolverton Street, had either turned round and walked back the way he had come, or turned sharp left and walked away in the direction of Breck Road.

There was, and is, a theory that Wallace timed his return to Wolverton Street to coincide with the Johnstons leaving their house, the idea being that he had them in mind as witnesses. This theory presupposes that Wallace, as well as knowing that his next-door neighbours were going out that night, also knew the time they would be leaving. But it is impossible to reconcile these pre-suppositions with Mrs Johnston's statement that she and her husband did not decide definitely to go out until after Mr Johnston returned from work at about half-past six.

Yseult Bridges rejects this particular theory,[1] but only to leave

[1] *Two Studies in Crime.*

the way clear for a variation on it. She suggests that, although Wallace had no prior knowledge that the Johnstons were going out, "he would be able to guess from a little observation what their intended movements were likely to be. He would know that the children were put to bed at 8 P.M. or 8.30 . . . and if, just after that, there were no lights upstairs he could conclude that the Johnstons were spending the evening at home; if, on the other hand, he saw lights in their bedroom he could as easily deduce that they were on the point of going out. There were lights in their bedroom that night; therefore . . . he would know that he had only to lurk in the shadows of the unlighted alley in order to intercept them as they made their exit." Yseult Bridges goes on to cite the evidence given by Mrs Johnston at the trial: "Her husband, she stated, went downstairs and soon afterwards called out to her to 'hurry up'; she called back, 'I'm coming', extinguished the light, and joined him downstairs. Even as Mrs Johnston had heard Wallace knocking on his back door almost directly below her bedroom window, so could Wallace have heard her calling to her husband that she 'was coming'. That would inform him that the Johnstons were on the very point of going out."

This theory—like so many of the theories concocted by 'anti-Wallace' writers—is based upon a complete reversal of the facts.

Fact number one: The Johnstons had two children, both of them girls. The elder daughter was married and living in West Derby; the Johnstons were on their way to visit her when they met Wallace in the entry. The younger daughter, who was in her teens, had not been 'put to bed' before her parents went out. She was still up when, about half an hour later, her mother returned to the house and sent her to inform Amy Wallace of the murder.

Fact number two: There were *no* lights in the Johnstons' bedroom that night—at least, not at a time when Wallace could have observed them.

Fact number three: Neither at the committal proceedings nor at the trial did Mrs Johnston say what Yseult Bridges quotes her as saying. In her statement to the police Mrs Johnston said: "I and my husband were getting ready to go out at about twenty minutes to nine. *We were in our living room at the back of the house*, and I heard Mr Wallace's usual knock at the back door leading into his house."

Addendum to fact number three: Even if Mrs Johnston *had* been in her bedroom when Wallace knocked at his back door, it is unlikely that she would have heard him. Unlike the Wallaces—who slept in the middle bedroom, overlooking the back yard—the Johnstons slept in the room at the front of the house.

During Thursday evening, while Wallace was sitting in Hubert Moore's office at police headquarters, Detective-Superintendent Charles Thomas came into the room and told him that the Qual-trough telephone-call had been traced to a public call-box "some-where in the Anfield district", and that it had been put through at "about seven o'clock". Wallace listened with interest, but without showing any sign of the alarm he must have been feeling if, as the police believed, it was he who had made the call.

It might be wondered not only what prompted the police to divulge this information to Wallace, but why it was imparted by Thomas, an officer with no real connection with the case, whose duties were almost wholly administrative; also, why Thomas was so vague about the location of the call-box and so inaccurate about the time of the call. There can be no doubt that Thomas, who was a stickler for protocol, would not have spoken to Wallace about the telephone-call without first consulting with Moore, the officer in charge of the case. Possibly—and, indeed, there seems no other feasible explanation—the two detectives hoped that, at some later date, Wallace might become confused between what he had been *told* about the telephone-call and what he already *knew*—and let slip some item of information known only to the investigating officers and to the murderer himself; if this were to happen, then Thomas's high rank, coupled with the fact that he was not *officially* working with the murder team, would strengthen the efficacy of his testimony as to Wallace's guilty knowledge.

It was about a quarter past ten when Wallace left police head-quarters and walked the short distance to the tram-stop at the corner of Lord Street and North John Street.

Already waiting at the stop were Samuel Beattie, James Caird, and Mr Baruch, who had just left the City Café, after attending the usual Thursday evening meeting of the Central Chess Club.

The three men were talking about the murder as they waited for their respective trams to arrive. It was Caird who first noticed Wallace approaching. He thought that Wallace was "very much changed, and terribly upset and shaken. He was dressed in mourning, and to me he looked ghastly."

Caird touched Beattie's arm to warn him of Wallace's presence. "Here he is now," he said quietly. Then, in his normal voice: "Good evening, Mr Wallace."

Wallace was not given the chance to return Caird's greeting. Administering, as it were, a civilian equivalent of the police caution to an accused person, Beattie said, "Now, Mr Wallace, don't say anything about this trouble, as anything you say may be misconstrued."

Caird noticed that "Wallace's lips were quivering, and he could hardly speak in reply". Ignoring Beattie's warning, Wallace said, "That telephone message—can you remember definitely what time you actually received that message?"

"Well, seven or shortly after," Beattie said.

"Can't you get a bit nearer than that?"

"I'm sorry, but I can't."

"Well, it's important to me," Wallace insisted, "and I should like to know if you can get nearer to it than that."

"I'm sorry," Beattie repeated, "but I can't."

There was a moment of embarrassed silence; then Wallace said, "I've just left the police; they've cleared me."

"I'm very pleased to hear it," Beattie said, "very pleased."

Caird and Baruch murmured that they too were pleased.

"When is the funeral to be?" Caird asked.

"Saturday, I think," Wallace said, "but I don't want any fuss."

The first tram to arrive was bound for Smithdown Road, and Wallace, after saying good night to the three members of the chess club, boarded it. He was followed on to the tram by another man— a plain-clothes policeman who had trailed him from police head-quarters and overheard most of the conversation at the tram stop. When Wallace alighted from the tram the policeman also alighted; he followed Wallace to Ullet Road and watched him entering his sister-in-law's flat. Then he returned to police headquarters and reported the gist of the exchange between Wallace and Beattie.

The following day (Friday) the police took statements from Beattie, Caird, and Baruch as to what had occurred at the tram stop.

Wallace had received permission from the police to return to work, and he spent the day collecting insurance money in Clubmoor. When he arrived at police headquarters at about half-past six in the evening he was at once taken to an office where Moore and Inspector Gold were waiting.

Moore wasted no time on preliminaries. He waited just long enough for Wallace to sit down, and then said, "You saw Mr Beattie of the chess club last night?"

"Yes," Wallace agreed, "on the footway in Lord Street while I was waiting for a tram."

"You asked him about the telephone message and about the time he received it?"

"Yes."

"You told him the time was important?"

"Yes."

"In what way did you mean the time was important?"

"I have an idea," Wallace answered, and added, rather lamely, "We all have ideas. It was indiscreet of me."

"I wish you would tell me what your idea was," Moore said. "It might help me with the inquiry."

Wallace said, "I cannot explain any further. I recognize now it was an indiscretion on my part."

Moore did not press the point. As with gambling, so it is with interrogation: the astute interrogator is the one who gets out while he is winning. By further questioning a man after he has made some injudicious remark the interrogator may make additional gains; but it is equally likely that he will provoke a reply which destroys—or, at least, undermines—any success he has already achieved. Moore was well satisfied with the result of the short interview. It seemed to him that Wallace had now made three mistakes—three mistakes which, added together, provided an inference that he was guilty of the murder of his wife.

Wallace was to pay a high price for ignoring Samuel Beattie's warning that anything he said might be misconstrued. At the trial, in the opening speech for the Crown, prosecuting counsel placed great importance upon three remarks made by Wallace—two of them in conversation with Beattie at the tram stop; the other during the interview, the following day, with Moore.

"Now you may think," prosecuting counsel said, "that that request to Mr Beattie [to try to remember the exact time of the telephone-call] and this subsequent conversation with the police rather suggests that the prisoner at that time was already very much on the defensive. Why should he imagine himself in any danger? . . . What does he mean by saying, when he was asked what might have been a perfectly simple question of Mr Beattie, 'I have an idea, we all have ideas, it was indiscreet of me'? If the facts are, as the Crown suggest, that it *was* indiscreet of him, that was an admirable description of that conversation. There is one other curious feature about that conversation with Mr Beattie. . . . He said to Mr Beattie that he had just left the police when he asked those questions, and he said, 'They have cleared me' . . . At that time no charge whatever had been made against him, certainly nothing had been said to him to suggest that they had suspected him, and he was now cleared; not at all."

This last point—the suggestion that if Wallace was innocent he had no reason to think that he was a suspect—was completely invalid. Wallace was an intelligent man who must have realized, right from the start of the investigation, that he was the No. 1 suspect—indeed, the *only* suspect. He had any number of reasons for thinking this. Why, for example, if he was not a suspect, did the police go to all the trouble of arranging the identification parade on the Thursday morning, attended by those people who had encountered him on his way to, and in, the Menlove Gardens area?

As for the remark to Beattie about being cleared, Wallace himself explained:[1]

"Well, I had just come from the police station. . . . During the evening Superintendent Thomas had come into the room, and had a conversation with me regarding the telephone message which had been received. . . . It was suggested to me that it was made from near my home. If that was so, and the time was stated to be about seven o'clock, I was in this position: I felt that if I had left home at a quarter past seven, and the telephone-call had been made at seven o'clock, and if the police up to that moment had believed all my statements to be true, and I had no reason to doubt otherwise, then that automatically cleared me of having sent that message."

(It has since been suggested that when Wallace said that he had no reason to doubt that the police believed his statements, he was, in effect, saying that he had no reason to believe that he was suspected. This is nonsense, of course. In his next breath Wallace spoke of being "automatically cleared"; if he thought that he was cleared it follows that he must also have thought that he was suspected.)

Wallace went on to explain why, in the interview with Moore, he had said that it was "indiscreet of him" to have questioned Beattie about the time of the telephone-call:

"When Superintendent Moore put these questions to me, I realized that . . . I must have been followed, my movements must have been under observation. If I had been under observation, I was therefore, to my mind, a suspected person, and the argument that went through my mind was, it was indiscreet of me, if I was a

---

[1] In direct evidence at the trial.

suspected person, to be talking to a man who may be called as a witness in any charge made in this case. I realized that it was an indiscretion, and that was why I was unwilling to say anything further about it."[1]

Wallace's explanations were at least credible; they fitted the circumstances. The same could not be said for the explanation given by the police, in the person of Inspector Gold, for the round-the-clock observation which was kept upon Wallace, beginning on the Thursday and continuing until his arrest. According to Gold, Wallace was followed "because he was going round his block collecting the insurance money, and we were told that the people there were hostile to him, and we sent a man with him in case of necessity".

This was not the reason at all, but merely a hastily-thought-up and inadequate excuse.

Although, of course, the police were aware that a large and increasing number of people suspected Wallace of the murder, they had no grounds—apart, perhaps, from a few crank telephone-calls—for believing that anyone was likely to take the law into his own hands and harm Wallace in any way. Gold, moreover, said that Wallace was followed only while he was collecting insurance money in Clubmoor; but, in fact, he was under surveillance at all times. Furthermore, if Wallace was followed, as one cynical Liverpudlian put it, "for the good of his health", why did the police not tell him that he was to be followed and explain why, instead of letting him find out for himself and draw his own conclusions?

Wherever Wallace went, one of three plain-clothes men—Frederick Austin, Thomas Cleater, and Thomas Hudson—was never far behind. What was the true reason for the surveillance? Did the police hope that Wallace, unaware that he was being followed, would do something which might be used in evidence against him? If so, then they were soon rewarded by the incident at the tram-stop. Or did they hope that Wallace, realizing that he was being followed, under constant pressure, would lose his nerve, perhaps break down and confess? If this second reason was the true one, then the police must have been vastly disappointed: Wallace was, or affected to be, completely unperturbed by the constant surveillance.

During the time he was staying at his sister-in-law's flat he took to visiting, in the evenings, a local pub called The Brook

[1] *Ibid.*

House. The detective on the "late shift" was an exceptional member of the Liverpool City Police Force, in that he was practically teetotal. On four consecutive evenings he followed Wallace into the saloon bar of the pub and bought a glass of mild beer, from which he took very occasional sips, making this excuse for his presence last until Wallace decided to leave.

On the third or fourth evening, after Wallace and the detective had been in the bar for about an hour, Mr Yates, the landlord, came out from behind the counter and walked over to where the detective was sitting.

"Aren't you thirsty?" he asked.

"Not very."

"It doesn't look like it." Mr Yates indicated the almost-full glass of flat beer. Then, without lowering his voice, he said, "You're watching Wallace, aren't you?"

The detective did not reply.

"You *are*, aren't you?" Mr Yates persisted.

"If you must know—yes, I am," the detective whispered. "But that's strictly between ourselves."

"Between ourselves . . .?" Mr Yates said. "You must be joking. Everyone in the pub's guessed that you're watching Wallace. It's no secret."

In a matter of a few days it was almost common knowledge in Liverpool that Wallace was under police surveillance. As this news spread, so did the rumour that the police were watching Wallace because they believed him to be "another Rouse".

Alfred Arthur Rouse, whose trial for the murder of an unknown man commenced at Northampton Assizes on January 26th, 1931, was a commercial traveller who had managed, over a long period of years and with remarkable dual success, to combine the business of selling with the pleasures of philandering. If Rouse could obtain such a high sexual as well as financial reward from his work (said the Liverpool rumour-mongers), then so, too, could Wallace, who was an insurance agent, calling at dozens of houses each day, and nearly always at a time when the menfolk were away from home. Not only did his job provide philandering opportunities galore, but it was also a perfect camouflage: once he "got the nod" from a female client, he simply walked into the house, ostensibly to discuss matters of insurance, but in fact to satisfy his insane sexual lust; none of the neighbours—except, of course, those already seduced —had the slightest suspicion of what was going on behind the closed door.

But now, at last (the rumour went on), Wallace was exposed. The murder of his wife—motivated, no doubt, by her discovery of his extra-marital activities—had prompted a spate of confessions from the seducees of Clubmoor. The husbands and fathers of the district were up in arms, determined to exact an appropriate revenge upon the man who had violated so many marriage-beds, deflowered so many innocent young virgins. Wallace was so frightened that he had asked for police protection: hence the presence of the plain-clothes men—fully armed, as the rumour had it—who accompanied him on his insurance round.

There were plenty of other rumours going around. One of them drew a comparison between Wallace and Frederick Seddon (who, in 1912, was found guilty of the murder of his lodger, Miss Eliza Barrow, by the administration of arsenic). Like Seddon, Wallace was an insurance man. There was even a slight physical resemblance between the two men. Upon this flimsy foundation was erected the top-heavy story that Wallace, with the plan for his wife's murder already taking shape in his mind, had insured her life for a massive sum of money. The amount grew as the rumour spread.

All sorts of realistic little details were added: the policy contained a double-indemnity clause, so, by killing his wife, Wallace stood to gain twice as much as if he had waited for the poor, sick woman to die a natural death; a team of insurance investigators had arrived in Liverpool, and were working in close collaboration with the police; knowing that the medical examination prior to the granting of the policy would reveal his wife as a "poor risk" and thus increase the amount of the premiums, Wallace, cunning as a fox and as mean as sixpence, had deceived the company doctor by introducing another, much healthier woman (Amy Wallace, perhaps?) as his wife—the doctor had now viewed Julia's body at the mortuary, and stated that this was not the Mrs Wallace he had examined in his surgery. (It may be that this last-mentioned detail was the embryo from which grew the widely-circulated rumour that Wallace, as well as being a murderer, a lecher, and an insurance swindler, was also a multi-bigamist.)

There was not a single item of truth in the grandiose rumour that Wallace murdered his wife for the insurance money. During the first two or three days of the investigation the police conducted a painstaking inquiry into his financial affairs. They discovered that Mrs Wallace's life was insured for the meagre sum of £20, little more than enough to cover the funeral expenses. Even if Wallace had imitated the stingy Seddon—who gave Miss Barrow a cut-price funeral and claimed 12*s*. 6*d*. commission from the undertaker "for introducing the business"—he would not have had much change left over; certainly not enough to provide a motive for murder. And it was not as if he were in desperate need of money: his account with the Midland Bank, Breck Road, showed a credit balance of £152; Julia had £90 in the Post Office Savings Bank.

Another rumour had it that Wallace's motive for murdering his wife was a purely altruistic one; he had been cruel, but only to be kind. Julia was suffering from an incurable and increasingly agonizing disease; Wallace had decided to put her out of her misery, anticipating the inevitable end by a few short months. Perhaps because it was hard to reconcile the idea of mercy-killing with the distinctly unmerciful method of extermination, this rumour never achieved the popularity it deserved. As a Liverpool doctor pointed out:

"If Wallace wished to destroy his wife, as one might wish to destroy a sick family pet, he had the perfect means at his disposal. He used one of the upstairs rooms in the house as a laboratory, wherein he conducted chemical experiments, and, however elementary were these experiments, he must have possessed enough poison to kill his wife a hundred times over. . . . His wife was in poor health, and her death, if accomplished by the subtle administering of poison, would quite possibly be ascribed to natural causes."

Wallace was unfortunate in his choice of pastimes. If he had been interested in, say, philately rather than science, and had played ludo instead of chess, then two of the most prejudicial rumours about him would never have been conceived.

The first of these painted a nightmare picture of Wallace the mad scientist—or of Wallace the sadist, using science as the cover for his perversion. He sat night after night in his laboratory, amidst a paraphernalia of bubbling test-tubes, tormenting insects and small animals, watching through his expensive microscope the magnified image of dumb and defenceless agony. This form of sadism, however, served only to whet his appetite; before long the desire to inflict physical pain upon a fellow human being became irresistible: he satisfied this desire by brutally slaying his wife.

There were several variations on the laboratory theme. One of them suggested that Wallace used his chemical apparatus to concoct aphrodisiacs (a tie-up with the "Rouse rumour"). Another—fostered, perhaps, by the news that he had spent a number of years in the Mysterious Orient—said that he was a drug-fiend who used the laboratory as a private opium den. By coupling these two stories, yet another variation was created—one which said that Wallace was a disciple of Aleister Crowley, and that he practised black magic in the small back room.

As for Wallace being a chess-player: this was interpreted to mean that he was able to devise a far more cunning murder plan than the average citizen. It was reported that he was "a master player; a man with a mind as brilliant as it was perverted, trained to think ahead to the next moves, and to anticipate the moves which his opponent would make".

Before long people were saying that only a brilliant chess-player such as Wallace could have conceived and carried out the scheme to murder his wife; therefore, unless the police discovered another suspect equally expert at the game, Wallace's guilt was a foregone conclusion.

The only people, it seems, who did not subscribe to this notion were those who had had the misfortune to play chess with Wallace. They knew that, far from being "brilliant" at the game, he was a very poor player indeed. His victory over Mr McCartney, the night before the murder, gave him tremendous pleasure—and no wonder, considering the novelty of the experience. At the time of the case a member of the Central Chess Club called Wallace a "chess-vandalist", adding that "the best one can say about him is that he is an enthusiastic duffer". Another member—a true devotee, this one—remarked, "The murder of his wife apart, I think Wallace ought to be hanged for being such a bad chess-player."

The idea that Wallace planned his wife's murder like a game of chess was still very much in the air when he stood trial for his life. Afterwards (and in all seriousness, apparently) a Liverpool barrister asked Wallace's solicitor why the defence did not call expert evidence to prove how poor a player Wallace really was.

Not all the rumours connected with the case suggested that Wallace was the guilty party.

There was, for example, a story that Julia had been having an affair with a married man. After a while the man decided to break off sexual relations with Julia and return, full-time, to the bosom of his family. But Julia was not having any of this. She threatened to write to the man's wife, spilling the beans and wrecking his marriage, if he did not either continue his visits or pay her cash in lieu. So he was forced to buy silence on the instalment plan. Each week he sent Julia money; each week brought him closer to financial ruin. At last, with bankruptcy staring him in the face, he realized that there was only one solution to his problem—namely, the destruction of his tormentor.

He telephoned the bogus message to the City Café, and, the following night, as soon as Wallace was out of the way, called at 29 Wolverton Street. Julia was surprised but delighted to see him —especially when he told her that he wanted to continue their liaison. Without further ado, they went upstairs to the front bedroom and made love (hence the disordered state of the bed-clothes). Then, returning downstairs, they entered the parlour. While Julia was lighting the gas fire the man picked up the iron bar from the hearth and proceeded to "do her in". Before leaving he searched the house for, and found, some letters he had written to Julia.

While he was searching the kitchen he came across the money in the cash box; thinking that it belonged to Julia, and was there-fore part of the blackmail proceeds, he pocketed it without the slightest qualm of conscience. Incidentally, the thirty shillings found in Julia's corset was probably the remainder of the final blackmail payment. And another thing: Wallace was reported as saying that he had no idea that his wife had as much as £90 in the Post Office Savings Bank. How else, then, could she have amassed such an amount, if not by blackmailing an ex-lover?—she certainly could not have saved all that by putting a little aside each week from the housekeeping money.

It was a good rumour, this one; very expertly contrived. There was no denying that, with a few tight squeezes here and there, it succeeded in fitting the facts. There were only two possible objec-tions, and both of these were easily turned aside. Firstly, if some-one pointed out the unlikelihood of any man finding Mrs Wallace attractive enough to want to sleep with her, the answer, usually accompanied by a knowing wink, was: You don't look at the mantelpiece when you're poking the fire. And secondly, if some-one said that Mrs Wallace seemed to be the last person in the world to have committed adultery or blackmail, the answer was equally simple and also metaphorical: You can't judge a book by its cover.

The picture of Julia as a licentious, extortionate woman was contradicted by the briefest yet perhaps most evocative of all the stories. A spiritualist lady claimed to have heard Julia's voice from the dead. In a tone more of sorrow than of anger the disembodied voice had said:

"Herbert, how could you? . . ."

Convinced that Wallace was responsible for his wife's death, and hoping that there might be truth in the saying that "no-one suddenly becomes a murderer", the Liverpool police compiled a dossier on his past life, and then rummaged among the facts in search of some symptom of violence in his nature, or, better still, some pointer towards a possible motive for the crime.

They found nothing.

Since Wallace's death, however, writers on the case have drawn some pretty staggering conclusions from these selfsame facts. This does not mean to say that the writers have been more percipient than were the police; once Wallace was out of the way, there was no-one to contradict the inference-manufacturers, and, more important, no-one to sue them for libel: they were able (literarily rather than literally) to get away with murder. Inference is the by-no-means-fine art of taking an acorn and turning it into a chestnut-tree. There are several instances in books and articles about the Wallace case where it would seem that the writers—determined to provide a solution to the mystery, but without a single acorn in sight—have thought up a suitable inference, and then invented the "fact" necessary for its support.

Briefly but truly, and without any inferential frills, Wallace's antecedents were as follows:

He was born on August 29th, 1878, at 44 Newton Street, Millom, a small town on the western outskirts of the Lake District, north of Barrow-in-Furness. His parents, Benjamin and Margery Wallace (*née* Hall), were working-class people. Benjamin was a none-too-successful printer; a part-time Prudential agent; an amateur but ardent geologist.

Wallace had a brother, Joseph Edwin, who was two years younger than himself, and a sister, Jessie, who was several years younger. The brothers, as well as being devoted to each other, bore a striking facial resemblance—so striking that they were known in the district as "the Wallace twins".

(Neither the devotion nor the resemblance diminished as the years went by. As soon as Joseph received the news of his brother's arrest he sailed half-way round the world, from Malaya to England, to assist in the defence, and to contribute a large sum towards the costs. A reporter noted: "Seeing them together is like observing a double-image. . . . Only the marked difference in height—Joseph is as much as six inches shorter than his brother—distinguishes them. Why, even their voices are similar!")

Under the old school-board system Wallace's attendance at the local school cost his parents a weekly fee of fourpence. If the task of education is to teach children to learn, then, in Wallace's case, it was fourpence a week well spent. "He was always asking questions," one of his boyhood friends recalls. "He could only have been about eight or nine years of age, but already he was interested in botany, natural history, and allied subjects. He joined the Public Library, and I remember that the late Mr Ernest Beck, then Chief Librarian, became one of his closest friends. I have never known anyone with such a thirst for knowledge."

In 1888 the family moved to Blackpool. It was in this same year that Wallace was taken ill with typhoid fever, his only serious childhood illness. The stay in Blackpool was a short one: by 1890 the Wallaces had returned to the Furness district and were living at 27 Victoria Street, Dalton, near Barrow.

Leaving school at fourteen, Wallace obtained employment as a linen-draper's assistant with Messrs Tennants of Cavendish Street, Barrow. He was paid three shillings a week during his first year as a wage-earner, with annual increases, over the next five years, of two shillings a week.

Here it is necessary to pause for a moment to destroy two of the most widespread and widely-accepted assumptions about Wallace: the first being that "the only apparent result of his intellectual interests was that they seem to have made him faintly disliked by most of his acquaintances";[1] the second, that "he never took the least interest, or part, in athletics and popular pastimes".[2] From these two assumptions, added together, comes the inference that Wallace was "murderer material"—for, as every red-blooded Englishman must know, an unpopular person who has no interest in sport is far more likely to commit murder than someone who, when not being the life and soul of the party, is engaged in some healthy outdoor pursuit.

The trouble, though, is that neither of the assumptions is true. Although Wallace was reserved and shy, he was well-liked by practically everyone he came in contact with. There is a vast amount of proof of his popularity in statements made by members of the Central Chess Club, neighbours in Anfield, Prudential

[1] *William Herbert Wallace*, by F. J. P. Veale.
[2] *Two Studies in Crime.*

colleagues and clients.[1] To assist in the destruction of this first
assumption, and to destroy completely the second, here are the
words of J. T. Ferguson, a Barrow businessman:[2] "I knew Wallace
intimately when he was in Barrow. That was more than thirty years
ago, and he became acquainted with a group of shop assistants—
of whom I was one—who used to camp on Walney.[3] After business
hours a group of us would meet and walk around the Abbey.[4]
Wallace was a delightful fellow, and all of us liked him immensely.
He was fond of football, cricket, and other sports. . . ."

After six years in the employment of Messrs Tennants, by which
time he was twenty and earning about 13s. a week, Wallace handed
in his resignation and set off for Manchester, where he obtained a
similar but higher-paid job with a wholesale firm.

By now Joseph had married Amy Blackwell, a Dalton girl, and
was working in Shanghai, as a printer for the Chinese Government.
It may be that his letters home persuaded Wallace to seek employment in the Far East. Anyway, Wallace applied for a job as a salesman at the Calcutta branch of the famous trading firm of Whiteway,
Laidlaw and Company; in 1902, at the age of twenty-three, he set
sail for India.

Since his late teens he had been troubled by a kidney ailment, for
which he had received treatment at hospitals in Barrow and
Manchester. After a few years in India the ailment worsened; he
underwent four operations at the German Hospital in Calcutta,
but remained uncured. Possibly at the suggestion of his brother
—who was, at this time, still working for the Chinese Government—he left Calcutta and moved farther eastwards, to Shanghai.
Excessively weakened by his illness, he was able to work only part-
time, as the advertising manager in a general store—a position which
in those pre-Madison Avenue days, was little more than a sinecure.

Despite a further operation, his condition was rapidly growing
worse, so he returned to England, and on April 7th, 1907, was

[1] During the investigation the police interviewed many people who
were acquainted with Wallace; but only one of these—a retired Prudential
agent named Alfred Mather—stated that he found Wallace dislikeable.
Also, the police were able to trace only one person to contradict the
impression that the Wallaces were a happy and devoted couple: this was a
Mrs Wilson, who, in 1923, had nursed Wallace through an attack of
pneumonia, and was now matron of a Liverpool police remand home.

[2] From an interview published in the *Barrow News*, May 23rd, 1931.

[3] A small island off the Furness Peninsula.

[4] Furness Abbey, now ruins, sited roughly half-way between Barrow
and Dalton.

admitted to Guy's Hospital, London, where his left kidney was removed.

A long period of convalescence was followed by an even longer period of unemployment. Eventually, eighteen months after the removal of the diseased organ, he was "back to square two", employed by the Manchester wholesale firm for whom he had worked before leaving for India.

His parents, with his young sister Jessie, were now living at Harrogate, and he visited them regularly at weekends. It was not long, however, before he found an entirely different reason for spending his weekends in the Yorkshire spa town.

He had become interested in politics—more particularly in the cause of Liberalism. At this time the Liberal Party headquarters for the Ripon Division, West Riding of Yorkshire, were at 5A Raglan Street, Harrogate. Wallace turned up there one day and offered his services as a voluntary worker. "He threw himself, heart and soul, into the work," recalls Mrs J. G. Rydel, who was one of his fellow-helpers. "You could be assured that whenever he was there, there was plenty of activity."

The local Liberal hierarchy must have been equally impressed by Wallace's ability and enthusiasm, because in 1910 he was appointed Liberal agent for the Division. Although the position was more prestigious than remunerative, he must have been a very happy man indeed.

And even happier when, in the summer of the following year, he met Julia Dennis, the thirty-three-year-old daughter of William Dennis, a veterinary surgeon, and his French-born wife, Aimee. Both of Julia's parents were now dead, and her sister Amy was working in Brighton, so she lived alone at 11 St Mary's Avenue, Harrogate, occasionally taking in paying guests. She is remembered (again by Mrs Rydel) as being "a rather timid young woman . . . who fluttered around like a rather drab butterfly. She was employed in an office in the town. I have an idea that it was an estate agent's office, but I can't be sure of that."

What else is known about Julia before her marriage? Very little, really. She was a regular church-goer, and took an active part in parochial affairs; she painted; she played the piano and sang (one of her favourite songs, which she often rendered at church socials, was entitled *No-one Knows Why*).

A year after his first meeting with Julia, Wallace began to court her in earnest. As far as is known, this was his first serious romance; Julia's, too, it seems. The courtship lasted for two years; then, on

March 24th, 1914, they were married at the parish church of St Mary.

Yseult Bridges suggests that Wallace married Julia for her money. Maybe he did—but, if so, he was in no great hurry to lay his hands on the loot. A year getting to know her, a further two years of courtship . . . perhaps he was using the slowly-slowly, catchee-money technique. It has generally been assumed that Julia, at the time of her marriage, was quite well off: one writer describes her as "a lady of independent means"; another says that she was "comfortably independent". But there is no evidence to support this view. It is true that the house in St Mary's Avenue was registered on the Burgess Roll in Julia's name, but it was owned jointly by herself and her sister Amy.

After a brief honeymoon Wallace moved his few possessions from 9 Belmont Road, where he had been living with his family, and set up residence with his wife at 11 St Mary's Avenue. A few weeks later Benjamin and Jessie Wallace also moved there. (Wallace's mother had died in the December of the previous year.)

With less than a year of marriage behind him, Wallace resigned his position as a Liberal agent, and he and Julia set off for Liverpool, where—through the good offices of Norman Allsop, a friend of his father—another job was waiting for him, again as an agent, but this time for the Prudential Assurance Company.[1]

Yseult Bridges suggests that Wallace was given the sack by the Liberal Party. Wallace himself said that "when the Great War commenced, this job ceased to be worth keeping up"; and he surely deserves the benefit of the doubt, not only because his earnings as a Liberal agent were only forty-three shillings a week, but also because many other of his verifiable statements were examined by the police, and *not one of them* was found to be untrue.

Yseult Bridges also suggests that Wallace was a cold-hearted, Simon Legree-type character. She writes that "on 22nd March 1915, Benjamin Wallace died of cerebral haemorrhage, aged 79, *in the workhouse infirmary at Knaresborough*". And concludes: ". . . savouring of that callousness which was so to strike observers

---

[1] It is worth remarking how the Wallaces followed in their forebears' footsteps. Benjamin was a Prudential agent: so was Wallace; Benjamin was a printer: so was Joseph. Jessie was a nurse: Joseph's son, Edwin, qualified as a doctor. Like his father and his uncle, Edwin worked in the Far East—and, like his father again, he was in Government service. At the time of his death, in December 1960, he was a member of the Colonial Medical Service, stationed at Kuching, Sarawak.

on the night of his wife's murder is surely Wallace's action in arranging for his dying father to be removed to meet his end in the infirmary of a distant workhouse."

The facts of the matter are as follows:

1. The "distant workhouse" was (and is[1]) only a mile or so outside Harrogate.

2. In 1915 there were three hospitals in the Harrogate district—the General Hospital in the town itself; the Thistle Hill Infectious Disease Hospital; and the Workhouse Infirmary, Knaresborough. At that time the majority of aged and infirm patients were treated at the Infirmary.

3. It is likely that Jessie Wallace requested that her father be sent to the Infirmary, since she was then working there as a nurse.

4. Wallace was already living in Liverpool when the arrangement was made "for his dying father to be removed to meet his end", etc. He began working as a Prudential agent in the first week of March 1915; Benjamin Wallace was not admitted to the Infirmary until a couple of days before his death on the 22nd.

Most of the main facts about Wallace's life in Liverpool have been mentioned in earlier chapters.

Although, nearly sixteen years after joining the Prudential, he was still only an agent, and was still working in a district that provided few opportunities for earning large sums in commission, he seemed perfectly content. During the first two or three days of the investigation into his wife's death the police interviewed Joseph Crewe, a Prudential superintendent. Crewe gave Wallace a glowing character reference:

"I have known Wallace for over twelve years as an agent under my supervision. He bears the highest character—absolutely, in every respect. To say that he is a kindly gentleman would be putting it mildly; no form of words would be too high praise for Wallace in that respect . . . Mr Wallace's world, and Mrs Wallace's world, were confined to their two selves. No-one else mattered. They were all in all to each other."

So far, so good—so far, *too* good, as far as the police were concerned. But they brightened up when Mr Crewe went on:

"I have lived at my present address, 34 Green Lane, Mossley Hill, for the past three and a half years." (It will be remembered that Wallace, during his search for Menlove Gardens East, walked along Green Lane. It was at the corner of Green Lane and Allerton Road that he spoke to P.C. Sargent.) "About two years ago Mr

[1] Considerably modernized, it is still in use today.

Wallace visited my house five times, in five successive weeks. I cannot fix the month in which these visits occurred,[1] but it was definitely winter, invariably about 8 P.M. He suggested he would like to play the violin . . . and I said I would give him a few lessons. That is how he came to call at my house. He came at no other time."

From this second paragraph from Mr Crewe's testimony the police extracted three points to assist their theory that Wallace made the journey to Menlove Gardens in order to provide himself with an alibi.

Point number one: If Wallace knew how to get to Mr Crewe's house in Green Lane, then he should also have been able to find his way to the Menlove Gardens area, adjacent to Green Lane, without needing to pester the tram conductors, Phillips and Thompson.

Point number two: Admittedly, it was two years since he had last visited Mr Crewe's house; but, if he knew Green Lane, it followed that not only should he have known where the Menlove Gardens were, but also that there was no such place as Menlove Gardens East.

Point number three: If he was really seeking insurance business rather than fabricating an alibi, why did he not call at Mr Crewe's house and ask his assistance in finding the address of R. M. Qualtrough?

The police, it seems, fell in love at first sight with the tripartite strengthening of the alibi theory. So enamoured of it were they, so determined that it should remain unsullied, that they turned a blind eye to the rest of Crewe's testimony.

They completely ignored, for instance, his statement that, before the first violin lesson, he gave Wallace explicit instructions on how to get to the house. If Wallace followed these instructions he did not travel along Menlove Avenue, but boarded a tram at Smithdown Road which took him along Allerton Road to the southern corner of Green Lane, where he alighted, more than a quarter of a mile from where Menlove Gardens North enters Menlove Avenue. Mr Crewe could not swear to it, but he was sure in his own mind that this was the route Wallace always used; he remembered accompanying Wallace, after each of the five lessons, to the tram-stop in Allerton Road: on one of these occasions they had a cup of coffee together in the restaurant of the near-by Plaza Cinema (a fact which Wallace thought important enough to record in his diary:

[1] It was December 1928. (The visits were recorded by Wallace in his diary.)

"After the lesson we went into the Plaza Cinema, a wonderfully well-got-up place").

Also ignored by the police was Mr Crewe's statement that, until now, he had no idea whether there was such a place as Menlove Gardens East or not. If Mr Crewe, who had lived in Green Lane for three and a half years, knew so little about Menlove Gardens, it was unreasonable to suggest that Wallace, after five visits to Mr Crewe's house, always at night, should know more.

As for the third point—that if Wallace had been truly concerned with finding the address of R. M. Qualtrough, he would have sought the assistance of Mr Crewe—Wallace explained that he *had* called at Mr Crewe's house, but received no reply. Why, then, he was asked, did he not mention this fact to the police when he was queried about the people he had met and spoken to in the Menlove Gardens area? The answer, Wallace replied, was implicit in the question: the police were only interested in the people he had actually *encountered* during his wanderings—the people who might be traced to confirm his story. There was support for Wallace's explanation in the statement he volunteered to Inspector Gold on January 22nd: after referring to three encounters he had not mentioned in his earlier statement, he concluded: "I think these are all the people *I spoke to* that night in Allerton." (Author's italics.)

At the trial prosecuting counsel suggested that Wallace invented this explanation after learning that Mr and Mrs Crewe were out at the pictures on the night of the murder. If this suggestion was true, and Wallace did not call at the house, one is left with a question that has no apparent answer:

Why didn't he?

After all, whether he was innocent or guilty of his wife's murder, whether he was out to get insurance business or an alibi, there seems no reason why he should not have called upon Mr Crewe; if he was alibi-seeking, Mr Crewe was an ideal witness to his presence in the neighbourhood.

There is another question—more difficult to answer, perhaps, than the first.

Why, with the whole of Liverpool at his disposal, and knowing that Mr Crewe lived within a stone's throw of the three existing Menlove Gardens, did he decide to invent a fourth?

There can be no doubt that he must have pondered the murder plan for weeks, maybe months, before putting it into effect. Did it not occur to him that the police would find out about his visits to

Mr Crewe—visits which conflicted, or, at least, seemed to conflict, with the all-important idea that he was "a complete stranger" in the district? Did it not occur to him, either, that by choosing Menlove Gardens he ran the risk of the whole plan collapsing at the outset? He knew that Samuel Beattie, as captain of the chess club, was the most likely person to take a telephone message for one of the members; he knew, too, that Beattie lived in Mossley Hill: but what he did not know, and could not possibly know, was whether Beattie—or any of the other members, for that matter[1]—was well enough acquainted with the Menlove Gardens area to be able to say that there was no such place as Menlove Gardens East. If Wallace was the murderer, then he certainly believed in pushing his luck.

The police found, in Wallace's diaries, what they took to be a further indication that his anxious reminders to the two tram conductors were not only unnatural in their persistence, but also unnecessary. Once or twice a year, "the time the roses were out", Wallace and his wife had visited Calderstones Park; they had also, on two occasions, been to Woolton Woods. To get to these places they almost certainly travelled by tram along Menlove Avenue. The inference drawn by the police was summed up in the rhetorical question: "Why, if not for some sinister reason, did Wallace need to ask the way to a place he must have known quite well?"

This point was completely invalid. Wallace never stated, or even intimated, that he did not know Menlove Avenue, which is one of the main thoroughfares of Liverpool, running nearly two miles from Queen's Drive to Woolton Road. When he was given the telephone message by Samuel Beattie he asked, "Is it Menlove Avenue?" and Beattie replied, "No, Menlove Gardens East." Not once in his remarks to the tram conductors did he mention Menlove Avenue, but always Menlove Gardens East.

In a letter to the author a life-long resident of Mossley Hill says: "The suggestion was put forward that because Wallace knew the whereabouts of Menlove Avenue he must also have known where Menlove Gardens were situated. Nonsense! This was the same as saying that, after looking at his new violin a few times, Wallace ought to have been able to find a particular note on it without assistance from a musician."

* * *

[1] E. B. Deyes (see p. 23) lived in Henley Road, a turning on the opposite side of Menlove Avenue to the Gardens. If one enters the Avenue from Henley Road, Menlove Gardens North is to the right and Menlove Gardens West to the left, neither of them more than a hundred yards away.

During the first three days of the investigation articles of clothing from Wallace's wardrobe were handed over to William Roberts, the Welsh-born City Analyst, to be microscopically examined for traces of blood; any suspicious stains were submitted to the benzidine test. On the morning of Saturday, January 24th, while Wallace was attending his wife's funeral,[1] Roberts received from Inspector Gold the remainder of the clothes; and, later that day, he sat down and wrote a report on his findings—which did not take long, since there was hardly anything to say.

He reported that Wallace's clothes were "free from blood, with the exception of two minute old bloodstains in the right-hand trousers pocket [of the suit he was wearing on the night of the murder]. These stains have nothing to do with this case; they are too old."

Now, everyone who had visited the parlour at Wolverton Street —a room which was to be described by prosecuting counsel as "a jam pot"—was convinced of one thing: the murder could not have been committed without the assailant being splashed with blood. Roberts's findings—or non-findings—provided the police with an enormous riddle. How could they reconcile the idea that Wallace committed such a brutal and messy murder with the fact that his clothes bore no vestige of blood? Looking back on the case, a retired Liverpool policeman recalls: "I remember one of my colleagues remarking that if Wallace was the criminal he had not only committed a crime but performed a miracle. To have escaped from the murder room as clean as when he went in was like taking a shower-bath and not getting wet."

Asked by the police if Wallace could have washed the blood from his clothes, Roberts said that this was out of the question. No amount of scrubbing could have removed all traces of blood; the benzidine test would still have given a positive reaction.

For a while the police toyed with the idea that Wallace might have disposed of the bloodstained clothing. But how? And where? The only opportunity he had had was during his walk from the house to the tram-stop opposite St Margaret's Church. Yet the whole area of Richmond Park had been searched for the murder

---

[1] At Anfield Cemetry. There were three mourners: Wallace, his sister-in-law, and his nephew. The funeral was kept secret from the Press; apart from the clergyman and the undertakers, the only other person to witness the burial was one of the triumvirate of detectives on surveillance duty. During the sermon Edwin noticed that his uncle "was unable to control his emotions and wept copiously".

weapon, and it was inconceivable that a bundle of clothing had escaped notice.

The structure of suspicion against Wallace was on the point of collapse when Roberts and Professor MacFall came up with a possible solution to the riddle.

They reasoned, first of all, that there were only two explanations as to how Wallace could have killed his wife without getting a single spot of blood on his clothes: *either he had worn no clothes at all, or he had worn something over his clothes to protect them.*

After a short discussion they rejected the idea that Wallace had stripped himself stark-naked before committing the crime. Apart from the ambiguous clot of blood found on the lavatory-pan, there was no evidence to suggest that Wallace had even washed any blood from his face and hands, let alone from his whole body; on the contrary, what evidence there was pointed towards the negative conclusion.

So Roberts and MacFall turned their combined attention to the second, and only other possible, explanation.

Until now hardly any thought had been given to the mackintosh which was found beside, and partly beneath, the dead woman's right shoulder. Roberts had examined it and noted that it was "extensively and heavily stained with human blood, inside and out". He had noted, too, and with more interest, that "a considerable portion at the bottom of the right side had been recently burnt away". In his opinion the burning had taken place on the night of the murder, because "the hearthrug of the parlour was the only place in the house where burnt fragments of the mackintosh were to be seen. . . . If it had been shaken or hung up anywhere else, portions would have been found there."

The fact that both the mackintosh *and* the front of Julia's skirt were severely burnt lent support to Mrs Johnston's impression that Julia was wearing the mackintosh over her shoulders when she was struck down; there was no doubt that the burn on the skirt was caused by contact with the gas-fire, probably by her falling against it after the first and fatal blow was delivered—and it was reasonable to assume that the burn on the mackintosh was caused in the same way.

How else?

For the time being Roberts and MacFall disregarded this question. They were concerned with a different question—a rhetorical one:

Was it not possible that the mackintosh was worn, not by Julia, but by her husband—*as a protection from the blood that gushed untidily from the arterial wound. . . ?*

They measured the mackintosh. It was fifty inches long. If worn by Wallace during the commission of the crime, and buttoned at the neck, it would have protected all but his hands and face, his boots, and twelve inches or so of trouser-leg. Admittedly, the most vulnerable parts of his body would have been his legs and feet . . . but this point had to be ignored if the theory was to survive.

They made a detailed examination of the bloodstains on the mackintosh. Out of dozens of stains—many of which were undoubtedly caused by contact with the blood on the hearthrug—they found two stains which, they believed, assisted the theory.

The first of these was on the front of the left sleeve, between the elbow and the shoulder, and it provided MacFall with an opportunity to use his favourite adjective. The stain on the sleeve, he said, was "characteristic of a mark of projected blood". The circular shape of the stain, and the tiny splashes which surrounded it, indicated that the blood had struck the material directly rather than from an acute angle. But even if the stain *was* a "projection mark" (and Roberts was by no means as definite as MacFall on this point), it did not necessarily follow that Julia was not wearing the mackintosh over her shoulders when she was killed: if, for instance, the loose sleeve had swung away from her body as she lurched forward, a spot of blood might have fallen directly upon the sleeve, causing a similarly-shaped stain to the one which was found.

The other suspicious stain was inside the mackintosh, slightly above the right armpit, and Roberts and MacFall suggested that it could have been caused after the murder, by Wallace withdrawing his blood-soaked right hand from the sleeve. There was, however, nothing in the shape of the stain to support this construction; apart from a small amount of blood within the cuff (which might have seeped through the material from the outside), the inside of the sleeve was completely clean.

With the two equivocal stains providing their theory with its only visible means of support, Roberts and MacFall turned to the problem of the burn on the mackintosh; and, after what can have been only a very short discussion, without reference to what was likely and what was not, devised an explanation which, although consistent with the theory, was certainly deserving of the description later applied to it by a Liverpool doctor—"a far-fetched, indeed ludicrous, piece of hypothetical hocus-pocus".

According to the opinion of Roberts and MacFall, the two burns

—one on the front of Julia's skirt, the other on the mackintosh—were both caused during the commission of the crime, but at different times and in different ways. The burn on the skirt, they opined, was caused accidentally, by Julia falling against the gas-fire—but the burn on the mackintosh was the result of a deliberate act of arson. After killing his wife Wallace took off the mackintosh; then, realizing that the police would question how it came to be so bloodstained, decided to destroy it *by burning it on the gas-fire*. He held the incriminating garment against the hot clays—but only for a moment or two; as soon as it began to smoulder and catch fire he pulled it away and extinguished the flames.

Why the abrupt change of mind? . . . Well, there were any number of possible reasons for that: you paid your money and you took your choice. Perhaps he foresaw the danger of the police discovering that his mackintosh was missing, and the difficulty of explaining its disappearance, since it was not the sort of thing a thief was likely to remove; or maybe, anxious to get away from the house as quickly as possible, he decided that he could not spare the time to clean up and dispose of the charred remains; or maybe he suddenly became frightened that the strong smell of burning rubber would be detected from the street . . . or that the flames might get out of control, burning down the house, cremating his wife, and, most serious of all, destroying his carefully-prepared alibi.

The "truncated-arson explanation" was, to say the least of it, highly disputable. Even allowing for post-murder panic, was it credible that Wallace had thought of using an ordinary gas-fire as an incinerator? . . . And wasn't it more than a trifle odd that Wallace—the arch-schemer, the "chess murderer"—had not considered the question of the tell-tale stains until after their tale was told? As a defence against questions like these, Roberts and MacFall enlisted the aid of sophistry to provide a blanket answer: Murder (they said in effect) is an abnormal act—therefore one cannot expect a murderer to behave completely normally.

On the morning of Sunday, January 25th, the mackintosh theory was presented to the police, in the person of Superintendent Moore, who received it gratefully and without remarking upon its obvious weaknesses. With the whole case against Wallace depending upon an explanation for the absence of bloodstains on his clothing, this was not the time to look a gift horse in the mouth.

Days before—perhaps as early as Wednesday; certainly no later than Thursday—the investigation had reached its point of no return; after that, if the case against Wallace broke down, the chance of finding a solution to the mystery was virtually non-existent. There was no each-way bet: no case against Wallace meant no case against anyone; it was too late to start looking for an alternative suspect.

For Hubert Moore the prospect of failure in this, his first major case as Head of the C.I.D., was enough to keep him awake nights, or to overcrowd his sleep with nightmares. There can be no doubt that he believed in Wallace's guilt—but there can be no doubt, either, that this belief was more emotional, or volitional, than intellectual. He *had* to believe in it. To change his mind was to admit defeat—and defeat was unthinkable at this crucial stage in his career.

Now it was a straightforward contest between himself and Wallace: both their futures were at stake; one of them had to lose. Now it was a matter of selecting the facts which told against Wallace—of disregarding, or finding a way round, the facts in his favour. Possibly to a police mind wanting to solve a crime, he could have thought that it was less important to find the solution to the mystery than to collect enough evidence to justify Wallace's arrest.

Once the arrest was made, Moore could breathe easily again: the buck would be passed to a prosecuting solicitor, then to a magistrate, and on to a barrister appointed by the Crown, to a jury, perhaps to three judges sitting in the Court of Criminal Appeal.

When, on the Sunday, the mackintosh theory was explained to Moore he was not concerned with the many flaws in its construction. It might be severely mauled, destroyed even, by whoever defended Wallace—but that would be some time in the future, after the arrest. For the present Moore saw the theory only as a means of side-stepping a giant obstacle in the path to the arrest; and, using it as such, he pressed on to the last obstacle of all:

The time factor.

In the afternoon of the same day Alan Close, the self-styled "missing link" in the case, was collected from his home above the dairy in Sedley Street and taken to Anfield Police Station.

How long was he kept there? ...

Who conducted the interview? ...

What form did the interview take?

These questions, put to police witnesses at the trial, received either no answer at all, or answers so evasive as to be meaningless.

All that is known is that something happened during the interview which caused the milk boy's memory to improve in one respect and to deteriorate in another.

Now he remembered (he said) that, on the night of the murder, during his milk round, but before delivering at 29 Wolverton Street, he had looked at the illuminated dial of the clock of Holy Trinity Church, at the corner of Richmond Park and Breck Road, and noticed that the time was twenty-five minutes past six. But as for his encounter, the following night, with Elsie Wright, Douglas Metcalf, Harold Jones, and Kenneth Caird, he could only vaguely remember (he said) the conversation that had taken place: he was sure, though, that he had not told the other children that he had seen Mrs Wallace alive at about a quarter to seven.

As soon as, or perhaps before, Close's statement was written out and signed, a detective called at the Vicarage of Holy Trinity Church, where he obtained the name—John Patterson—and the address—in West Derby—of the man whose job it was to regulate and wind the clock. Questioned at his home, Patterson said that he had set the clock correctly on Friday, January 16th; when he had visited the church again, on the following Friday (January 23rd), he had noted that "the time shown on the clock was correct to within a matter of seconds".

Having established the accuracy of the clock, the next, and all-important, task for the police was to determine the time that had elapsed between when the milk boy passed the church and when he left 29 Wolverton Street, after delivering the milk to Mrs Wallace. Accompanied by Inspector Gold and Sergeant Bailey, both armed with stop-watches, Close set off from opposite the church and (as Bailey explained at the trial) "retraced his steps over the route he took on the night in question, calling at the houses and going through the actions of delivering the milk and so on, eventually arriving at Wolverton Street".

Close's route was as follows:

1. From the church, he walked along Breck Road and turned left into Sedley Street, where he stopped at the dairy to deposit a dozen empty milk-cans and to collect a fresh supply.

2. Continuing to the bottom of Sedley Street, he used the entry beside the Parish Hall to take him through to Richmond Park.

3. After delivering milk to a house in Letchworth Street he left two bottles of milk in the garden of a house in Richmond Park and picked up a couple of empties.

4. Lastly, he crossed Richmond Park and walked through the

entry to Wolverton Street, where he called at Nos. 31 (the Johnstons) and 29 (the Wallaces).

According to the police test, the whole operation took just six minutes to complete. Therefore, assuming that the milk boy's delayed-action memory was reliable, and that the test was accurate, Mrs Wallace was still alive at 6.31 on the Tuesday evening. With the "tram tests" establishing that Wallace could not have left the house any later than 6.49, this meant that he had had *a maximum time of eighteen minutes* in which to kill his wife, get rid of any traces of the crime upon his person, clean the murder weapon (which, for some reason or other, he did not want to leave in the house), fabricate the evidence of robbery, and do a few other little jobs, such as turning off the light and the fire in the parlour.

Eighteen minutes . . . a maximum of eighteen minutes. Not long.

Long *enough*, though, the police decided. Working fast (and Wallace would certainly not have dawdled), he could have done all that was necessary, and still have had a couple of minutes to spare before starting out for the "alibi area" of Menlove Gardens.

But was it really as early as 6.31 when Mrs Wallace said good-night to the milk boy and closed the front door? . . . Was the timing of the milk round conducted fairly by the police?

To answer these questions it is necessary to examine in more detail the calls made by Close and to put a *minimum* time to each of them:

1. *In Sedley Street.* He walked into the dairy, deposited twelve empty cans beside the counter, collected a fresh supply, walked out. *25 seconds.*

2. *In Letchworth Street.* He rang the customer's bell, waited for her to answer the door, handed her a can of milk, and again waited while she took the can through to the kitchen at the back of the house, emptied the milk into a jug, and came back to the front door with the empty can, which she returned to him. *40 seconds.*

3. *In Richmond Park.* He walked into the garden of a house, set down two bottles of milk, picked up two empty bottles, and, putting them in the crate he was carrying, walked back to the street. *8 seconds.*

4. *In Wolverton Street.* He knocked at the door of No. 29, put a can of milk on the step, then went next-door to No. 31 (without returning to the street: it was his habit, he said, to step over the intervening parapet between the two houses); he knocked at No. 31, waited for Mrs Johnston to come to the door, handed her

a can, and again waited while she took it through to the kitchen, emptied the contents into a jug, and came back to the front door. Then he returned to No. 29, where Mrs Wallace—who, while Close was serving Mrs Johnston, had emptied her milk into a jug—was waiting to give him the empty can. She advised him to "hurry up home because he had got a cough"; she said that she had a cough, too. After an exchange of good-nights Mrs Wallace closed the front door. *60 seconds.*

Altogether, then (and remembering that the times given above are absolute minima), Close spent more than two minutes on the calls. If this time is subtracted from the six minutes recorded by the police there is the undeniable fact that Close had less than four minutes of *actual walking time* to get from the church to the house, a distance of 503 yards.[1]

This means that if the police timing was an honest and accurate reflection of the milk boy's movements on the night of the murder, Close must have travelled at an average speed of at least 5 m.p.h.—amazingly fast progress for a fourteen-year-old, considering that the average *adult* walking speed is $3\frac{1}{2}$-4 m.p.h., and that Close was carrying a cumbersome and quite heavy crate of cans and bottles.

On February 19th, three and a half weeks after the first timing of the milk round, Close took part in a re-run. On this occasion he completed the test in five minutes dead (at an average speed of more than 6 m.p.h.). But by then the police were not the only people interested in the time of Close's departure from 29 Wolverton Street. Wallace's solicitor was gathering evidence from several quarters to show that not only was the police timing of the milk round incorrect, but that when Close passed Holy Trinity Church on the Tuesday evening it was a good deal later than twenty-five minutes past six.

On Monday, January 26th, a conference was held at police headquarters. In addition to the officers engaged in the investigation, the conference was attended by Lionel Everett, the Chief Constable of Liverpool; Colonel Winstanley, the Assistant Chief Constable; and J. R. Bishop, the Assistant Prosecuting Solicitor to Liverpool Corporation. The conference lasted throughout the day and into the early hours of the following morning.

On Tuesday a further conference, of shorter duration and minus the presence of Everett and Winstanley, preceded Bishop's depart-

[1] Not 60 yards, as Yseult Bridges says. Even for a crow the distance from the church to the house is 110 yards.

At the main bridewell Wallace was again cautioned and charged. He made no reply. His pockets searched and emptied, he was put in a cell for the night.

Moore walked to one of his favourite pubs, where he stayed until closing-time. He had good reason for celebration.

The Committal

> *"You will observe the Rules of Battle, of
> course?" the White Knight remarked,
> putting on his helmet too.
> "I always do," said the Red Knight,
> and they began banging away at
> each other with such fury that Alice
> got behind a tree to be out of the way
> of the blows.*

The Liverpool grapevine was marvellously efficient. Although no mention was made of the arrest in the Tuesday edition of the local morning paper, the *Daily Post*, the news was circulating the city long before Wallace appeared before the stipendiary magistrate, Stuart Deacon, at 10.30 A.M.[1]

"Half an hour before the court was fixed to open, the public gallery in the stipendiary's court was crowded with spectators. The police had to disperse a crowd of 200 that filled the ante-room in the hope of getting into the court.

"There was a stir in court when Wallace's name was called. He stepped into the dock calmly, and, holding his bowler hat in his hand, leaned on the dock rails while the charge was being read. . . . He looked interestedly around the court, and then, when Mr Bishop, at whose left sat the Chief Constable and Supt. Moore, began his statement, Wallace listened attentively.

"Once or twice he shook his head, and smiled slightly in contradiction of something Mr Bishop was saying. . . . As Mr Bishop proceeded, Wallace fingered his moustache and scratched his head."[2]

In perplexity, no doubt. As he listened he must have wondered

---

[1] Late on the Monday evening William Armstrong, the producer at the Liverpool Playhouse, was telephoned at his home by a member of the repertory company, who told him that the performance had gone well—"and Wallace has been arrested!"

[2] *Liverpool Echo* (3.2.31).

where Bishop had obtained much of the information contained in his speech; he must also have wished that he had retained a solicitor to represent him at the hearing.

As prosecuting solicitor, Bishop should have presented a dispassionate summary of the evidence which tended towards the presumption of Wallace's guilt, together with such comment as he thought fair. It is perhaps unfortunate that, in the light of the full facts, as we now know them, his opening speech contained *eighteen* misstatements of fact.

The speech is given here in full, just as it was reported in the two Liverpool evening papers, just as it was read by thousands of people in South-west Lancashire, included among whom were the men and women who would form the jury at Wallace's trial.

Bishop began:

"The accused was arrested about seven o'clock last night. He is accused of murdering his wife on the night of January 20th last. Between 6.30 and 8.45 that night this woman was murdered in her house. She lived there alone with the accused, there being no children and no servants resident in the house.

"His business takes him about Liverpool at various times in the day. [*Misstatement No. 1: Wallace's business was confined to the small area of Clubmoor, contiguous to Anfield.*]

"He usually returned about midday for a meal, and in the evening for his tea. His story is, that on this particular evening he arrived home about 6.5 and had tea, and left again about 6.45, and when he returned about 8.40 he discovered that his wife had been murdered.

"After the accused, the last person to see the unfortunate woman alive was a milk boy, at 6.31, and it is the suggestion of the prosecution that after this boy had called at 6.31 the accused murdered his wife, and left the house at about five minutes to seven.

"He had an appointment—so he says—which required him to leave the house about seven o'clock, and it is a fact that he was seen at a short distance away [*2: When Wallace boarded the tram at the junction of Lodge Lane and Smithdown Road he was more than two miles from his home*] at about ten past seven. [*3: The tram left the junction at about six minutes past seven.*] To get to that spot he may have left the house at any time from five to four minutes to seven. [*4: The police "tram-tests" showed that he could not have left the house any later than 6.49.*]

"When he made the discovery at fifteen minutes to nine, he had with him two neighbours. I attach considerable importance to that point.

"The police were sent for at once, and they arrived very shortly afterwards—some few minutes after nine o'clock—and they began to make their investigations, and as a result the accused appears in the dock.

"Now, when he left the house, on the evening of the murder, he says he went to keep an appointment which had been made with him. In fact, on the previous evening, at about 7.45, the accused was in a café, and while he was there a friend of his gave the accused a message which had come over the telephone, requesting him to go the next night to a house in the Sefton Park district [5: *Not Sefton Park, but Allerton*] and call upon some person who wished to be a client.

"It is the suggestion of the prosecution that this message was sent to the accused by himself. In fact, it will be proved that the message emanated from a call-box two or three hundred yards from the house. [6: *Actually, 400 yards.*]

"It would have taken him just as long to get from that call-box, in time to reach the café where he received the message, as did time elapse between the time the message was received and accused arrived at the café. [7: *This was pure guess-work. The police never bothered to ascertain the duration of the journey from the call-box to the café.*]

"One curious fact is this—but for the fact that that message was sent from a call-box, and that the number to which it was sent was engaged [8: *The number was not engaged. Neither Gladys Harley nor any of the members of the chess club had used or answered the telephone that evening*], one could never have traced the call-box from which the message was sent. So it was that this message was noted, and particulars of it will be proved.

"It is the case for the prosecution that this message was a bogus one and the person who sent it was careful to disguise his voice when speaking to the person who eventually delivered the message to the accused. We suggest that the accused disguised his voice because his normal voice would have been recognised by the person who took the message.

"While the message was given to the telephone official in one voice, a totally different voice was assumed on speaking to the gentleman who received the message. [9: *There was no evidence to support this statement.*] I say that it is the suggestion of the prosecution that the accused sent that message so that on the following night, after he had carried out his preconceived intention of murdering his wife, he would be able to establish an alibi as to his position on or about the time of the murder.

"He says he left at 6.45. The prosecution say at some time before seven o'clock [*10: See 4 above*] he went to keep this appointment which he said had been made in Menlove Gardens. [*11: There was a great deal of difference between Menlove Gardens, which existed, and Menlove Gardens East, which did not.*] He made elaborate enquiries. He was most persistent, not only in asking for the address, but told a policeman at which house his business was. He explained he had received a message, and gave the address to which he was going—sufficient, according to the prosecution, to enable him to say later: 'At the time the murder was committed, I was in Menlove Gardens.'

"He says that having been unable to find this address, he became suspicious and felt that something was wrong, and so he returned home. Why should he become suspicious that something was wrong at home because some address that had been given to him turned out to be wrong? I suggest that he, in fact, knew what was wrong, and that the time had come for him to make the discovery. He says he hurried home, but as a matter of fact, he was seen in conversation with some man within a very few yards of his home, apparently standing and talking. Then he says that on arriving at his home he went to the front door. That is a curious fact, as he said later that he was always in the habit of going in by the back door. [*12: He said nothing of the sort. What he, in fact, said—in a statement to the police (28.1.31)—was this: "When I returned home at 8.41 p.m. on Tuesday the 20th inst., I went to the front door because it was my usual practice if I was out late at night. It was my usual practice to use the back door in daylight."*]

"He says he could not open the front door, so he went round to the back, and found he could not open that. He thought perhaps it was bolted. After that, he went round to the front door again, tried that, and then rushed round to the back door, but before he could reach the back door he met two neighbours.

"It is suggested by the prosecution that he was waiting until he could meet one or two persons who would go into the house with him to make the discovery.

"Then he goes to the back door, which was not bolted or locked, and he goes in. Now, downstairs there are two rooms—a kitchen and a front sitting-room—and three bedrooms upstairs. It is a curious thing that the accused, having gone into the house, asked

I

his neighbours to wait in case there was anything wrong. [*13: It was not Wallace but Mr Johnston who suggested that he and his wife should wait.*]

"He goes into every room in the house before he goes into the front sitting-room, where his wife was battered to death.[1] When he comes out, he calls his neighbours in and Mrs Johnston goes in. There they find the woman. She is dead, and lying beside her on the carpet is a mackintosh which belonged to the accused, and which he had been wearing earlier in the day. For some reason, when he went out afterwards, he did not wear the mackintosh, but his coat. Perhaps because it was colder. [*14: Wallace did not wear his mackintosh in the afternoon or evening, for the simple reason that it was no longer raining.*]

"This mackintosh, which was lying by the side of the woman, had been hanging up on the rack. Accused immediately remarks to the neighbour, 'What is my mackintosh doing here?' [*15: It was not until Wallace and Mrs Johnston went into the parlour the second time that he mentioned the mackintosh.*]

"When the police came and saw this mackintosh they held it up and examined it. It was covered with blood, and was burnt to some extent at the bottom, towards the right side. There was blood all over it and blood up the sleeves. [*16: It may be thought that when Bishop said there was "blood up the sleeves" he was not misstating a fact, but speaking ambiguously. In his opening speech at the committal proceedings, however, he made it clear that what he meant was that there was blood inside the sleeves. In fact, apart from a few small stains within the right cuff, the insides of the sleeves were clean.*]

"When this was held up by the police and shown to the accused it was not until he saw two patches on it that he identified it as his. I suggest that that mackintosh was used to protect the murderer from the blood of his victim. That an attempt was made to destroy it by fire afterwards.

"Accused discovered that his house had been robbed. He found that four £1 notes had been stolen from the cash-box, quite a small thing, which had been kept on a high shelf where one would not expect to look for a cash-box. [*17: After checking his insurance*

---

[1] Later it was suggested by the prosecution that an innocent man would have looked in the parlour *before* going upstairs. But as Wallace himself explained, it was natural that he should have left the parlour until last, since it was the last place he expected to find his wife. The parlour was the "best room", only used for musical evenings, or when visitors called.

books Wallace had informed the police that the cash-box had contained a £1 note, three 10s. notes, thirty or forty shillings in silver, a postal order for 4s. 6d., and a crossed cheque for £5 17s. od.]

"He found, strangely enough, that the money had been stolen, and the tray replaced, cash-box closed and replaced on the shelf. I suggest it is a most unlikely thing for any thief who broke into the house to do. Later it was found that four £1 notes were in a vase, in a bedroom upstairs, and on one of these notes there was some human blood. I need say no more about that.

"In the bathroom of the house, on the first floor, there is a water closet, and on the top rim of that there was found a bloodstain which, there is no doubt at all, was of the same period of time as the murdered woman's death. [*18: The only undoubted facts about the stain were (a) that it was of human blood, and (b) that it was not of menstrual origin.*]

"The suggestion of the prosecution is that whoever murdered the woman went up into the bathroom, and washed away all stains of blood from his person. It is suggested that no person—or stranger—who broke into the house with robbery as his motive would have gone upstairs into the bathroom, when there was plenty of hot water in the kitchen below.

"No weapon could be found. I suggest that that is a most significant fact. The suggestion is put forward that if a stranger broke in and robbed and murdered the woman, he would not take his weapon away."

Bishop adjusted his pince-nez, consulted his notes to make sure that he had covered all the points, then sat down. He did not stay sitting for long. As soon as Inspector Gold had related the details of the arrest Bishop was on his feet again, applying for a remand in custody for the maximum period of eight days.

"When the stipendiary asked the accused if he had anything to say Wallace gripped the rails of the dock tightly with his long hands, and, pulling himself up to his full height, said, dramatically, 'Nothing, sir, except that I am absolutely innocent of the charge'."[1]

The remand was granted.

As Wallace was being led down the stairs from the dock there was a sudden outburst of laughter at the back of the court, provoked by a remark from a spectator:

"Wallace, the chess-murderer, got rid of his queen, but now he's having trouble with a Bishop."

* * *

[1] *Liverpool Echo* (3.2.31).

Before being taken to the hospital block at Walton Gaol, Wallace was allowed to telephone a solicitor.

The man he chose to take charge of his defence was Hector Munro, of the Dale Street firm of Herbert J. Davis, Berthen & Munro.

A dapper, boyish-faced man in his early thirties, Munro had been practising in Liverpool for four years. Before that he and Miss Edith Berthen—one of the first women to be articled as a solicitor—had held a joint practice in London. In 1927 the ageing Herbert J. Davis had offered Miss Berthen a partnership in his old-established firm, an offer which she had accepted, on condition that Munro was included in the partnership. Davis had willingly agreed, and now, in 1931, the newly-constituted firm was already recognized as one of the foremost general law practices in the North-west.

Hector Munro was a man who worked hard and played hard. He had many other interests besides the Law. One of his main fascinations was chess, a game at which he excelled; he represented Lancashire in matches against other counties, and played in tournaments all over the country.

He was a member of the Liverpool Central Chess Club.

His attendances at the twice-weekly club meetings were infrequent, and he had never had the misfortune of playing chess with Wallace—indeed, he had never even spoken to him; all that he knew about Wallace was that his initials were W.H., having seen the name on tournament sheets pinned to the notice-board at the City Café. Wallace must have known a good deal more about Munro than Munro knew about him—enough, at any rate, to convince him that he was choosing the right man for what lawyers call "the temporary post of life-saver".

It was the captain of the chess club who had given Wallace the message which sparked off the train of events leading to his arrest; now the club's star player was presented with the task of securing his freedom.

Munro, newly married, had returned from his honeymoon only a few days before, so he knew practically nothing about the case, apart from what he had gleaned from the brief accounts in the national Press. He had no idea of the intense interest the case had aroused on Merseyside; he had heard none of the rumours, none of the theories that were circulating.

Without delay, he set about acquainting himself with the details of the case, first of all obtaining a copy of Bishop's speech at the preliminary hearing, then driving to Walton to hear Wallace's side of the story. Later, accompanied by his wife, May, and his clerk, Norman Wheeler, he visited the scene of the crime.

Munro was quick to appreciate the crucial importance of the time factor. According to Bishop's exposition of the police theory, Wallace had murdered his wife some time between 6.31, when a milk boy had called at the house, and about five minutes to seven. Was it possible, Munro wondered, that the milk boy was *not* the last person to have seen Mrs Wallace alive?

There was one way of finding out.

He spent several evenings in and around Wolverton Street, questioning the Wallaces' neighbours in the hope of tracing someone who had called at the house after the milk boy. One of the people he contacted was James Caird, whom he knew slightly, having met him once or twice at chess-club meetings. In the course of their conversation Caird mentioned that, the night after the murder, his son Kenneth had set out for the library, but had returned shortly afterwards, bubbling over with the news that a milk boy named Alan Close had seen Mrs Wallace at quarter to seven the previous night.

Munro asked if he could speak to Kenneth Caird, and the boy was called into the room. "I have a clear recollection of the talk between Jones, Elsie Wright, Metcalf, Close, and myself," he said, and went on to give a detailed account of the incident.

With Kenneth Caird's assistance Munro had little difficulty in tracking down the other three children.

Harold Jones confirmed Kenneth Caird's statement.

So did Elsie Wright. She was positive that Close had said that he had seen Mrs Wallace at a quarter to seven.

She was equally positive that he had been nowhere near Wolverton Street at 6.31. "When I was out delivering milk on Tuesday evening, 20th January," she stated, "I came into Breck Road and heard the bells of the Belmont Institute ringing for half-past six service. I then went to the Vicarage of Holy Trinity, and was kept there for about five minutes. Before I got to the Vicarage the bells had stopped. When I left the Vicarage I went to Letchworth Street. I passed Alan Close while I was in Letchworth Street. He was going in the direction of Wolverton Street. When I passed him it would be about twenty to seven. The next evening, when I saw him in the dairy, we talked about the murder, and he said he had been on his way to Mrs Wallace when he met me."

Of all the children, Douglas Metcalf was the one with the clearest recollection of the conversation with Close. But the most valuable part of his statement ran as follows: "On the night of the murder . . . I was in the Parochial Hall in Richmond Park giving Mr Davies, the Caretaker, a paper, and there was a Lantern Lecture going on. I asked one of the men the time, as I wanted to go to a football match, and he said it was twenty-five to seven. I then had to go across to Campbell's Dance Hall in Richmond Park, and when I came out of there I talked to some boys for a very short time, and then walked down the passage into Wolverton Street. I had just crossed over to 23 Wolverton Street when I saw a boy named Allison Wildman walking down the entry towards Redbourn Street."

On Wednesday, February 18th, Hector Munro called upon Allison Wildman at his home in Twickenham Street, Anfield, and received the following statement:

"I am 16 years of age . . . In my spare time I deliver newspapers for my uncle. . . .

"I always glance at the Holy Trinity Church clock in passing. When I passed on the evening of 20th January, it was twenty-five to seven. Having passed Holy Trinity, it takes me about two minutes to get into Wolverton Street. I remember the time quite clearly because when I read of the murder next morning I thought over what time I had passed Holy Trinity. I told my mother about it.

"When I delivered the paper at 27 Wolverton Street, it would be about twenty-two or twenty-three minutes to seven. The door of No. 29 Wolverton Street was wide open and a milk boy was standing on the top step with two or three cans in his hand. He was wearing a Collegiate cap. When I left, the milk boy was still standing there."

It didn't take Hector Munro long to find out that Alan Close was a pupil of the Collegiate School. Elsie Wright stated that the boy was definitely wearing his school cap on the night of the murder (and, at the committal proceedings, Close himself admitted that this was so).

Munro was well pleased with the results of his investigation into the time factor. He had collected strong evidence—indeed, well-nigh conclusive evidence—that Close had said that he had seen Mrs Wallace at a quarter to seven. The combined statements of the four children showed that Close had mentioned this time not once, but on three separate occasions: first of all at the dairy, in conversation with Elsie Wright; secondly, replying to Douglas Metcalf's question; thirdly, when he had spoken to the policeman at 29 Wolverton Street. There was the evidence of Elsie Wright that she had seen Close walking in the direction of Wolverton Street at "about twenty to seven" on the night of the murder. And there was Allison Wildman's evidence that Close had been standing on the doorstep of 29 Wolverton Street at twenty-two or twenty-three minutes to seven.

So far Munro had interviewed three newspaper boys—Harold Jones, Douglas Metcalf, and Allison Wildman—but he still had to trace the boy who had delivered the evening paper which was found lying open on the kitchen table after the discovery of the murder. As it turned out, this newspaper boy was not a boy at all, but a man in his middle-twenties named David Jones. Munro eventually caught up with him in a neighbourhood pub.

David Jones stated: "I have delivered 'Echoes' to the Wallaces for 4 or 5 years. On 20th January last I delivered there at about 6.35 P.M. I thrust the 'Echo' through the letter-box."

(If Jones's estimate of the time was accurate it was reasonable to assume that Mrs Wallace was still alive at twenty-five minutes to seven. Either she or her husband had picked up the newspaper from the mat and taken it through to the kitchen, and she was more likely to have done this than Wallace—who, if he was getting ready to murder her, or had already committed the crime, would surely not have been the least bit interested in reading the day's news.)

David Jones went on: "I did not notice any lights in the house. I did not hear any noise or commotion of any kind.

"I was seen by the Police on the Thursday evening after the murder, when I was in Wolverton Street at 6.35. I made a statement to them on the lines of the foregoing."

Munro was more than slightly puzzled by those last two sentences in David Jones's statement. By now the committal proceedings had begun, and he had seen the list of witnesses to be called by the prosecution. *David Jones's name was not included on the list.* Munro wondered why. Was this an unintentional oversight or a deliberate omission on the part of the police, whose duty, as laid down by the Court of Criminal Appeal, was "to ensure that *all* the known facts and *all* the arguments in a case are presented, irrespective of whether or not these facts and arguments assist in proving the guilt of an accused person"?

The more Munro pondered this question, the more his suspicions grew that the police were bending the rules—or, rather, disregarding them—in order to secure Wallace's conviction. Deciding to put his suspicions to the test, he wrote to Superintendent Moore, suggesting that David Jones and Allison Wildman, copies of whose statements he enclosed, should be interviewed by the police and called as prosecution witnesses.

Moore did not reply to the letter, but on the day that it was delivered at police headquarters Inspector Gold called at Allison Wildman's home and took a statement from him; the following day Gold interviewed Wildman's employer and the headmaster of the school he had attended—clearly in the hope of learning of some episode in the boy's past which might provide a reason for disqualifying him as a witness of credit. But unfortunately for the police, Wildman was a person of excellent character. And so was David Jones, whose past was also scrutinized.

Although the police had no excuse for excluding them as witnesses, neither Wildman nor Jones was called to give evidence at the committal proceedings.

Munro's suspicions were confirmed: the police were presenting a one-sided case against Wallace. He was refused permission to see the statements of people who had been interviewed during the investigation but were not being called as witnesses; the police were compelled to provide their names and addresses, but Munro lacked the time and the resources to contact all the people named on a list which covered several foolscap pages.

From now on always at the back of his mind was the disquieting thought that the police were holding back other witnesses like David Jones, whose evidence was relevant to the case but damaging to the accusation against Wallace.

Sydney Scholefield Allen was the barrister chosen by Munro to represent Wallace at the committal proceedings.

He was a young man, only a year or so older than Munro, and of a similar height and build to the solicitor. (By the end of the case, however, the similarity of build was a good deal less marked: Scholefield Allen expended so much nervous and physical energy on Wallace's behalf that he lost more than a stone in weight.)

Munro had briefed Scholefield Allen several times in the past, in cases of a comparatively minor nature, and he knew that, quite apart from his talents as an advocate, he was a man of courage and perseverance—a man who believed in justice in the fullest sense of the word, and who was willing to make great personal sacrifice in order to attain it and to uphold it. There were several barristers

in Liverpool with a wider experience of criminal law than Scholefield Allen; but few, if any, who could match his ability to identify
himself with his client and contest a case as if his own future
depended upon the verdict.

At the committal proceedings fighting spirit would count for
far more than forensic skill on the part of defence counsel. With
this in mind, Munro had little hesitation in deciding that Sydney
Scholefield Allen was the best man for the job.

One of Scholefield Allen's closest friends was Dr Robert Coope,
a tall, strongly-built man in his late thirties, who, as well as
carrying on a successful practice in Rodney Street (the Liverpool
equivalent of London's Harley Street), held several official
medical posts, including those of Physician to the Liverpool
Hospital for Diseases of the Chest, Honorary Assistant Physician
to the Liverpool Royal Infirmary, and Lecturer in Clinical
Chemistry and Demonstrator in Medical Pathology at the University of Liverpool.

In the evening of the first day of the committal proceedings
Coope arrived at Scholefield Allen's house in Prince's Park to keep
a dinner date that had been arranged some weeks before. He
entered the living-room to find Scholefield Allen squatting on the
floor, surrounded by a mass of papers—witnesses' statements,
newspaper cuttings, and sheaves of notes taken at interviews with
Wallace at the prison. When Scholefield Allen explained that he
was working on the Wallace case Coope offered to leave; but he
was told that, far from being in the way, he could not have arrived
at a more opportune time. In the next day or so, Scholefield Allen
explained, the prosecution were calling their medical witnesses,
and he asked for Coope's assistance in framing the questions to
put to them in cross-examination.

Coope sat down and listened, occasionally chipping in with
questions, as Scholefield Allen outlined the main facts relating to
the medical evidence in the case. By the time dinner was served,
however, the roles were reversed, with Coope doing most of the
talking, while the barrister sat concentrating on his words, only
interrupting to query a particular point, or to ask that a remark
be amplified.

They were still at the dinner-table when the conversation turned
from the general subject of methods used in estimating time of
death to the question of the bloodstain found on the lavatory-pan
in the bathroom at Wolverton Street. Scholefield Allen said that the

prosecution were placing great importance on this item of evidence: if Wallace was the murderer he must have washed himself before leaving for Menlove Gardens, and the bloodstain was the only indication that he had done so.

"Have you any idea of its size and shape?" Coope asked.

"None at all."

"How long did Wallace have at his disposal?"

Scholefield Allen said that, according to the evidence of Alan Close and the police witnesses who had taken part in the "tram tests", the maximum time available to Wallace was eighteen minutes (6.31–6.49), but the defence had evidence to show that Julia was still alive between 6.37 and 6.38, which reduced the maximum time to approximately twelve minutes.

Coope was silent for a moment. Then: "The dimensions of the bloodstain are important," he said. "It would be well worth putting some questions on this point."

Scholefield Allen frowned. "But I don't see how this information could help us."

Coope asked him to get a needle; then the two men left the dining-room and went into the bathroom. Coope pricked his finger and let a few drops of blood fall from different heights on to the rim of the lavatory-pan.

"Now you can see for yourself," he said. "When dropped vertically from even up to a foot in height the drop of freshly shed blood invariably takes on a circular shape, and remains almost perfectly flat. Looked at from the side, it is like a very shallow inverted saucer. It gradually dries into a circular red flake of dried blood, its depth negligible. On the other hand, a piece of firm, solid clot would be three-dimensional. Hence the importance of knowing the measurements, because if the spot was a piece of firm clot and not a drop of freshly shed blood, it must have been away from the victim's body for a good deal longer than eighteen minutes, the maximum time available to Wallace."

A couple of days later Superintendent Moore gave evidence at the committal proceedings, and, as soon as the case was adjourned for the day, Scholefield Allen and Hector Munro, both of them in a state of high excitement, rushed round to Dr Coope's consulting rooms.

Munro read from the notes he had taken of the detective's answers in cross-examination:

"The blood in the bathroom was a clot, not a blood splash. . . . When Dr MacFall removed it on a small piece of paper at 1 A.M., the inside of it seemed quite moist and more of a blood colour than the outside. . . . The clot had the appearance of a small pea, cut in two, with a circular top."

Coope did not keep the two lawyers in suspense. "If this description is correct," he said quietly, "the blood found on the lavatory-pan could not have been dropped there by Wallace."

"But can you be sure of that?" Scholefield Allen asked.

"As sure as one can be sure of anything in Medicine," Coope replied calmly. "I cannot envisage any circumstances which would cause a drop of fresh blood to take the shape of a split pea."

Munro asked Coope if he would make some experiments to ascertain the approximate age of the blood when it was deposited on the lavatory-pan. Coope agreed. He pointed out, though, that before commencing the experiments he would need more information than was contained in Superintendent Moore's testimony. He provided a list of questions, which, the next day, Scholefield Allen put to Professor MacFall.

Replying to these questions, MacFall stated that "the circular clot of blood was three-sixteenths of an inch in diameter and one-eighth of an inch in height. From this there was a light streak of blood in the direction of the pan centre." The temperature of the bathroom, MacFall said vaguely, was "ordinary", adding that it was "not very cold—about the same as the room down below".

As soon as Coope received a copy of MacFall's deposition he began a series of experiments—118 in all—using drops of blood or blood clots ranging from a few minutes to four hours in age, dropping them on to porcelain from different heights, and varying the surrounding temperature.

The results of these experiments more than confirmed his original opinion, and he reported to Munro:

"The spot of blood . . . could not possibly have been a fresh blood spot. . . . Such a fresh blood spot . . . would dry into a flat, 'dry varnish' type of mass which could then be scraped off in hard flakes.

"Firm clots, carefully removed from the serum surrounding them, could be used to give 'spots' of the conical mass required. These dry first upon the surface, and later begin to wrinkle; as they dry inside, the blood becomes crumbly, rather like truffle chocolate.

"It seems clear that the blood found in the bathroom was a piece of *firm* clot, and, if it came from the deceased, that it must have been transferred from the clot around the body some time after death. I think it is fair to guess that the clotted blood around the body would not be firm enough to give a cone of clot such as was described, before at least an hour after death; and in view of the experiments showing the drying of firm clot, it might be argued that the clot may have been deposited less than 3 hours before 1 A.M., when it was removed, wet inside.

"The slight creeping of blood in the direction of the pan centre is probably due to a thin film of moisture on the top of the pan . . . which would tend to cause creeping of the red colouring matter of the blood."

While he was engaged on the experiments Coope consulted his friend and colleague, James Henry Dible, Professor of Pathology at the University of Liverpool. After reading MacFall's deposition and carrying out some experiments of his own Dible—a small, neat, quiet-spoken man, whose reputation as a pathologist was second to none—came to the same conclusion as Coope.

"Professor MacFall's measurements of this clot of blood," he wrote, "are three-sixteenths of an inch in diameter by an eighth of an inch high. This, it will be noticed, indicates an elliptical or conical mass of blood, the ratio of whose height to diameter is 2:3, which is greater than that of a half sphere (1:2). . . . It is impossible to form a blood spot of the stated dimensions with fresh blood."

Having established the irrelevance of the clot of blood to the case against Wallace, Coope and Dible turned their attention to the other medical evidence. Although neither of them had much regard for MacFall's abilities as a forensic expert, they were astonished at the slipshod way in which he had performed the examination; what astonished them even more was the number of examples contained in his deposition of dubious inferences masquerading as definite facts.

Much of MacFall's deposition was taken up by his answers to questions concerning the time of Julia's death, which he said had occurred about four hours before his arrival at the house at 9.50. This estimate, Dible pointed out, was based upon MacFall's observation of (a) the presence of rigor mortis in the neck and upper part of the left arm and (b) the exudation of "a small amount" of serum from the blood on the hearthrug—two processes so variable in time occurrence as to give little help in ascertaining the time of death with any degree of accuracy.

MacFall was guilty of a large number of errors of omission in his handling of the medical examination; but by far the most glaring of these, it seemed to Dible, was his failure to note the temperature of the body—the method universally accepted among medico-legal experts as being "the best and most constant guide to the number of hours since death".[1] Without the evidence of the rectal temperature, it was impossible to be at all exact as to the time of death.

Answering a question from Sydney Scholefield Allen, MacFall said, "The degree of accuracy in estimating post-mortem rigidity is within one hour and three-quarters of an hour." Which was nonsense, Dible said; depending upon the circumstances, rigor mortis might appear "as early as two hours or as late as eight hours after death".

(Incidentally, it was difficult, if not impossible, to reconcile another of MacFall's statements—"Progressive post-mortem rigidity assisted me in saying how long she had been dead"—with the eccentric behaviour-pattern of the rigor mortis in Julia Wallace's body. In the two hours between 9.50 and 11.50 the rigor made no progress at all; at 12.10, according to Pierce, it was "about the same"; but in the fifty minutes between 12.10 and 1 A.M., when MacFall and Pierce took their last look at the body before it was removed to the mortuary, the rigor really got a move on, spreading to the extremities of three limbs. How MacFall was "assisted" by the stop-go policy of the rigor—140 minutes spent loitering in the vicinity of the left shoulder, then 50 minutes of remarkably speedy advance through the whole body—remains one of the minor mysteries of the Wallace case.)

"In estimating the time deceased had been dead," MacFall stated, "I relied mainly on the post-mortem rigidity, but this evidence was corroborated by my observation at 9.50 of the large blood clot on the edge of the hearthrug, from which there was a small amount of serum exudation, the appearance of which was very characteristic. The evidence of the blood clot," he added, "is not quite so reliable as post-mortem rigidity." In other words, he used the extremely unreliable evidence of the blood clot to substantiate the slightly less unreliable evidence of the rigor mortis.

Noting that MacFall's only reason for believing that the blood had been standing for about four hours was the separation of a small amount of serum, Dible commented, "This again is very variable in time occurrence. . . . The only opinion which can be hazarded is an estimate of the shortest time in which it is likely to take place. In a very guarded way I should say it is not likely to be very evident earlier than two hours."

[1] *Taylor's Principles and Practice of Medical Jurisprudence* (8th edition).

Dr Coope agreed with Dible's comments, and added, "The amount of blood shed gave such a mass that its weight would help greatly in the squeezing out of serum." He believed that the small amount of serum observed by MacFall indicated that the blood had probably been standing for no more than three hours.

During the period between the committal proceedings and the trial something happened in Liverpool which helped to confirm this belief. A man committed suicide by throwing himself from one of the top-floor windows of Lewis's department store in Ranelagh Street: his skull was smashed; death was instantaneous. As soon as Coope heard of the tragedy he telephoned Dible, and the two doctors were waiting at the Royal Infirmary when the body was brought in. For several hours they observed the changes in the state of the body and in the condition of the blood from the head wound, noting the time of each change in relation to the time of death, which was known to the minute.

The most important of their observations was this—that in two and a half hours there was "a very abundant" exudation of serum from the blood around the head. If the serum could appear and spread so rapidly in the suicide case, then it was reasonable to suggest that the serum in Julia Wallace's blood might have separated from the clot at much the same speed. There were marked similarities between the two cases: the injuries were similar, and so were the amounts of blood under observation; the same accelerating factors were present (but there were probably more of them in the parlour at Wolverton Street than in the sterilized conditions of the hospital mortuary). If nothing else, the observation of the suicide's blood showed that MacFall's estimate of the age of the blood clot might be astray of the truth by as much as two hours.

Neither Coope nor Dible was willing to hazard a guess as to the exact time of Julia Wallace's death; they both believed that there were too many unknown factors involved, any one of which might have accelerated or retarded the post-mortem signs. All that Dible would say was that the murder might have been committed at the time estimated by MacFall . . . but it was just as likely to have been committed after seven o'clock, when Wallace was away from the house.

Beginning on Thursday, February 19th, the committal proceedings lasted for seven days, during which time the prosecution called thirty-five witnesses, whose evidence—about 50,000 words of it—was taken down in longhand, in the form of depositions, by the Clerk of the Court, Henry Harris.

Reflecting—and magnifying—the public interest in the case, the Liverpool evening papers devoted yards of space on their main news pages to verbatim reports of the proceedings . . . or to *supposedly* verbatim reports: only rarely did their two versions of the evidence coincide, word for word. Less obtrusively, but certainly more accurately, the *Liverpool Daily Post* provided its morning readers with a summary, contained in a column or two, of the previous day's evidence.

Each day the public gallery was jam-packed with spectators. They came from all over Liverpool, but especially from Anfield, and from all walks of life, but mainly from what the papers called "the labouring class". Their pockets stuffed with bags of sandwiches and buns and Thermos flasks, their minds filled with rumour-inspired prejudice against Wallace, they came to the committal proceedings, not because they were particularly interested in hearing the prosecution case, but for the thrill of seeing Wallace in person—the double thrill of seeing a man who had committed a brutal murder and who was now on the first stage of the journey to the scaffold.

But the thrill was disappointingly short-lived, lasting only for as long as it took Wallace to enter the court and take his place; from then on all that the people in the public gallery could see of him was the back of his head, and there was nothing very exciting about that.

Needing some form of entertainment to while away the hours, they listened for hidden meanings in the evidence, for innuendoes that could be used as the excuse for laughter. They roared when MacFall said that the clot of blood found on the lavatory-pan was "not of menstrual origin"; they split their sides when a police witness said that Wallace's diaries contained "many entries relating to the illnesses of himself and his wife"; but the best joke of all—at least, the one which provoked the loudest laughter—was concocted from Inspector Gold's statement that Julia's artificial hair-pad "was hair that had been worn by a lady".

On the first day the *Liverpool Echo* reported:

"Half an hour before time, hundreds of persons had gathered in the courtyard. . . . When the doors of the stipendiary's court were opened, about half of the crowd managed to obtain standing room in that court, the remainder being shepherded back into the street. But the accused appeared in No. 2 court, where few, besides witnesses, had gone."

No. 2 Court was presided over by a lay magistrate, an elderly gentleman named R. J. Ward, who was the proprietor of a music business which specialized in supplying band instruments to the Salvation Army and the Boys' Brigade. It seemed almost unbelievable to many people (and still does) that while the stipendiary, a qualified lawyer, sat in No. 1 Court, meting out fines to drunks, careless drivers, and petty thieves, the case against Wallace, a man charged with the gravest crime in the calendar, was heard (but none too clearly, for Mr Ward was rather deaf) by someone with only a meagre knowledge of the law.

According to a court official, Mr Ward "was aged, somewhat egotistical and not possessed of a logical or a judicial mind. Furthermore, he was inclined to the view that if a person was brought before the court by the police, he must be guilty."

Hector Munro was well aware that, even with the stipendiary sitting, the odds against Wallace being acquitted in the magistrates' court were astronomically high: in the three years from 1928 to 1930, of 191 persons prosecuted for murder, only six were not committed for trial. With Mr Ward on the bench, Wallace didn't stand a chance.

The first-day spectators were quick to realize that they were in the wrong court. As the stipendiary took his place on the bench and a man charged with some small offence was led into the dock, there was a rising murmur from the public gallery—then a wild but concerted rush for the doors, a stampede across the lobby and into No. 2 Court.

The court was quiet again, the crowd settled, when J. R. Bishop rose to make the opening speech for the prosecution.

A fortnight before, applying for Wallace's remand in custody, Bishop had included eighteen misstatements in his speech . . . an average of one for every eighty words, which must be something of a legal record. Now, in his second speech, he repeated most of these misstatements—and added a few more.

The most spectacularly incorrect of the new additions appeared when he suggested that Wallace had lied when, after receiving the telephone message from Samuel Beattie, he said that he did not know where Menlove Avenue was. (Which, it will be remembered, was itself a misstatement, carried over from the first speech: Wallace had said no such thing.)

Bishop found the remark which Wallace never made "curious for this reason—that his chief lives at a house, 34 Green Lane, which runs out of Menlove Avenue. Menlove Gardens North,

POST CARD

17a Villa
Cemaes Bay
Anglesea

This is a lovely place
and we have such a
nice place to stop.
Isn't what a journey! 10 hours

Mrs Johnston
31 Wolverton St
Anfield
Liverpool

e 64558

Postcards sent by Julia Wallace to her neighbour, Mrs Johnston, while on holiday at Port Padrig, Cemaes Bay, Anglesey; postmarked (above) July 23rd, 1926, and (below), July 6th, 1928

Richard Whittington-Egan Collection

A page from Detective-Inspector Herbert Gold's insurance book, with entries made by Wallace

Wallace's appearance was not in his favour

A sketch made by Sir Frederick Bowman after attending the committal proceedings.

South, and West all run out of Menlove Avenue, on the opposite side. The accused has been in the habit of visiting his chief for some time past at this house, and must know the district well—apart from the fact that he has lived in Liverpool for many years, and that, when his chief has been laid up, as he was some two years ago, he went there regularly two or three times a week."

Three sentences: three misstatements. One can accept that the first two misstatements (saying that all three of the Gardens ran into the Avenue, when in fact only two of them did; and that Wallace had been "in the habit of visiting his chief for some time past", when in fact he had visited him only five times within a period of a couple of months, and not at all in the previous two years), were unintentional errors, caused in the first instance by faulty map-reading, and in the second by a mistaken idea of the meaning of the word 'habit'.

But there can be no possible doubt that the third misstatement—"when his chief has been laid up, as he was some two years ago, he went there regularly two or three times a week"—was based on an audacious piece of fabrication by someone connected with the prosecution for whom Bishop was an unwitting spokesman. Joseph Crewe, in his own words, "had never been ill a day in his life"; his statement to the police contained no reference to his health and he later assured Hector Munro that, when, interviewed by Inspector Gold, "the subject of his health never arose".

Clearly, then, someone connected with the prosecution invented the illness for Joseph Crewe. Clearly, too, necessity was the mother of the invention. Wallace's few night-time visits for violin lessons were not enough to support the assertion that "he knew the district well", so Crewe's illness—a pretty severe and prolonged one, if Wallace visited him "regularly two or three times a week"—was devised to meet the need.

Continuing his speech, Bishop started to outline the mackintosh theory: but he did not get very far with it. As he was saying ,"The reason, I suggest, that Wallace was not wearing his mackintosh at Menlove Avenue is because it had played some part in the crime," Scholefield Allen leapt to his feet to make the first objection, to speak the first words in Wallace's defence.

Trying, not altogether successfully, to keep the anger out of his voice, Scholefield Allen said, "Time after time, Mr Bishop is suggesting things. It is his duty to present this case fairly, without

K

bias, and on the facts. Wallace is on trial for his life, and my friend seems to forget that. I protest strongly about this."

"I do not know how far I must curb my opening remarks," Bishop said.

"Address to the jury, was it not?"

"You can take it from me," the magistrate chipped in, "it is having no effect on me."

Scholefield Allen had been waiting for just such a cue as this. His voice quieter than before, more controlled, he said:

"There will be full reports of Mr Bishop's speech in the Press tonight. It will be read by people wise and people ignorant. It will also be read by people who have a logical faculty and people who have not. It is from among those people that the twelve men and women will be selected to try this man for his life. Surely Wallace is presumed to be innocent until he is proved guilty, and Mr Bishop is not entitled to give his opinion. What we must have are the cold, hard, logical facts." Then, turning to Bishop, he added, "If any."

Silence in the court. Even the people in the public gallery were quiet. Bishop and Scholefield Allen looked towards the bench, waiting for the magistrate to speak.

Blinking through his spectacles, owl-like, Mr Ward thought for a few moments. And then for a few more. The silence began to prickle with suspense. At last, inspiration came to Mr Ward, and in the voice of a man who expects his words to be passed down through the ages and quoted in all the standard law-books, he said:

"It must be realized that there is a prosecution and a defence."

A pause—just long enough for Scholefield Allen to search the remark, but in vain, for some hidden pearl of legal wisdom—then: "I appreciate that," he said (meaning that he understood it; not that he was grateful for it), "but knowing the serious responsibility that lies upon Mr Bishop and upon me, I submit that it is his duty as a cold, remorseless instrument of justice, to present the facts which tell against the accused man, and not to attempt to flare up the imagination of the public."

Bishop retorted: "I am sorry if I am attempting to flare up the imagination of the public. I am attempting to put the case before the magistrate. . . ."

He was about to say something else, but Scholefield Allen interrupted: "Then tell the magistrate, who will act legally, as advised, on the cold facts." And with that, Scholefield Allen sat down.

This was only the first of many arguments—or "BREEZES BETWEEN COUNSEL", as the newspapers gleefully headlined them. As the proceedings wore on, the breezes increased both in number and in force, until, on the penultimate day, when Scholefield Allen rose to tell Bishop not to put words into a witness's mouth, Bishop's temper was so frayed that, without thinking of legal niceties, he shouted at the defence counsel to sit down.

But by then Bishop had another reason, and a far stronger one than the annoyance of being continually put off his stroke by objections, for feeling bad-tempered: the prosecution case was so diminished as to be almost non-existent. The way Scholefield Allen had assaulted it was little short of vandalism; he had torn apart most of the misstatements and thrown the pieces back in Bishop's face . . . he had pricked the giant bubbles of speculation . . . he had exploded the theories with ridicule.

Wallace's defence was in good hands, and no-one was more aware of this fact than Wallace himself. His confidence in Scholefield Allen's method of advocacy was emphasized by his calm manner as he sat in the well of the court, leaning forward so as not to miss a word of what was said, but without showing the slightest sign of worry or emotion. This calmness of Wallace's must have been as disappointing and frustrating for the pleasure-seekers in the public gallery as it undoubtedly was for the reporters who sat for six long days, their eyes glued on him in the hope that he might give them an excuse for using a more exciting adjective than "collected" to describe his demeanour.

It was not until just before the lunch-time adjournment on the seventh and final day that the reporters' hope was realized, their patience rewarded, and Wallace—for the first and only time in public—lost his composure and broke down.

Inspector Gold, the last prosecution witness, was being cross-examined by Scholefield Allen. Earlier, in direct evidence, Gold had referred to, and produced as an exhibit, the small Prudential "give-away" diary containing Wallace's note of the Qualtrough telephone message. He had made no mention, however, of the other diaries—the four personal diaries which Wallace had kept from the beginning of 1928 until the Sunday before his wife's murder. Noting this omission, and remembering that Bishop had questioned none of the other C.I.D. witnesses regarding the diaries, Scholefield Allen concluded that the prosecution were once again attempting to withhold evidence which was helpful to Wallace.

One of his first questions to Gold was: "Are the police in possession of other diaries belonging to the accused?"

The inspector hesitated for a moment, then produced from his jacket pocket three small diaries, held together by an elastic band. "There are these business diaries which were kept by the accused," he said casually.

"But there are *other* diaries?" Scholefield Allen persisted, his voice steely now. "Are there other diaries of events, thoughts and opinions?"

Once again Gold hesitated before admitting, "Yes, and of daily occurrences." Then, looking like a glum-faced magician whose first trick has misfired, he produced one, two, three, four large diaries from various pockets and laid them on the ledge of the witness-box. As he placed the last diary on top of the others, he blurted out: "There is an entry relating to a falling-out with his wife on January 7th, 1928."

Scholefield Allen made no commment. None was necessary. If the diaries provided a full and accurate record of Wallace's life over the past few years, then it was hardly surprising to find in them at least one reference to a "falling-out" between him and his wife; what *was* surprising—and indicative, surely, of an uncommonly happy marriage—was that Gold could find nothing worse to say about the diaries than that they contained a reference to an argument which had taken place more than three years before the murder. In trying too hard to assist the prosecution, Gold had succeeded only in making a point for the defence.

Asked by Scholefield Allen to read aloud the entry on December 5th, 1930, Gold read it to himself and then gave the court his version of what Wallace had written. "It relates", he said, "to an anxious time Wallace spent during the evening, because it appears that his wife had gone to Southport, and she was very late getting back because there had been an accident on the railway. He says in his diary that he went to the police station at 1 A.M. to see if there was any news of her."

Scholefield Allen, preferring that the court should hear Wallace's own words rather than Gold's interpretation of them, asked to see the diaries. They were handed down to him. After quickly scanning the entry concerning Julia's late return from Southport he pointed out that Gold's version of the story was "oddly incomplete".

"This entry," he said, "goes on: 'I went back home and found her ladyship had just turned up. It seems a laundry van had been smashed up on the railway line, the train derailed, and the line blocked. Julia waited at Southport Station until after ten o'clock, and as she had apparently no hope of getting a train she decided to take a bus. She arrived in Liverpool at 12.30 and reached home at 1. It was a relief to know she was safe and sound, for I was getting apprehensive, fearing that she might have been run over by a motor-car or something.' "

As his counsel read the last sentence in this passage, Wallace suddenly lifted his hands to cover his eyes; his shoulders shook as he tried to fight back the tears.

A small sound, a sound like the rustling of tissue-paper, ran through the court, as first one person, then another, noticed that Wallace was crying and whispered the news to a neighbour.

The only person unaware of Wallace's distress was Scholefield Allen, whose attention was completely taken up by an entry he had found while leafing through the few completed pages in the 1931 diary.

"There is an entry on January 7th, 1931—three years after the one entry about the falling-out with his wife," he said, and went on to read the account of how Wallace and Julia had been "equally charmed" by the effects of frost in Stanley Park.[1]

Although, as Scholefield Allen commented, this was "a word-picture of a beautiful and tender incident", it must have been the last thing in the world that Wallace wanted to hear at that particular moment. The *Liverpool Echo* reporter noted that "during the reading of this extract, Wallace was overcome with emotion, and wept freely, holding his handkerchief up to his face". And the reporter for the rival *Express* wrote that Wallace "was so affected . . . that he sat for a few minutes after the magistrate had adjourned for lunch, and then slowly walked to the cells as his solicitor said to him: 'All right now, Wallace?' "

When he was brought back to the court after the adjournment Wallace looked perfectly composed again. As he resumed his seat he was seen to smile slightly at a remark made to him by Hector Munro.

There was very little left to be done. Scholefield Allen completed the cross-examination of Inspector Gold; Bishop told the court that the prosecution case was closed; the clerk read out the charge; and the magistrate informed Wallace that if there was anything he wanted to say, now was the time to say it.

Wallace rose to his feet. In a quiet but firm voice, he said:

[1] See page 69.

"I plead not guilty to the charge made against me and I am advised to reserve my defence. I would like to say that my wife and I lived together on the very happiest terms during the period of some eighteen years of our married life.[1] Our relations were of complete confidence in, and affection for, each other.

"The suggestion that I murdered my wife is monstrous; that I should attack and kill her is to all who know me unthinkable, and the more so when it must be realized that I could not possibly obtain one advantage by committing such a deed, nor do the police suggest that I gained any advantage.

"On the contrary," Wallace continued—and he was speaking with emotion now, "in actual fact I have lost a devoted and loving comrade, my home life is completely broken up, and everything that I hold dear has been ruthlessly parted and torn from me. I am now to face the torture of this nerve-racking ordeal. I protest once more that I am entirely innocent of this terrible crime."

The magistrate waited until Wallace had sat down, until the court was silent again . . . then: "I have followed the evidence very clearly," he said, "and taken notes, mental and otherwise, from the beginning to the end." Having explained how he had passed the time for the last seven days, Mr Ward paused a moment, and then, as if as an afterthought, committed Wallace for trial at the Liverpool Spring Assizes.

In the public gallery someone let out a cheer.

Hector Munro was responsible for Wallace's defence. He was also responsible for finding the money to pay for it.

In one of his early interviews with Wallace at the prison Munro questioned him as to his financial state. Wallace said that he had about £150 in his bank account, and that he could probably raise a few pounds more by cashing two small endowment policies he held. This sum—although, in those days, quite a reasonable nest-egg for a man in Wallace's position—was ludicrously small compared with the amount which would be needed to cover the defence costs.

Somehow, from somewhere, the extra money had to be found: at least eight hundred pounds, Munro reckoned, and this estimate did not include his own charges, which were bound to be considerable.

---

[1] Wallace miscounted. He and Julia were married on March 24th, 1914; so, at the time of her murder, they were approaching their seventeenth wedding anniversary.

He decided to approach Wallace's employers, the Prudential Assurance Company. It was a matter of Hobson's Choice: he doubted if the company would help—they were concerned with life protection of a different sort from that needed by Wallace—but, apart from the Prudential, who else was there to turn to? No-one that Munro could think of.

Often, in sensational and widely-reported murder cases, the defence costs were paid by a national newspaper, in exchange for the right to publish, after the trial, the accused person's "own and exclusive" story; but the Wallace case, while attracting tremendous newspaper coverage in Liverpool itself, received surprisingly little attention from the national Press.

Munro considered, but quickly rejected, a suggestion put to him that a public appeal be launched. He knew by now that the general consensus of opinion in and around Liverpool was that Wallace was guilty. Even his clerk, Norman Wheeler, normally the most unbigoted of men, had allowed rumour to affect his reason, and strongly supported the majority view. Every morning, first Munro's in-tray, then his waste-paper basket, was filled with indignant but nearly always anonymous letters ("Signed: Vigilante" . . . "Signed: Blind Goddess") from people who accused him, among other mostly unprintable things, of "siding with a clear-cut murderer" or of being "a dirty Wallace-lover". With so much prejudice against Wallace, Munro felt sure that a public appeal would only be a waste of time and effort—and perhaps also of money, for the response to such an appeal might not even cover the expenses of launching it.

One of the less remarkable coincidences in a case which contained so many of them was that the offices of Herbert J. Davis, Berthen and Munro were in the Prudential Building, Dale Street. At his first opportunity Munro arranged an appointment with James Wild, the Prudential Chief Clerk for the Liverpool district, with whom he was slightly acquainted, having met him occasionally in the building. As he walked into the insurance man's office he knew that Wallace's whole future might depend upon the outcome of the meeting; his mission was truly a matter of life and death. Earlier he had spent a long and worrying time trying to decide which method of approach was most likely to succeed with Wild.

But, as it turned out, he need not have bothered. Wild was so anxious to help Wallace, so verbose with his anxiety, that Munro could hardly get a word in edgeways. It was a pleasant surprise. It was also something of an anticlimax. Oddly enough, for a second or two, instead of being elated, Munro felt almost let down by so much enthusiasm.

Wild said that his desire to assist Wallace was shared by the other members of the Prudential indoor staff. On February 3rd, the day after the arrest, Wild had discussed the matter with Arthur Evans, the local secretary of the Prudential Staff Union, and had asked him to organize a collection among the branch members to help Wallace with his defence costs; he had also asked Mr Evans to write to the union headquarters in London, suggesting that "the strongest consideration should be given to the proposition that Mr Wallace should receive financial aid out of Union funds".

The possibility of union assistance was something that had not occurred to Hector Munro. He knew, of course, that the Prudential was a vast organization, but he had had no idea that there were enough employees to support their own separate union. Only later did he learn that Wallace had been a union member for almost as long as he had been with the company, and that, in 1919, he had been chairman of the Liverpool branch.

Wild showed Munro a copy of the union reply. Signed by the joint national secretaries, E. T. Palmer (M.P. for Greenwich) and W. T. Brown, the letter expressed "deep concern at Mr Wallace's predicament", and went on: ". . . the case may go no further than the Hearing before the Magistrates. If, however, the case is sent for trial, you may rest assured that the Executive Council will consider ways and means of helping our brother member."

Munro agreed with Wild that the reply gave grounds for optimism. Then, seizing his chance during a lull in the torrent of words from the chief clerk, he broached the question which had brought him to the office in the first place: Could Wallace expect any financial aid from the Prudential?

Wild looked blank at this. Hastily, Munro pointed out that if one accepted Wallace's innocence, then one also had to accept that he was engaged on company business—or, at least, that he *thought* he was—when his wife's murder took place; the true murderer had used Wallace's profession as the means of getting him away from the house, and if Wallace had been less conscientious the crime would not have been committed, Wallace would not now be in peril of dying upon the scaffold.

Having said his piece, Munro waited for Wild's reaction. The chief clerk slowly shook his head . . . but not to deny the force of Munro's argument. "I never thought of it," he said in an astonished voice. He promised to write at once to the Prudential head office in London.

A couple of days later a reply was received from the Prudential solicitors' department. Like the union, the company wished to defer their decision until after the committal proceedings.

There was little that Munro could do except wait. Towards the end of February he had several meetings with Arthur Evans, the local secretary of the P.S.U.; and with Norman Allsop, a union member with a rather special interest in the case: a native of Barrow-in-Furness, and a close friend of Wallace's father, he had been responsible for Wallace's joining the Prudential back in 1915. Now he proved to be one of Wallace's staunchest allies, sharing with Mr Evans the collecting job, and, as he himself put it, "treating the rumours like bluebottles, and swatting them whenever they came anywhere near".

On March 4th, the day after Wallace's committal for trial, Mr Evans wrote a long and eloquent letter of appeal to the union headquarters, and Mr Wild wrote similarly to the Prudential head office. Hector Munro let a few days go by, then followed up these letters with letters of his own.

Writing to the joint national secretaries of the P.S.U., he outlined the situation as follows:

"The Crown may brief very eminent Counsel, and it will be desirable for the defence to be placed in a position to instruct a leader of equal eminence. We have been in communication with Mr Roland Oliver, K.C., and he would require a fee of 200 guineas on the Brief, and refresher fees of 50 guineas a day for each day beyond the first. If the case lasts five days, his fees would therefore be very substantial, and it must be remembered that junior Counsel is entitled to remuneration at the rate of approximately two-thirds of the leader's fee. . . .

"We could not advise that any less sum than £800 to £1000 would be adequate to ensure the briefing of the best Counsel and the bringing of really competent scientific evidence."

Munro finished up by echoing, though in a less emotional tone, the appeal made by Mr Evans, and by making the perhaps not altogether valid point that "The reputation of insurance men generally is involved in this case".

At the time when this letter, and the one to the Prudential, was written, there was slightly less than £450 in the defence kitty: just about enough to cover the pre-trial expenses. The odd £50 was the total of the collection made among the local P.S.U. members (a surprisingly large amount, considering the limited scope of the collection—and remembering, of course, that a pound in 1931 was worth about three and a half times what it is today); £100 had come from Wallace himself; the rest—£300—was contributed by Wallace's brother, Joseph, who had by now arrived from Malaya (and was trying so hard to help Wallace that he was causing a good deal of hindrance to Munro: he was in and out of the solicitor's office all day long, asking questions, putting forward suggestions, calling conferences, and generally making a well-intentioned nuisance of himself. When he was not in the office or on the telephone to Munro or visiting Wallace at the prison, most of his time was spent wandering the streets of Anfield, searching for information which might throw new light on the mystery. One day he came rushing into the office, hardly able to contain himself as he told Munro that he had heard that two window-cleaners had seen Julia alive after the time given by Alan Close. Munro set about tracing the men. It was a long job. When, eventually, they were found they said it was true that they had seen Julia alive at about 7 P.M.—but not on the night of the murder.)

Within a fortnight of Wallace's committal the defence kitty was boosted to £600. The Prudential, "having taken into consideration Mr Wallace's long and faithful service with the Company", agreed to "make a grant not exceeding the sum of £150" towards the costs.

Meanwhile the joint national secretaries of the P.S.U. had devised a novel plan to resolve the question of how much assistance the union was going to provide. Letters were sent to union officials all over the country, asking them to attend—and form the jury, as it were—at a mock trial to be held at Holborn Hall, the union headquarters in Gray's Inn Road. They would hear both sides of the case—that presented by the prosecution at the committal proceedings, followed by the defence's answers to it—and would then be asked to say whether they believed Wallace to be guilty or innocent of the charge. To protect Wallace from the prejudicial effect of a guilty verdict leaking out to the public, and to prevent the prosecution from learning the full strength of the defence case in advance of the actual trial, the mock trial would be held in camera, and all who attended would be sworn to secrecy.

On Thursday, March 26th, long before the proceedings got under way at half-past ten, the council room was packed with officials representing branches of the union from every part of the country.

The mock trial lasted all day. The case was brought before the union jury by Norman Allsop. Then, after a union official, standing in as clerk of the court, had read aloud the transcript of J. R. Bishop's opening at the committal proceedings, Hector Munro put the case for the defence.

A short break for refreshments—or, rather, in this context, an adjournment—then the union officials were allowed to question Munro, and to argue the pros and cons of the case among themselves. This discussion period went on for two or three hours, and it was starting to get dark outside when J. C. Kinniburgh, the president of the P.S.U., called the meeting to order and asked for the vote to be taken.

The next few minutes were anxious ones for Hector Munro: if the vote went the wrong way, then Wallace's defence would almost certainly have to be conducted "on the cheap"; no counsel of any eminence was likely to accept the defence brief without some assurance that his fees would be paid in full. Munro had done his quiet best, first of all in his speech, and afterwards, answering questions, to convince the union officials that Wallace deserved their support—now he could only sit and wait and hope that his best was good enough.

The voting slips were completed, collected, counted. The man responsible for the count had cleared a space on his desk large enough to take two piles of slips—the votes for Wallace, the votes against. But he need only have made space for one pile. One after another the slips were examined and placed on the right-hand side of the desk. The union officials watched the count in silence at first; then, as the pile grew and the left-hand side of the desk remained empty, an excited murmur ran through the council room . . . someone at the back of the room started clapping his hands in time with the counter's unhurried, unchanging movements, and soon the people around him were clapping, too.

As the last few slips heightened the pile, practically everyone in the room was either clapping or stamping the floor or shouting, "Yes! Yes! Yes! . . ." Some of the more excited ones were clapping, stamping, *and* shouting.

Lifting his hand for silence, the president announced the unanimous verdict in Wallace's favour, and, without preamble, cramming his words into a few seconds of comparative quiet, said that *the executive council would guarantee the whole cost of the defence*.

Then the applause broke out—no ordinary applause, but an

ear-shattering, ceiling-shaking, window-rattling expression of approval, untidily fashioned from shouts and cheers and whistles, clapping hands and stamping feet.

The executive council's decision made trades union history. Never before—and, as far as is known, never since—had a union guaranteed the defence costs of a member, except in cases concerned with union activities. The fact that, at that time, the P.S.U. was a comparatively small and by no means affluent union made the decision even more noteworthy, praiseworthy.

The day after the mock trial "The W. H. Wallace Defence Fund" was set up, and a circular letter was sent to all P.S.U. members, setting out the broad facts of the case and stating the executive council's decision.

At once contributions began to pour into the union treasurer's office—sackfuls of them, mostly of small amounts ranging between two and five shillings. Of the 7000 members of the P.S.U., more than 4000 responded to the appeal, and the eventual total of their contributions (which continued to dribble in long after the case was over: the treasurer was still acknowledging contributions in the March 1932 issue of the union magazine) was in the region of £550. When the defence costs were totted up it was found that a further £250 was needed to settle the bill, and this sum was provided out of union funds.

During the committal proceedings, anticipating the magistrate's decision and already thinking ahead to the trial, Hector Munro had made a tentative offer of the leading defence brief to Roland Oliver, K.C.

Munro's first action, following the successful outcome of the mock trial, was to make the offer firm; and on Tuesday, March 31st —after a couple of days of um-ing and ah-ing by Oliver's clerk, who was concerned that the dates of the Wallace trial might conflict with those of a civil case in which his principal was instructed to appear—Munro was able to announce to the Press that Oliver had accepted the brief and would lead for the defence, with Sydney Scholefield Allen as junior counsel.

At the time of the Wallace case Roland Giffard Oliver was one of the leading figures at the English Bar. "He was an all-round man," says Edgar Lustgarten,[1] ". . . constantly briefed in 'fashionable' jury suits, 'society' divorces, and so-called 'heavy' crime." He was no stranger to sensational murder cases: exactly

[1] *Verdict in Dispute* (Wingate, 1949).

PRUDENTIAL STAFF UNION.

Joint General Secretaries :
E. T. PALMER, M.P.
W. T. BROWN.

Telephone :
HOLBORN 6798.

Registered Office :

30 & 31, HOLBORN HALL,

GRAY'S INN ROAD,

LONDON, W.C.1.

April, 1931.

W. H. WALLACE DEFENCE FUND.

Dear Colleague,

We are, as we write, sitting in session of Executive Council in Holborn Hall and have had under our urgent consideration a matter of life and death. One of our members, an agent, MR. WILLIAM HERBERT WALLACE, of Liverpool, is in Walton Gaol, charged with the murder of his wife. The Press of the country has given this case some publicity. He is committed to the Assize for trial. He is unable to finance the necessary legal assistance, briefing Counsel, etc. Executive Council, having given careful consideration to all available relevant information, which was supplied by MR. A. EVANS, of Liverpool, MR. N. ALLSOP and the lawyer engaged on the case. Messrs. Evans and Allsop know Mr. Wallace well. Mr. Allsop started him in service of the Prudential. Both bear witness that he is an educated and cultured man, not robust in health, who lived in complete happiness with his wife. A man sober, quiet in his habits, respectable in every sense and respected by all who know him. He is held in high esteem by his Prudential colleagues and was at one time chairman of Liverpool Branch. Those who know him think it inconceivable that he could be capable of such an atrocious murder. No motive has been assigned or suggested, except robbery, which would clear Mr. Wallace. Executive Council recognises that our duty to Mr. Wallace does not arise out of the fact that we are a Trade Union and he is our member, although that makes us stand related as brothers, but on the broader, stronger ground of human brotherhood and Christian charity. Executive Council has agreed to guarantee the whole cost of his defence and to raise what money will be required. We therefore, hereby call on all our members to contribute by sending direct to our Treasurer, T. U. WILSON, at Holborn Hall, Grays Inn Road, London, W.C.1. We have placed a duty on the conscience of each member and trust wholeheartedly that there will be a response, immediate and ample, to the needs of this supremely serious occasion. Every person is held innocent, until guilt is proved, in British law and equity.

Yours sincerely,

E. T. PALMER, M.P.,
W. T. BROWN,
General Secretaries.

J. C. KINNIBURGH,
President.

twenty years before, as a young barrister of twenty-nine, he had been second junior to Edward Abinger at the trial of Steinie Morrison, and since then had appeared with Sir Thomas Inskip at the trial, in 1922, of Edith Thompson and Frederick Bywaters, and, in the same year, with Sir Henry Curtis-Bennett, defending Ronald True; in 1923 he had been junior to Curtis-Bennett and Sir Edward Marshall Hall in the defence of Madame Fahmy, and in 1926 had again been led by Marshall Hall, when that greatest of all defence advocates had made his last appearance in a capital case at the trial at Maidstone Assizes of Alphonso Smith.

Although, among fellow members of the Bar, Oliver was generally respected and admired for the sharpness and clarity of his legal mind, and for his ability to grasp complicated facts and communicate them, simplified but undistorted, to judges and juries, there were few people who found him likable as a person. He was a cold, austere, apparently unemotional man, who carried the atmosphere of the courtroom around with him as a snail carries its shell; no matter whether he was questioning a witness in court or conversing with a companion at the dinner-table, his speech was almost entirely free of contractions—invariably he would say, "is it not . . . ?" rather than "isn't it . . . ?"; always "I do not"; never "I don't".

His face was lined, but not as a result of laughter, for there were not many things that amused him—least of all, jokes concerning the Law. The Law was his religion, the statute book his Bible; the Law was majestic, well-nigh perfect, almost almighty . . . or so he believed.

Paradoxically, if he had had slightly less respect for the Law, he would have achieved far greater success as a jury advocate. Whereas the great defenders—men like Marshall Hall, Curtis-Bennett, and Hastings—used the Law as a guide-line, letting go of it if they saw a chance of taking a legitimate short-cut to a winning verdict, Oliver used the Law as if it were a tight-rope stretched from the beginning of a case to the end: at times so intent was he upon keeping his balance that he failed to notice what his opponents were up to.

But, oddly enough, it was as much for his defects as a jury advocate as for his virtues that Roland Oliver was chosen to lead for the defence at the Wallace trial. Clearly, the main task for the defence would be to convince the jury that the Crown case was "a hotch-potch of half-baked hypotheses",[1] that there was little, if any, evidence against Wallace that could be accepted as true legal

[1] Not Hector Munro's words, but a fellow-solicitor's.

tender. To Hector Munro, considering the choice of counsel, it seemed that Oliver, with his unwavering, indeed almost fanatical, insistence upon keeping to the strict letter of the Law, was ideally suited to the task of cutting the Crown case down to its proper, paltry size. The other defect in Oliver's favour, Munro believed, was that his style of advocacy—bleak, clinical, quiet-spoken— would help to lower the temperature of the case by a few degrees.

At the Wallace trial, then, Roland Oliver would have the unusual, if not unique, opportunity of employing his two greatest weaknesses as a jury advocate—his rigid devotion to the Law plus the frigidity of his courtroom manner—as important weapons for the defence.

Or so Hector Munro believed.

It was as if the prosecution had been waiting for the defence to show their hand. The day after Munro made known the defence arrangements for the trial the local papers reported that the Recorder for Liverpool, Edward George Hemmerde, K.C., would lead for the Crown.

The announcement appeared on April Fools' Day.

"If this is someone's idea of a practical joke," barked an elderly member of the bench of magistrates, "I can't say that I appreciate his sense of humour."

There were plenty more people who thought it no laughing matter. Indeed, the choice of prosecutor in the Wallace case caused almost as much commotion in Liverpool as the case itself, for Edward Hemmerde was probably the most controversial figure ever to grace the northern legal scene.

Few barristers, by their out-of-court behaviour, can have aroused more interest and argument among the general public than Hemmerde; few men, no matter what their calling, can have been the object of as many different descriptions as were applied to him. Among the ordinary people of Liverpool, the readers between the lines of the newspaper accounts of his activities, he was variously depicted as "a profligate", "a wastrel", "a martyr to the establishment", "a stormy petrel", "a soured man", "a good-time Charlie", and "a man who was much maligned and misunderstood"; he was also (stringing a few of the adjectives together and finishing up with the most-used noun) "an irrepressible, loudmouthed, honourable and outspoken braggart".[1]

[1] These descriptions are taken from letters from Liverpool people to the author.

By his friends—and there were a good many of them, who knew him by the onomatopoeic nickname of "Haemorrhoid"—he was thought to be "his own worst enemy . . . generously endowed with courage but lacking in discretion".

Hemmerde was a remarkably handsome man, wide-browed, aquiline-featured; and at fifty-nine, his age at the time of the Wallace case, his physique still bore witness to his youthful prowess at sport—particularly rowing, at which he achieved greatness, winning the Henley Diamond Sculls of 1900.

His physical perfection was marred by only one thing—or, rather, two things: his feet. They were enormous. In profile, straight-backed and vastly-booted, Hemmerde was shaped like the letter L. He was very conscious of the size of his feet, and standing in company, especially female company, he had a habit of leaning forward to make the bottoms of his trousers cover as much leather as possible.

He was conscious, too, of the unloveliness of his speaking voice, which, when he was at all excited, rose to a high-pitched screech. Since it took very little to get him excited, his voice, almost as often as not, was up in the higher registers, causing distress to sensitive ear-drums and threatening disaster to any wine-glasses that happened to be near.

At Oxford in the early 1890s, Hemmerde was a fellow student of F. E. Smith and John Simon. All three joined the Bar at about the same time, and took silk on the same day. There were many people who believed that, of the three, Hemmerde was the most brilliant, the one most likely to reach the summit of his profession; and during his early years at the Bar, Hemmerde did plenty to justify this belief. The future could hardly have looked more rosy. As his reputation grew, so did the size of the fees marked on the briefs that were offered to him, and in a very short time he was able to pick and choose his cases, thinking more in terms of publicity and prestige than of his purse.

In 1906, when he was thirty-five, he was elected Liberal Member of Parliament for East Denbigh, and in 1909 the Liberal Government nominated him as Recorder of Liverpool. During the next nine years, until his defeat in the parliamentary contest for the North-west Norfolk constituency, Hemmerde worked like a beaver. Goodness knows how he managed to find the time, let alone the energy, but on top of his duties as Recorder and M.P., and as well as making frequent appearances as counsel in civil and criminal cases, he wrote a number of plays: one of them, *A Butterfly on the*

Left: Mr Justice
Wright

The judge who
tried the case.
*Photo Syndication
International*

Right: Roland
Oliver

Counsel for the
Defence.
*Photo "Radio Times"
Hulton Picture Library*

Edward Hemmerde
Prosecuting Counsel.
Photo Liverpool Court of Passage

Left: Sydney Scholefield Allen

The barrister chosen to represent Wallace at the committal proceedings.

"He expended so much nervous and physical energy on Wallace's behalf that he lost more than a stone in weight."

Right: Professor J. E. W. MacFall

Expert witness for the Prosecution.

"More of a placard than a person".

Photo Liverpool Daily Post and Echo

Wheel, which he wrote in collaboration with another M.P., Francis Neilson, was presented at the Globe Theatre, Shaftesbury Avenue, in 1911, and ran for a respectable total of 119 performances.

It is impossible to hazard even a rough guess as to how much money Hemmerde earned before he reached the age of fifty, but it must have been a pretty tidy sum, for in addition to his fees as a barrister there were royalties coming in from his plays, and his salaries as Recorder and M.P.

Yet he was unable to make both ends meet.

By the early 1920s he was not merely broke; he was up to his ears in debt. His financial predicament was caused by a mixture of bad luck, bad judgment, extravagance, and—the main ingredient— sheer irresponsibility. He was a born gambler, the sort of man who, if he had only two halfpennies to rub together, would toss you for a penny, double or quits. There were no half-measures with Hemmerde: he gambled high; he lost heavily.

It would not have been so bad if he had restricted his operations to the gaming-table, the race-track, but he became fascinated, indeed obsessed, by the thought of the profits that could be made in that greatest of all betting shops, the Stock Exchange. Using his reputation as collateral, he borrowed large sums of money to finance his quest for more; it never seemed to occur to him that, whether he hit the bonanza or not, the borrowed money would have to be repaid.

In March 1921, Hemmerde appeared in court—not as counsel this time, but as defendant in an action (Spencer *v.* Hemmerde) for the recovery of a debt of £1000 and interest at 7 per cent. He pleaded that the debt was barred by the Statute of Limitations, but the judgment of the court went against him. Despite the entreaties of his friends, who realized that the publicity of the case was doing him great harm, Hemmerde decided to appeal. And he won. But that was not the end of the matter: the plaintiff, Spencer, took the case to the House of Lords, and the original verdict was confirmed. The popular Press, which reported the case in the manner of a serial story, complete with "cliff-hanger" endings and recapitulations of "the story so far", treated the Lords' decision as if it were the happy ending to a fairy-tale, with Right, embodied in Spencer, triumphing over Wrong, in the person of Hemmerde.

The costs of the prolonged action, the thousand pounds—plus the interest on it, almost half as much again—all this had to be paid by Hemmerde. But the price in pounds, shillings, and pence was small compared with the expense to his reputation. At the

L

beginning of 1921 he was a rising star; by the end of the year he was a fallen idol.

Hemmerde's life for the next ten years was like something out of the pages of Greek tragedy. He had rubbed the Gods up the wrong way; now they clubbed together to teach him a lesson. Yet, in an odd sort of way, and without any apparent sign of self-pity, Hemmerde seemed almost to enjoy his misery. When things were at their blackest he was still able to smile and make a joke or recite in his high, squealing voice the first couple of lines of Kipling's *If*. Maybe there was a large streak of masochism in his nature; or maybe, as a playwright, a romantic in an unromantic age, he appreciated the drama of the situation and got some kind of perverted pleasure from playing the role of a tragic figure. Whatever the reason, he not only accepted the cruel turns of fate—but appeared to go out of his way to make things even worse for himself.

His troubles came thick and fast. While the action for the recovery of the borrowed money was making its much-publicized journey to the House of Lords, his other creditors—frightened to death that if they waited any longer for him to honour his debts he would plead the Statute of Limitations against them, too—began pestering him for repayment. In no time at all there were more bills coming into his chambers than briefs. But somehow—usually by a miracle of persuasion, only rarely with the aid of money—he managed to forestall anyone from following Spencer's example.

(The story is told of how Hemmerde wiped off his debts to a group of Liverpool money-lenders. These gentlemen were being plagued by the activities of an expert on legal punctuation who was putting his very special knowledge at the disposal of recalcitrant money-borrowers: in return for a small fee, he would examine an agreement drawn up between lender and borrower, and almost invariably find some error of punctuation which made the whole document legally invalid. Before long he was doing a roaring trade, and making large dents in the money-lenders' profits. The money-lenders, banding together to prosecute for alleged common barratry, chose Hemmerde, one of their best clients, to appear as counsel on their behalf, on the understanding that the total of his fees would be divided between them and deducted from what he owed. When the action came to court it was soon apparent that the money-lenders had virtually no case . . . but Hemmerde kept the proceedings going for a couple of weeks, taking up the court's time with reams of largely irrelevant questions to witnesses, elongating pauses into lengthy silences, and getting the judge to adjourn early each day. When, at last, the case ended, with the inevitable verdict in the defendant's favour, the money-lenders owed so much to Hemmerde in refreshers [legal overtime payments] that it was no longer he who was in debt to them, but they who were in debt, and quite considerably, to him.)

Within a few months of his legal battle with Spencer, Hemmerde was in court again, and in the news again, when his wife, after being married to him for nineteen years, sued for divorce. As far as is known, this was the first and only time Hemmerde appeared in court without raising a single objection to the opposition evidence.

In 1922 he re-entered politics. Switching his allegiance from the declining Liberals to the surgent Socialists—and thus giving his enemies the excuse for adding "turncoat" to the lengthening list of his supposed faults—he contested and won the seat at Crewe. (At the meeting of the Crewe Labour Party to choose the parliamentary candidate Hemmerde's main rival was a local man named Hills. Paraphrasing Shakespeare, Hemmerde pleaded with the selection committee to "scorn the 'Ills you have and fly to another that you know not of".)

When the first Labour Government was being formed in January 1924, Hemmerde confidently expected to be appointed either Attorney- or Solicitor-General. And he had good reason to feel confident, for as far as legal and political experience was concerned he was way ahead of the other contenders. It looked like a cast-iron racing certainty, a perfect each-way bet, that he would be offered one or other of the Law offices. While he waited for the call to 10 Downing Street he told his friends, "I know that this will be the big chance of my life—and I have no intention of muffing it."

But the big chance never came: Hemmerde was passed over. Although, of course, no official reason was ever given, it was generally accepted that Ramsay MacDonald's decision not to include him in the Government was a direct though belated sequel to the Spencer *v.* Hemmerde case. A lot of mud had been thrown at Hemmerde, and was still being thrown—the Prime Minister did not want to risk getting splashed.

After this disappointment, as Hemmerde himself said, "Either I gave up politics, or politics gave me up—I'm not sure which way round it was." For the next couple of years he concentrated all his efforts on trying to rebuild his legal practice. During this time he and his clerk worked almost as hard at acquiring briefs as at carrying them out. If the Bar Council had learned that Hemmerde was touting for business he would have been in serious trouble, perhaps even disbarred, but somehow or other he managed to get away with it. By the beginning of 1926 a fair volume of work was coming into his chambers—nothing like as much as he had been getting five years before, but enough to suggest that complete recovery was not too far away.

Then things started to go wrong again.

First of all, he was faced with the heart-breaking news that his twenty-three-year-old son had been killed in an accident in East Africa. Soon afterwards, sorrow at his son's death turning to tetchiness, he fell out with Sir Thomas White, the Leader of the Liverpool City Council, and started off one of the longest running and most publicized squabbles in local-government history—a squabble which went on and on and on, not just for months but years, for practically a decade.

Most people in the public eye, and especially most members of the legal profession, would have done their utmost to keep the matter quiet. But not Hemmerde. He was, it would seem, incapable of having a private argument: the slightest disagreement with someone, and he treated it like an action between parties, bringing it before the court of public opinion in the expectation of getting a coherent verdict from a jury composed of everyone. It has been said that Hemmerde was his own worst enemy; it might also be said, and with as much truth, that he was his own worst advocate, his own worst client.

His argument with Sir Thomas White provides an excellent, though by no means singular, example of his unhappy knack of creating storms in teacups and making mountains out of molehills; it provides an example, too, of his I-don't-give-a-damn attitude to the washing of dirty linen in public. Instead of trying to sort out the trouble behind closed doors. Hemmerde had to go and air his grievances to the Press; the Leader of the Council had no alternative but to answer back; then it was Hemmerde's turn again. So it went on.

Never happier than when he had something to be righteously indignant about, Hemmerde now appeared to be thoroughly enjoying himself—unconcerned, it seemed, at the damage the publicity was doing to his practice, unaware that people were saying that he was "petty-minded", "a man who argued simply for the sake of arguing".

Certainly, to the average man in the street, depending for his knowledge of the affair upon the alternating statements of Hemmerde and the Leader of the Council, there seemed scarcely enough reason to justify even a small tiff, let alone such seemingly ever-lasting conflict. According to what Hemmerde told the Press, he bitterly resented the Liverpool Corporation's "policy of ceremonial and professional boycott", which, he alleged, dated from the time when, defending Sinn Fein prisoners, he criticized the methods of the Special Branch of the Liverpool Police, led by Hubert Moore. Asked to be more specific in his allegations, he cited the order of precedence on ceremonial civic occasions: as Recorder of Liverpool, he said, his rightful place in processions was alongside the Leader of the Council—not behind, which was where the Corporation insisted upon putting him.

But there was more to it than that. Although the public was given the impression that the argument was mainly over a question of protocol, it was, in fact, not so much "ceremonial boycott" as "professional boycott" which Hemmerde was up in arms about. And it does seem as if he had good grounds for complaint. In all his years as Recorder, stretching right back to 1909, he had not received a single important brief from the Liverpool Corporation. Such neglect can hardly have been unintentional.

In March 1931, when he was offered the leading prosecution brief in the Wallace case, Hemmerde was jubilant, triumphant. He assumed—no doubt rightly—that the brief was offered as an olive-branch; a symbol of the Corporation's wish to put an end to the long-drawn-out feud. Now, if he played his cards right, the years ahead could be peaceful and prosperous ones.

He believed that a lot, perhaps everything, would depend upon his handling of the prosecution of Wallace. When the case came to court Wallace would not be the only person on trial: a verdict against Wallace would be a verdict in favour of Hemmerde—and, God forbid, vice versa. Success in the case would mean further briefs from the Corporation, an increase in other work, an un-troubled future. The stakes were enormous. He could not afford to lose.

While one can understand Hemmerde's motives for pressing the prosecution case so hard, it is impossible to excuse the methods he employed in order to achieve his goal. Not only did he ignore the long-established English legal tradition that it is the duty of Crown counsel to present the known facts of a case accurately, impartially, and without appealing to the emotions of a jury, but he was guilty of hiding evidence and exhibits which would have assisted the defence, and of attempting to elicit from witnesses evidence which he knew to be untrue.

* * *

Edward George Hemmerde and Roland Giffard Oliver.

At the Wallace trial they provided probably the most spectacular example of Carrollesque back-to-frontedness that has ever been seen in an English court of law. While Hemmerde presented the prosecution case in the manner of a battling, pugnacious defence counsel, a counterfeit presentment of Marshall Hall (even down to the trick of using hand exhibits like theatrical props), Oliver behaved as if he were briefed by the Crown to prosecute the prosecution, rarely raising his voice above a conversational tone, preferring sarcasm to anger, and always being most careful to observe legal niceties.

But this apparent transposition of roles of the opposing advocates was not the only thing that might have been conceived by Lewis Carroll.

The Wallace trial—indeed, the whole case, for that matter—contained any number of oddities, incongruities, downright absurdities: more than enough to justify its being sub-titled "Wallace in Wonderland".

The Trial—I

> *"Chorus again!" cried the Gryphon, and the
> Mock Turtle had just begun to repeat it, when
> a cry of "The trial's beginning!" was heard in
> the distance.*

The Liverpool Spring Assizes began on April 13th and lasted
for two weeks.

On the Monday morning of the second week Wallace, with a
motley collection of other prisoners awaiting trial, was driven from
Walton Gaol, on the outskirts of Liverpool, to St George's Hall,
in the centre of the city, where he was lodged in a basement cell
to await the decision of the Grand Jury. At about five o'clock,
informed that a true bill had been returned against him and that
he would face trial the following Wednesday, he was driven back
to the gaol.

Wallace cannot have derived any pleasure from his first outing
for seven weeks; but at least he was given a foretaste of the routine
which would be observed by the prison officers during the course
of the trial.

"In the morning, before we stepped into the Black Maria," he
afterwards wrote, "a warder gave me my little personal belongings:
my watch, finger ring, cigarette case (empty) and my fountain pen.
In the evening when we returned I gave them up again. Then I
was searched. . . . During all the time I was being tried for my life
the only human association I had—excepting, of course, the
official guards—was with the men in the infirmary or observation
ward. That is the regulation governing the treatment of prisoners
on trial for murder."

St George's Hall, the grandiose setting of the Wallace trial, has
been described as the finest Greco-Roman building in Europe.
Standing—or, rather, lying, like a giant's sarcophagus—on a plateau

opposite Lime Street Station, the building took sixteen years—from 1838 until 1854—to complete. Contained within the vast structure, almost lost within it, is the Liverpool Crown Court, which, says Gordon Hemm, is "imbued with academic grace in proportion and detail. . . . The sharp and crisp profiling of the numerous suites of mouldings that go to the making of architraves, friezes, cornices, and other numerous classic motifs are worthy of close inspection, for they give life and character, and an interplay of light and shade which is pleasant to behold."[1]

In such magnificent surroundings Mr Justice Wright, the judge of the Wallace case, looked very insignificant indeed—"like an old lady wearing a red dressing gown" is how one observer described him. Actually, he was not all that old: sixty-one, which is no great age for a judge. He was a little man, with small eyes set in a round face; above them, George Robey eyebrows; below them, heavy pendant bags. Although, before his appointment as a Judge in the King's Bench Division, Robert Alderson Wright was one of the most brilliant and successful silks in the country, his practice was exclusively concerned with civil cases, mostly in the realm of commercial law; he had no experience of criminal work.

This was unfortunate for Wallace. At the magistrates' court, the case against him had been heard by a retired music-salesman with no legal training, little legal knowledge; now, at his trial, the judge was a man who, until his elevation to the bench, had hardly ever set foot inside a criminal court. It would be wrong to say that Wallace was put at any grave disadvantage by Mr Justice Wright's presence on the bench, but there can be no doubt that his chance of acquittal would have been improved had the judge been an all-rounder rather than a specialist in commercial law.

It would have been better for Wallace, too, if Mr Justice Wright had not been so anxious to get the case over as quickly as possible. Before the trial opened the judge called the two leading counsel into his room to tell them that he wanted to give the case to the jury by Saturday at the latest. The reason for the haste, he explained, was that he was due at Manchester Assizes the following Tuesday, and he did not want his timetable upset. During the trial, whenever he thought the pace was slowing, or that counsel were asking too many questions of a witness, he inserted terse little reminders of the Saturday deadline.

The Wallace case was a legal jigsaw which needed care and patience to solve, and Mr Justice Wright's insistence upon hurrying

[1] *St George's Hall, Liverpool* (Northern Publishing Co., 1949).

it along, cramping it into four days of court time, gave an unfair advantage to the prosecution, who were only too happy to have the cross-examination of certain of their witnesses cut short or diluted in strength by the demands of a clock-watching judge. In this case more haste meant less justice.

In the seven weeks which elapsed between the end of the committal proceedings and the beginning of the trial the public interest in the case, instead of cooling off, only increased; and on Wednesday, April 22nd, the *Liverpool Evening Express* reported:

"Two hours before Mr Justice Wright took his seat in the Crown Court a public queue had begun to form under the massive walls of St George's Hall. Hundreds more stood about on St George's Plateau and watched the arrival of legal representatives and court officials.

"A soft drizzling rain fell steadily, but this did not prevent large additions to the queue, and it was noticeable that a large number of women were included in the many hundreds."

The report continued:

"In the courtroom, a number of people watched the proceedings from the seats usually occupied by the Grand Jury, and they were mainly women.

"The calling of the jury occupied a few minutes only, two women being called to serve. Mr Justice Wright took his seat promptly at 10 A.M., and there was a hush in court when the Clerk of Assize directed the chief warder to 'Put up Wallace'.

"Wallace stepped slowly from the stairs of the cells to the dock. He wore a smart dark suit, black tie, stiff linen collar. When the brief and formal terms of the charge of murder were read by the clerk, Wallace said in quiet but firm tones: 'Not Guilty.' He followed the swearing-in of the jury with interest, but occasionally he raised his eyes to the glass roof of the court."

By now Edward Hemmerde could hardly wait to get started. He fidgeted nervously in his seat, tweaking his peruke to an unintentionally rakish, almost comic, angle and pulling furiously at the sleeves of his gown, while the Clerk of Assize intoned the formal words of the indictment.

Simultaneously, as the clerk resumed his seat, the prosecuting counsel rose to make the opening speech. So quick off the mark was Hemmerde that, to an observer at the trial, it seemed as if "the first word of the opening overlapped the last word of the clerk's instruction to the jury". Mr Justice Wright, thinking of his date at

Manchester Assizes the following week, must have been mightily pleased at Hemmerde's apparent desire to keep the proceedings moving at a cracking pace.

Hemmerde spoke for two hours, and it was clear that he had put a lot of work into the composition of his speech. Hardly pausing, except for dramatic effect, he screeched out the prosecution case as if the words were red-hot, searing his tongue.

In the main, the factual and suppositional ingredients of the opening speech were much the same as those contained in Bishop's two speeches in the magistrates' court; but whereas the earlier speeches contained misstatements, however unintentional, which plugged the holes in the case, Hemmerde preferred to pretend that the holes did not exist. An example of this is the way in which he dealt with the question of how Wallace could have disposed of the murder weapon, telling the jury that "a thing like that would go into the ground anywhere; there is no difficulty at all"—but not mentioning that (a) large numbers of police, with the assistance of the Sanitation Department, had searched for the weapon for days; (b) there were remarkably few open spaces in the Richmond Park area that were not either paved or cemented; (c) the murder happened in the middle of winter when the earth was frozen hard, so Wallace must have been a good deal stronger than he looked if he was able to prod a twelve-inch iron bar out of sight beneath the ground.

At the beginning of the section of his speech devoted to the murder weapon Hemmerde made dramatic use of an iron bar similar to the one which, according to Mrs Draper, the Wallaces' cleaning woman, had disappeared from the parlour hearth since her last visit to the house on January 7th.

"There was in the room there, and had been for some time, by the gas stove,[1] an iron sort of poker thing, like *that*, amply sufficient to have done this deed."

As Hemmerde said, "like *that*," he suddenly picked up the iron bar and flourished it menacingly above his head; then, after adding "amply sufficient to have done this deed", he lowered the iron bar and let it fall with a resounding crash.

"The effect of prosecuting counsel's gesture was electric," says an observer. "I noticed that one of the women members of the jury was visibly affected. Although afterwards it was made clear that the iron bar produced in court was merely a facsimile of the original . . . it was hard to believe that a different weapon from that

---

[1] Hemmerde meant the gas *fire*, of course.

suggested by the prosecution was used to carry out the crime."

There was no respite for the sensitive lady juror. Still only partially recovered from the shock caused by Hemmerde's iron-bar histrionics, she was forced to listen to a spine-chilling revised version of the mackintosh theory. In the magistrates' court the theory advanced by the prosecution was that Wallace wore the mackintosh to protect his clothes from blood—but now Hemmerde took the theory a stage further, and introduced an element of sexual perversion into the case, by suggesting that Wallace wore the mackintosh *over his nude body while he committed the crime*.

"I draw your attention," Hemmerde said, "to the fact that there is no blood whatever anywhere on the stairs—because the Crown suggest to you that in this case whoever did this deed was taking elaborate precautions. The history of our own criminal courts shows what elaborate precautions people can sometimes take." A pause, prelude to the punch lines: "One of the most famous criminal trials was of a man who committed a crime when he was naked. A man might perfectly well commit a crime wearing a raincoat, as one might wear a dressing gown, and come down, when he is just going to do this, with nothing on on which blood could fasten, and, with anything like care, he might get away, leaving the raincoat there, and go and perform the necessary washing if he was very careful."

No doubt the reference to "a famous criminal trial . . . of a man who committed a crime when he was naked" was inserted by Hemmerde because he felt that the less original the "nude-murderer" theory could be made to appear, the more chance there was of the jury accepting the idea.

It seems a pity that Roland Oliver did not take him up on this point by asking him to *name* the trial—because the only famous trial in which a similar theory was adumbrated was that of Robert Wood at the Old Bailey in 1907. The jury in that case returned a verdict of Not Guilty, so Hemmerde was not talking of Rex *v.* Wood . . . or if he was he should not have been.

The generally accepted view is that Hemmerde was referring to the trial of François Courvoisier, in 1840, for the murder of Lord William Russell. If so, then one can only say that he was quoting an extremely dubious example. Although it seems probable that Courvoisier, a Swiss valet, was naked when he slit his master's throat, literally from ear to ear, there is no real evidence of this.

Hemmerde's display with the iron bar and, directly afterwards, his recital of the "nude-murderer" theory—these were the dramatic highlights in an opening speech which, though no master-piece of legal reasoning, was a remarkable demonstration of forensic sleight of tongue. Not only did Hemmerde show himself to be an expert at marshalling disparate facts into a seemingly homogeneous whole, but he somehow contrived to make a number of possibilities add up to what seemed like certainty.

Winding up the speech, his voice rasping now from the effort of two hours of continuous oration, Hemmerde said:

"If this man did what he is charged with doing, it is murder foul and unpardonable. Few more brutal murders can ever have been committed—this elderly, lonely woman literally hacked to death for apparently no reason at all." (A nice touch, this: using the absence of motive as a point for the prosecution—suggesting to the jury that the absence of motive did not conflict with the case against Wallace, but only increased the infamy of his crime.) "Without an apparent enemy in the world, she goes to her account, and if you think that the case is fairly proved against this man, that brutally and wantonly he sent this unfortunate woman to her account, it will be your duty to call him to *his* account."

As Hemmerde sat down, there was absolute silence in the court-room. But the silence lasted only for a second or so—then was broken by a buzz of excited conversation that swelled in volume as the groundlings in the public gallery and the more favoured spectators in the Grand Jury box and the Press-men and, of course, the members of the jury, began murmuring and muttering and whispering their assorted reactions to the opening speech.

Contributing to the buzz, but unexcitedly, a member of the defence team remarked to his neighbour that "some enterprising impresario should sign Hemmerde up to repeat his performance twice-nightly at the Empire Theatre in Lime Street".

After his labours, Hemmerde rested. The first few witnesses were taken through their evidence by Leslie Walsh, junior counsel for the Crown.

The first person to take the stand was *Harry Cooke*, the police photographer. In his short cross-examination Roland Oliver set out to show that, though the camera cannot lie, it can be used as an instrument of falsehood. According to Cooke, the two photo-graphs of the murder room had been taken "one after the other and approximately at one o'clock in the morning", and he was at a loss to explain how Photograph No. 6 showed an upright chair standing in the doorway and the mackintosh lying spread out between the body and the fender, while Photograph No. 7 showed the chair tucked in against the sideboard and the mackintosh bundled up and pushed under Julia's right shoulder.

Who else was in the room while the photographs were being taken?

Only Superintendent Moore, Cooke replied.

Oliver did not bother to stress the obvious: that if Cooke had not moved the chair and the mackintosh, then they must have been moved by the Head of the C.I.D. But why? Later on in the trial a possible explanation was provided for the chair being moved, when the prosecution suggested that it was in the doorway when Wallace returned from Menlove Gardens; and that he must have known that it was there, or he would have tripped over it in the darkness; and that if he knew that it was standing in such an odd position he must have been in the parlour earlier that evening— for the purpose of murdering his wife.

Harry Cooke, still frowning as he tried to puzzle out The Mystery of the Moving Objects, left the witness-box and was replaced by *William Harrison*, another formal witness, who was called to explain the various plans that had been drawn up by the City Surveyor's Department.

The evidence of the next seven witnesses was concerned, either completely or to a large extent, with the Qualtrough telephone-call.

Leslie Heaton, who was given the rather grand-sounding title of "telephone electrician in the employ of His Majesty's Postmaster-General", stated in evidence-in-chief that "the call-box, Anfield 1627, is one of several in the district", but "the other call-boxes are on enclosed premises". Cross-examined, he was not sure if the call-box was lit up at night. Hemmerde offered to check this point, and later told the court, "There is no light fitted in that telephone-box at all. The nearest light is twenty-four feet away."

The pace of the trial quickened as, one after another, the girls from the Anfield telephone exchange dashed into the witness-box, gave quick, chirpy answers to the prosecution's questions, and dashed out again, unimpeded by cross-examination.

It was not only dust that was left in their wake, but a sprinkling of question-marks; their combined evidence, instead of throwing light on the mysterious phone-call, the even more mysterious caller, only increased the difficulties of understanding what had happened to what sort of man and why.

During their short spells in the witness-box all three girls were asked the same question: "What kind of a voice did the caller have?" and all three gave the same answer: "Just ordinary."

So did *Gladys Harley*, the waitress at the City Café, when the question was put to her.

But the next witness, *Samuel Beattie*, had much more to say about it. Too much, perhaps. He employed so many adjectives to describe the voice that the jury might have been forgiven for believing that Qualtrough was not a single person but a massed choir.

First of all, answering Hemmerde, he said, "It was a strong voice, a rather gruff voice." Complications set in during his cross-examination, when Oliver said, "At the police court you said it was a confident and strong voice."

"That means it was not a hesitating voice, in answer to some question."

Mr Justice Wright found the place in the deposition. "You used the words 'It was a confident voice'," he told Beattie.

"Yes, in answer to a question; it was a confident voice, sure of himself."

"He says he was asked the question, and he said it was a strong, confident voice," the judge told the jury, in case they had missed that bit. Then, as if he could not believe his ears, he turned to Beattie. "Did you use confident and strong as well?" he asked.

"Yes, a strong, confident voice," Oliver put in.

The judge pounced on Beattie. "You missed out 'strong' just now," he said accusingly.

Beattie didn't answer.

"So far as you could judge," Oliver went on, choosing his words very carefully now, "was it a natural voice?"

"That is difficult to judge."

"I know it is—but did it occur to you it was not a natural voice *at the time?*"

"No, I had no reason for thinking that."

"Do you know Mr Wallace's voice well?"

"Yes."

Oliver's next two questions to Beattie were probably the two most important, and definitely the two most delicate, questions to be put to any witness at the trial. There is a legal maxim which says that an advocate should never ask a question in cross-examination unless he is absolutely sure of the answer. Oliver knew this; he knew perfectly well the risk he was taking; he believed the risk was justified. Perhaps he was right. It is impossible to say. If Beattie gave the answers Oliver wanted, then fine—it would mean a heavy score for the defence . . . but if Beattie gave the wrong answers, then there would be little point in continuing the trial—Wallace could virtually say goodbye to life.

The first question was spoken quite casually:

"Did it occur to you it was anything like his voice?"

"Certainly not," Beattie replied.

And the second question—just as casual in tone, perhaps more so:

"Does it occur to you now it was anything like his voice?"

The answer came promptly, firmly. "It would be a great stretch of the imagination for me to say anything like that."

The risk had paid off. But to look at Oliver one would never have thought that he had just wagered a man's life and won the bet. Most advocates would have scooped up the winnings in both hands and jangled them in front of the jury, made some show of the defence's sudden affluence. But not Oliver, who considered ostentation to be a deadly legal sin—something which, although it undoubtedly impressed juries, had no right to be displayed in a court of law. Without even a pause, without even a quick glance at the jury, Oliver continued the cross-examination.

Beattie's account of the events of the Monday evening and of the chance meeting with Wallace at the tram-stop the following Thursday was confirmed by *James Caird*, Wallace's chess-playing friend and neighbour.

As a prosecution witness, Caird made an excellent witness for the defence. Apart from a couple of opening questions about the chess-club meeting, Oliver restricted the cross-examination to questions relating to Caird's opinion of Wallace's character and temperament, and of the relations that existed between Wallace and his wife.

"With regard to his behaviour, is he a violent person or what?"

"Oh no, not at all—a placid man."

"Would it be fair to say that from your observation they were a devoted couple?"

"Yes."

"Would that be putting it too high? Use your own phrase."

"Well, I should say they were a happy couple—a very happy couple."

James Caird was the last of the witnesses called to testify to what happened on Monday, the day before the murder. So far there was no scintilla of evidence to connect Wallace with the crime. The prosecution case, opened so "high", seemed to be falling flat.

The next witness, *P.C. James Rothwell*, said that he had seen Wallace crying in the street about half-past three on the Tuesday afternoon.

It is surprising that Oliver bothered to cross-examine. Probably the best method of discrediting evidence which seems irrelevant is to ignore it, putting a wealth of meaning into the two words, "No questions". Few witnesses—least of all police witnesses—can be made to say what they do not want to say.

Only once during the prolonged cross-examination did Rothwell come anywhere near agreeing with a point made by Oliver, and that was when he said that it was "quite possible" that a person's eyes might water in cold weather. Again and again Oliver suggested that he was mistaken in thinking that Wallace's alfresco snivelling display was a sign of "distress occasioned by contemplating a crime", but Rothwell refused to budge. "He gave me that impression," he said, and added, "as if he had suffered from some bereavement."

"If I were to call about twenty-five people who saw him that afternoon about that time, and they said he was just as usual, would you say you had made a mistake?"

"No," Rothwell said stubbornly, "I should stick to my opinion."

If one were asked to name the prosecution's star witness, the choice would fall between the milk boy, Close, and the medicine man, MacFall. Close's evidence was so crucial to the case that the defence expected his examination-in-chief, conducted by Hemmerde, to occupy quite some time.

But that was not at all what happened.

When *Alan Close*, dressed for the occasion in his Sunday-best suit, replaced Rothwell in the witness-box, it was not Hemmerde but his junior, Leslie Walsh, who conducted the examination—and the examination, composed of no more than a dozen brief questions, was all over in a couple of minutes.

"Just a little more detail about this," Roland Oliver said drily as he rose to take up the questioning, and then proceeded to establish, step by step, action by action, the boy's movements from the time he passed Holy Trinity Church until he left the doorstep of 29 Wolverton Street, having delivered the milk to Mrs Wallace.

After a dozen questions, each of them relating to a different action during the first half of the journey, Oliver broke off to ask in an astonished voice, "Do you really say you did all this in five minutes?"

"Yes," the boy said, "I have been over the ground with two detectives and it took me five minutes."

Shaking his head ever so slightly, Oliver went on to reconstruct the second half of the incident-packed journey.

Then:

"You met Elsie Wright in Letchworth Street?"

"Yes."

"And if she says that the time was then something like twenty to seven you would not agree with her. Is that right?"

"No, sir."

"Do you remember this—that as you stood on Mrs Wallace's doorstep, was there a paper boy at the next house?"

"I do not remember."

Until now Close had seemed to be quite enjoying his spell in the witness-box. But as Oliver turned to questions concerning the meeting with the other children on the night after the murder, the boy's manner changed abruptly. His voice became faltering, at times hardly audible; he fidgeted with his hands; his gaze flickered about the court, as if he were searching for someone who might come to his assistance. He looked very uncomfortable indeed.

"We have now got to the 21st," Oliver said. "On the evening of the 21st did you have a conversation with Elsie Wright, and was there also there another boy named Metcalf?"

"Yes."

"Did he ask you this: 'What time were you there?' "

Before Oliver had completed the question Close was replying, "I do not remember."

"Just try and remember, will you?" Oliver snapped. "Perhaps this next thing will bring it back to your mind. Did you say, 'At a quarter to seven'?"

"No, sir," Close said quickly.

"*Think.* I suggest to you, in the presence of Kenneth Caird, Elsie Wright, and this boy Metcalf, you said that you were there at a quarter to seven."

"No," Close mumbled, "between half-past six and a quarter to seven."

"Did you say that?"

M

A pause; then, in not much more than a whisper, "I think so."

"You were there between half-past six and a quarter to seven. That was true, was it?"

"Yes."

"Why have you sworn today you were there at half-past six?"

The words came tumbling out as if he were reciting the theorem of Pythagoras: "Because I have been over the ground and it has taken five minutes to cover that ground and that added to twenty-five past six makes it half-past."

"When did you think that?"

Back to mumbling: "Later on."

"But when?"

"The following Sunday."

"Since you gave evidence before?"

"No, the following Sunday," Mr Justice Wright interposed. "That is what he says."

"I cannot catch everything he says because he is so indistinct," Oliver explained.

"Yes, it is a difficulty to everybody."

Continuing the cross-examination, Oliver said, "I must put this to you quite seriously: that you, in the presence of those other children, said that it was a quarter to seven when you were at Mrs Wallace's. Now you think hard. Is not that right?"

Not just a pause this time, but complete silence.

Eventually, leaning to his right and speaking in a grandfatherly tone, the judge broke the silence with: "What do you say about it?"

No reply. The boy shook his head slightly.

"Do not shake your head," the judge said, injecting a note of sternness into his voice.

Still no reply.

So the judge gave up. Leaning back in his seat, he suggested: "Perhaps he is tired."

"Are you feeling all right?" Oliver asked the boy.

At last: "Yes."

"Will you just apply your mind to what I put to you? Did you not say that you took the milk to Mrs Wallace at a quarter to seven?"

"No, between half-past six and a quarter to seven."

"It has taken you a long time to answer. You were not feeling ill, were you?"

"No."

"He shook his head several times and could not bring himself to speak," the judge said to nobody in particular.

"Do you remember," Oliver said, "still on the question of the quarter to seven, the boy Metcalf saying this to you: 'The police ought to know, because in the papers it is said Mr Wallace went out at a quarter past six, and if you saw her at quarter to seven people could not think Wallace had done it'?"

"No."

"Do you say you cannot remember—or he did not say it?"

"I am sure he did not say it."

"Are you prepared to swear he did not say that?"

"No. He persuaded me to go to the police."

"Yes, but do not you remember the newspapers had said quite wrongly Mr Wallace went out at 6.15?" Oliver insisted.

"No."

"Are you sure, then, that nothing of that sort was said?"

Another pause; another mumbled reply: "I cannot swear to it."

"That is quite honest," Oliver said. "You may have forgotten." His voice more relaxed now, he went on: "Did you rather make a joke about it that evening when they wanted you to go to the police? Do you remember you put your thumbs in your waistcoat like that"— he illustrated—"and said: 'Well, I am the missing link'?"

A pause.

"Well, did you?"

Close shook his head. "No."

"Nothing like that?"

"No, sir."

Oliver was speaking sharply again. "You have said they were present and persuaded you to go to the police. What I am putting to you is this—that you were rather reluctant to go to the police?"

"Well, naturally," Close answered.

"And said you were the missing link?"

"No."

"You say you were reluctant to go?" the judge asked.

"No."

Oliver did a double-take. "He said naturally he *was* reluctant."

"No, naturally I was *not* reluctant," Close said.

"If they were to say you used that expression, that is quite wrong, is it?"

"Yes, sir."

"It is a funny thing to invent, do not you think?"

Very funny, Close thought. He sniggered. "Yes," he said.

"Do not answer carelessly," Oliver thundered. "Just think if during that evening you did not use that expression."

Pouting now, Close muttered, "No, sir."

"Nobody is saying it is very wicked if you did. I am only trying to find out what you did say."

"Well, I did not say it," Close cried, desperation lending defiance to the reply.

"You *swear* you did not?" Oliver asked finally.

"Yes, sir."

Hemmerde rose to re-examine. "Did you know that it was said in the papers that the prisoner left at 6.15?" he asked.

Twice during his cross-examination Close had sworn one thing, only to be pressed into saying another. Now he contradicted himself again by answering, "Yes."

Doing his best to keep the surprise out of his voice, Hemmerde said, "You knew that?"

"Yes," the boy persisted.

As Alan Close left the box a barrister sitting next to Professor Dible remarked, "That's the fade-out of the Crown case." One wonders how Hemmerde felt at that moment. Whatever his feeling was, it certainly cannot have been a feeling of happiness.

While the tram conductor, *Thomas Phillips*, was in the box, Hemmerde saw a chance of repairing some of the damage caused by the milk boy's poor showing as a witness.

At the committal proceedings Phillips had given 7.6 as the time of the tram's departure from the junction of Smithdown Road and Lodge Lane; now Hemmerde managed to persuade him into saying that, because of congestion and a diversion of traffic earlier along the route, the departure time might have been four minutes later: 7.10.

A difference of only four minutes—but a vital difference. If the jury accepted Close's evidence as the truth, then they would probably also accept the prosecution's suggestion that the tram's departure time was 7.10—and add the extra four minutes to the time available to Wallace for the murder of his wife. If, on the other hand, the jury doubted the truth of Close's evidence, they might accept the later departure time in preference to the earlier one—in which case, the time at Wallace's disposal would be virtually unchanged . . . a few minutes subtracted at the beginning, four minutes added at the end.

Hemmerde had a lot to gain and nothing to lose, and if he had honestly believed that there was some doubt about the tram's departure time, there would have been nothing ethically wrong in his attempt to implant the later time in the jury's mind.

But he knew perfectly well that the earlier time was the correct one.

He had definite proof of this. Folded inside his brief was the time-sheet made out by Edward Angus, the ticket inspector who had boarded Phillips's tram in Smithdown Road. It showed that Angus had joined the tram at the Earle Road stop—*and left it at the Portman Road stop, which was four minutes away from the junction of Smithdown Road and Lodge Lane, at 7.10.*

Luckily for the defence, *Arthur Thompson* was positive that it was 7.15 when his tram left the Penny Lane terminus. Roland Oliver had no difficulty in establishing that the journey from one end of Smithdown Road to the other took ten minutes . . . and ten minutes subtracted from 7.15 left much the same answer as the prosecution had first thought of.

Hemmerde's trick misfired badly. After nearly half an hour of unnecessary questions and answers, he not only had to admit that "the first figure, 7.6, is most accurate", but was forced to produce the time-sheet as an exhibit. Perhaps because of his anxiety to acquire the extra four minutes, he failed to make any capital out of what he had referred to in his opening as Wallace's "unnatural conversations with the conductors".

The next four witnesses were the people who had encountered Wallace in the Menlove Gardens district. *Katie Mather*, the lady who lived at 25 Menlove Gardens West, was followed into the box by the young clerk, *Sydney Green;* then came *P.C. James Sargent;* and lastly there was *Lily Pinches*, the manageress of the newspaper shop in Allerton Road.

Once again the main argument between the prosecution and the defence was over the question of time.

Sydney Green provided a splendid example of how certain a witness can be that he is telling the truth—and yet how wrong. It was clear that Wallace could not possibly have alighted from Thompson's tram much before twenty minutes past seven; but Green, in direct evidence, stated that it was 7.13 when he met him in Menlove Gardens West. He told Roland Oliver that he was *confident* that it was ten past seven when he left his house;

that it was *exactly* ten past seven; that he was *sure* that it took only three minutes to walk to the spot where Wallace spoke to him.

"If he was sitting on a tram car at a quarter past seven, you could not be right?" Oliver suggested suavely.

"No, sir," Green murmured bemusedly.

According to Lily Pinches, it was about ten past eight when Wallace entered her shop, and ten minutes later when he left. If she was right about the time of his arrival, what on earth had he been doing since a quarter to eight, when he checked his watch with that of P.C. Sargent?

Clearly, Lily Pinches was wrong about the time of Wallace's visit to the shop. He was back at Wolverton Street at twenty to nine, after a journey which took at least half an hour, and it didn't need an arithmetical genius to work out that he must have left the shop, at the latest, by ten past eight.

The oddest thing about the argument concerning the duration of Wallace's stay in Menlove Gardens was that there ought not to have been any argument at all—for the prosecution, if they had wanted to, could have called evidence as to the time he left the district.

By coincidence, it was Arthur Thompson's tram, returning towards the centre of town, which Wallace boarded on the first stage of his journey home.

Thompson mentioned this to the police when he was interviewed, and it is impossible to imagine that his schedule was not checked to ascertain the time his tram passed near Menlove Gardens. There is a reasonable conclusion to be drawn from the fact that the prosecution kept this evidence to themselves, and that is that it did not fit in with the alibi theory, which depended to a large extent upon the suggestion that Wallace spent an unnaturally long time searching for Qualtrough. Unfortunately for the defence, either Wallace did not recognize Thompson when he boarded his tram the second time, or he recognized him but afterwards forgot about it: for one reason or the other, the defence were completely unaware that this important evidence was being withheld.

Lily Pinches was briefly re-examined by Hemmerde, who then called five members of "The Anfield Harriers" (the title, it will be remembered, which Scholefield Allen gave to the group of C.I.D. officers who took part in the "tram tests"). One after the other the detectives followed their notebooks into the witness-box, recited their evidence, closed their notebooks with a sound like the satisfied smacking of lips, and departed. It was all very professional; some of the lay witnesses could have learnt a lot from watching the performance.

Next into the box came *Joseph Crewe*, the Prudential superintendent. At the committal proceedings Crewe had given J. R. Bishop a lot of trouble by using the prosecuting solicitor's questions as excuses for making little impromptu speeches on Wallace's behalf, and no doubt Hemmerde had been warned to treat him with the utmost care and circumspection. He did just that, restricting the examination-in-chief to less than twenty questions concerning only two subjects. It was a clever piece of kid-glove advocacy. After establishing that Crewe's house was close to Menlove Gardens, he asked a few discreet questions about Wallace's visits for violin lessons; but as soon as Crewe began to warm up and show signs of becoming obstreperous Hemmerde handed him over to the defence.

Replying to Oliver, Crewe said that Wallace normally paid in the insurance money on a Wednesday, and that "anyone who knew him, or knew about his habits or employment, might expect him to have the bulk of the cash . . . anything from £50 to sometimes over £100 . . . by Tuesday night".

"Would he have any right to have business in such a district as Menlove Gardens?"

"Every right."

"What commission would he get on an endowment or life policy? Would it be something worth having?"

"Yes, twenty per cent of the yearly premium—that is, the first premium."

Every one of Crewe's answers was more or less helpful to the defence, and Hemmerde was forced to re-examine, to try to blunt some of the points made in cross-examination. But he succeeded only in making things worse for himself.

Hoping to suggest to the jury that, in an average week, Wallace's takings were small—too small even to provide a motive for robbery, let alone murder—he said, "The weekly cash return is made up from industrial subscriptions, pennies a week, and that sort of thing?"

"Yes, that's right," Crewe said—and added, before Hemmerde could stop him, "On the 5th January Mr Wallace paid in £55 2s. 11d. On the 12th January, that is for the Monday, he paid in £89 0s. 9d."

Mr Justice Wright wanted to know why some of the returns were far higher than others.

"The week of the 12th January," Crewe explained, "is what we call a monthly week. In this week, he collects weekly premiums and monthly premiums. That accounts for £89 being paid that week."

Hemmerde chimed in again: "But a collection of £30 is thought to be a fairly average debit?"

"Yes, that is a fairly average debit," Crewe agreed. "But I do not want you to overlook this point, that there are the ordinary branch premiums to collect also in the same week."

"I am taking merely the weekly debit."

"Yes."

Before Crewe could enlarge upon this Hemmerde hastily said, "No further questions," and called *Lily Hall* to take Crewe's place.

Miss Hall, the young typist who claimed that she had seen Wallace talking to another man in Richmond Park at 8.35 on the night of the murder, was the last witness of the day, and also the last witness to testify to events leading up to the discovery of the crime, so everything was left neat and tidy.

The prosecution, who had suffered so many setbacks with witnesses not coming up to proof, must have been praying that Lily Hall would put up a reasonable show.

Their prayers went unanswered.

Here is a short extract from her examination-in-chief, practically the whole of which reads like a Will Hay cross-talk routine. (Hemmerde speaks first.)

"When did you last see Mr Wallace before this tragedy?"

"On the 19th."

"That was the Monday?"

"No, the Tuesday."

"You mean Tuesday the 20th?"

"Yes."

"What time was that?"

"*About twenty past nine.*"

"Who was he with?"

"Talking to a man. I was on the other side and I crossed over."

Mr Justice Wright: "Which side was he?"

"The side of the entry."

"Which side were you?"

"The passage side."

"Which entry are you talking about?"

"The one I was standing by." (*Standing* by . . .?)

Hemmerde: "Are you living with your parents?"

"Yes."

"How many of you are there at home?"

"Two."

"Your sister and father and mother?"

"Yes, and me."

If ever a witness was self-destructive, that witness was Lily Hall. The cross-examination was brief:

"I suppose you saw a good many other people about the streets?" Oliver asked.

"Yes."

"You never gave those a thought at the time, did you?"

"No."

"No, why should you? Then there was a murder. How long after the murder did you give your statement to the police?"

"I think it was about a week, but I'm not quite sure."

"What made you wait all that long time before going to the police?"

"I was ill in bed for one thing."

Oliver might well have asked what the other thing was, but all he said was: "That would not prevent you from sending for them," and then sat down.

The long first day of the trial was over. The jury had heard an opening speech of two hours' duration; they had heard 25 witnesses giving 1079 answers to as many questions.

How much of what they had heard would still be in their minds when they were asked to decide whether Wallace should live or die?

Precious little, if the attitude of one of their number reflected the attitude of the rest of them. As they filed out of the box, each of them holding a twelfth part of Wallace's future in his or her hands, and trooped down the long stone corridor to a back entrance of St George's Hall, where cars were waiting to take them to a near-by hotel, one of the jurymen was thinking about "the injustice of the English trial system". It seemed all wrong to him that, for the duration of the trial, he and the other members of the jury were just as much prisoners as Wallace, "guarded day and night by the police, not allowed to talk to anybody, not even allowed to read a newspaper". All through the day, on and off, he had been thinking about this.

Something else which had occupied his mind during the afternoon session, and still did, was the worrying thought that he had smoked his last cigarette. Now he was dying for a smoke. He decided that as soon as they arrived at the hotel and were installed in their rooms he would ask one of the police guards "to pop out and get him a packet of cigs".

The Trial—II

> *"Consider your verdict," the King said*
> *to the jury.*
> *"Not yet, not yet!" the Rabbit hastily*
> *interrupted. "There's a great deal to come*
> *before that!"*

Day two. The picture hardly changed.

Wallace, pale-faced, dressed in black, the central figure of the case in the centre of the picture. . . on either side of him in the dock, a warder . . . behind him, the semicircular public gallery packed to capacity, many of the faces recognizable from the day before . . . to his left, the Press-box (a whispering gallery of pencils on paper), the jury-box (each juror sitting in the same place as yesterday, the two women next to one another in the back row), and the witness-box . . . to his right, the crowded Grand Jury box . . . in front of him, below him, the two rows of red-leather benches for the black-gowned barristers, the morning-suited solicitors; the well of the court where the officials and the shorthand-writers sat, and where the exhibits of the case were congregated (the smaller ones arranged, as if for some legal version of Kim's game, around the white, shining lavatory-pan); last of all, on the same level as Wallace and directly facing him, the dumplingesque, scarlet-gowned judge.

The weather had improved since the day before, and the court was brighter, more firmly etched; occasionally patches of sunlight emphasized the shadows.

The first witnesses of the day were the Johnstons: *John Johnston*, then his wife *Florence*. They told of how they met Wallace in the entry; of how they discovered the body in the parlour; of how Wallace reacted.

Asked to look at the two police photographs of the parlour, Johnston said that they both "appeared inaccurate". He was sure, he said, that when he first entered the room "there was no chair facing the doorway"; he was equally sure that the position of the body was different, and that if the mackintosh had been as clearly visible as the photographs made out he would have noticed it, although he might not have recognized it as a mackintosh.

"Is it essential to look at them?" his wife asked when she was handed the photographs during her examination-in-chief.

Prosecuting counsel told her that it was; then: "Is that like the room when you went in?"

"Well, the furniture is the same," Mrs Johnston answered, "but, of course, as I said before in the other court, it looks like a faked room."

Mrs Johnston made a delightful witness. She said what she thought—not what she thought she was expected to say.

Towards the end of her cross-examination Oliver asked:

"With regard to the position of the mackintosh under the body, you say it was under the shoulder. You did say so?"

"Yes, I did."

"Do you think it was possible, from the position it was in, that it had been thrown around her shoulders to go to the front door?"

Mrs Johnston hesitated a moment, then: "I could not say as to that," she replied.

"You mean she had thrown it on?" Mr Justice Wright asked Oliver.

"Yes, to go and open the door; that is my suggestion."

"That was my idea," Mrs Johnston blurted out. "I thought that was the object."

"You had the idea, too?" Oliver asked, and for the first time in the trial he sounded excited.

"It just flashed across my mind," Mrs Johnston said, "because it was a peculiar thing, a mackintosh."

"Did you know that she had seen the doctor for bronchitis some ten days before?"

"No, I did not, but I knew she had been very poorly."

Oliver left it at that. He turned to another point:

"Williams was the first police constable to arrive?"

"Yes."

"I understand he first knocked and you went to the door and could not open it?"

"Yes."

"Then Mr Wallace opened it?"

"Yes."

The last question—an important one: "If he says he undid the bolt, you would not contradict him, would you?"

"I do not know whether he did," Mrs Johnston said, "but I cannot remember that."

Hemmerde called *P.C. Frederick Williams* to the witness-box.

Seeking to suggest that the front door was not bolted, and that when Wallace returned from Menlove Gardens he could have got into the house by this entrance *if he had wanted to*, Hemmerde asked, "When you got there, what did you do?"

"I knocked at the front door," Williams replied.

"What happened?"

"After a few seconds' fumbling by somebody inside, the front door was opened by the accused."

"Did you or did you not hear any bolt drawn?"

"I did not."

Hemmerde had a large repertoire of significant sniffs. The one he used to punctuate P.C. Williams's last reply said to the jury, as clearly as any words, "There—what did I tell you?"

Much of Williams's cross-examination was taken up with questions concerning part of the statement Wallace had made shortly after the policeman's arrival at the house. According to Williams's notes, Wallace had said, "At 6.45 P.M. I left the house in order to go to Menlove Gardens, and my wife accompanied me to the back-yard door. She walked a little way down the entry with me, and she returned and bolted the back-yard door. . . ."

But Wallace denied saying that Julia had walked down *the entry* with him, or that she had bolted the back-yard door; what he had in fact told Williams, he said, was that his wife had walked down *the back yard* with him and let him out.

In itself the point was not worth arguing: whether Wallace said the entry or the back yard, it had little, if any, bearing on the case. But the prosecution made a great song and dance about "Wallace's reversal of his original statement". They had to. Between the time of the discovery of the murder and his arrest, Wallace answered hundreds of police questions and made several long statements—but without altering his story in the slightest detail. Which was remarkable—and intensely aggravating, so far as the prosecution were concerned. Needing, and needing desperately, to point out some contradiction in his story, some indication of untruthfulness, they made a little go a very long way, taking his denial that he had used the words ascribed to him in Williams's notebook and presenting it to the jury as a major reason for accepting his guilt.

"You may think it very curious," Hemmerde had said in his opening, "that in a matter where you would have thought that every detail of that last meeting would have been clear in his mind, he should have given those two different accounts."

In direct evidence, asked, "Did you make a note of the statement in the house?" Williams had replied, "I made a rough note of the statement in the first person." Accepting this splendid *non sequitur* without batting an eyelid, Hemmerde had turned to other questions.

But now Oliver wanted to know how long had elapsed between the statement being made and its being put into writing:

"Did you make your note after you had, so to speak, made your round with Wallace of the house?" he asked as a starter.

"I made my note when the first police officer arrived on the scene," Williams said.

"Who was the first?"

Williams thought for a moment or so, then: "Not Inspector Kelly," he substituted for an answer. (Inspector Kelly, whose only claim to fame seems to be that he was *not* the first police officer to arrive at the scene of the crime after Williams, is an even more mysterious figure than Qualtrough. If anybody else saw Kelly at Wolverton Street, they never mentioned it.)

"Who was the first to arrive after you?" Oliver persisted.

"Superintendent Moore. He came at half-past ten."

"What time did Breslin come?"

"About a quarter of an hour before that."

"Superintendent Moore was not the next one, then," Oliver said patiently. "The next after you was Breslin. Had you then made your note?"

"I made no notes outside till Superintendent Moore came in and took charge."

"You told my learned friend that at some time or other you made notes." Oliver sounded weary now. "I am only trying to find out when it was."

"I should say it would be about half-past ten when I made my rough notes of what I had ascertained." At last.

"So at half-past ten you sat down to record, quite properly, what had happened during the last hour and a quarter?"

"I did not sit down to it."

"Then stood up," Oliver snapped. "Now, are you sure he said she walked down the entry with him and not down the back yard?"

"I am emphatic that he said she walked down the entry."

Oliver put the stock question: "Have you never made a mistake?"

And got one of the stock answers to it: "I dare say I have." But Williams was not finished yet. Stung by Oliver's sarcastic tone, he went rushing on: "But I am confident I never made a mistake, because I thought of the probability at the time of somebody having sneaked into the house while the accused and his wife were a few yards down the entry. That is how I remember it."

"... *the probability ... of somebody having sneaked into the house ...*" This from a police witness. An unexpected gift horse for the defence. Oliver must have been in two minds at that moment, wondering which course to follow: whether to continue the attempt to make Williams admit that he might have made a mistake in his notes, or to accept his version of Wallace's statement —and with it the simple explanation of how a criminal could have entered the house.

"Sneaked in while they were in the entry?" he asked.

"It is a peculiar neighbourhood."

"Is it a peculiar neighbourhood? What is peculiar?"

Williams realized that he had said the wrong thing. "As regards the laying out of it, the planning of it," he improvised.

"But there have been troubles there occasionally, have there not?"

"I do not know," was Williams's reply. True? ... Surely not. Did Williams not know about the ubiquitous and elusive housebreaker who had committed between twenty and thirty crimes in Anfield, including two in Wolverton Street, but had ceased activities since the murder? Williams must have been reminded time and time again by his superiors to keep his eyes open for this character —and for other less industrious members of the Anfield housebreaking fraternity. If his memory was good enough to recall totally a 150-word statement an hour and a quarter after it was made, despite the fact that his mind was occupied during that time with dozens of other matters, then it hardly seems feasible that he could have forgotten about the wholesale house-breakings and burglaries that had turned Anfield, and especially the Richmond Park area, into a self-service bargain basement for thieves.

But Oliver did not pursue this point. "Perhaps someone else knows. At any rate, I am suggesting that you are mistaken about that."

One final question: "Are you quite clear that he told you she bolted the back-yard door?"

"Absolutely." (This, of course, did not make sense: if Julia walked down the entry with Wallace and then walked back, how could he know if she bolted the door or not?)

Williams's place in the witness-box was taken by *Mrs Sarah Draper*, the widow-lady who "used to go to Mrs Wallace's once a week to do a bit of cleaning". Asked by Hemmerde if she had noticed anything missing when she visited the house with Inspector Gold, she replied, "A poker out of the kitchen."

"Did you notice something else was missing?"

"A piece of iron out of the sitting-room fireplace, which was always kept there."

Cue for a repeat performance of Hemmerde's celebrated iron-bar display. But not with one bar, this time—with several.

"Can you give us any idea of the size and thickness of it?" he asked, opening a box which lay in front of him. "Perhaps it might help you if you would look at a few things here to give you some idea, because measurements are always vague", and with that he proceeded to extract four or five bars from the box. Whereas, in his opening speech, he had overplayed the act, milking it for melodrama in the manner of Tod Slaughter at a Saturday-night second-house, he now showed off his histrionic versatility by using the throw-away technique favoured by his friend Gerald du Maurier.

"Is there anything like the one?" he inquired.

"Like that one," Mrs Draper said, pointing to the bar he was holding discreetly unaloft.

Hemmerde appeared not to hear. He put the bar down and picked up two others. "Was it anything like these?"

"Like *that* one," Mrs Draper said, still pointing at the discarded bar.

So he picked it up again. "Shaped like that sort of thing?"

"It was a bit rougher than that."

Bless you, Mrs Draper—"But that sort of thickness?"

"Yes."

"Was it as heavy as this?" The bar was handed to a court official, who passed it on to the witness, who very nearly dropped it.

"Yes, about the same weight."

"Only rougher."

"Yes."

"I do not know if you would like to look at it or not, members of the jury, but you can," Hemmerde said generously.

Some of them did; some of them didn't. The two women jurors were in the latter category. When the bar was offered for their perusal they both shook their heads; one of them looked as if she would scream if the bar came anywhere near her. But some of the male members of the jury seemed to get quite a kick out of handling the thing, smacking it against the palms of their hands and making whispered remarks which made their neighbours giggle.

Cross-examining Mrs Draper, Oliver asked only one question about the iron bar—"You say it stood up where it could be seen and other times it was close under the kerb?" to which the answer was "Yes"—and then employed her as a witness to the apparent harmony that had existed between the Wallaces.

The next witness was *James Sarginson*, a locksmith. The Monday after the murder (January 26th) Inspector Gold had removed the locks from the front and back doors at Wolverton Street and handed them over to him for examination.

Hemmerde put twelve questions to Sarginson. The purpose of the first ten of these questions was to elicit evidence concerning the condition of the lock taken from the front door. Ten about the front . . . two about the back—a most unequal distribution of emphasis. But more than that—the emphasis was not only unequal but misplaced, truly back-to-front, since the condition of the front-door lock was *completely irrelevant* to the case. There was only one question to ask about the front door, and it was not a question that could be answered by any locksmith. Simply, it was this: *When Wallace returned from Menlove Gardens, was the door bolted—or was it not?*

When, at last, Hemmerde asked about the back-door lock Sarginson said, "I found that the locking bolt was rusty, but in good working order. It was stiff for want of oil. The crank which actuates the spring bolt was grinding on the base of the lock, so that when you turned the lock the spring bolt remained in. It required pressure to open it."

Sarginson was supposed to be an impartial witness; but he seems to have thought that because he had been called by the prosecution it was his duty to support the prosecution case, to make things as difficult as possible for the defence.

Asked by Oliver if the lock taken from the back door was "exceedingly stiff", he replied, "A *portion* of it is stiff."

"Is it erratic in its operation and at some times stiffer than at others?"

N

Sarginson did not want to answer this question. "It has been like that for some considerable time."

"I am sure of it," Oliver said, polite as an icicle, "but I want to get this from you: there are cases, are there not, where latches will open easily and sometimes with great difficulty?"

"But that would be in most cases due to rust."

Oliver pointed to the lock. "But that is rusty, is it not?"

"Yes, it is rusty," Sarginson was forced to admit.

"Whether it was rusty or not," Oliver said, approaching the subject from a different direction, "the question as to whether it worked freely or stuck might depend upon the condition of the strike of the lock, the part that fits on to the door?"

"Yes," Sarginson said, suddenly—and, in the context of the cross-examination, uniquely—helpful. "I had one on my own shop door like that and I had to lift the door to turn the key."

Encouraged, Oliver went on: "With regard to the possible grinding effect of rust or anything else on the strike, that might have the effect of making it sometimes difficult and sometimes easy?"

Back to his old self again, Sarginson replied, "I do not think so in this case, because the stiffness is due to the internal workings of this lock."

"Leave them out," Oliver said. He sounded weary, like the man in Chesterton's poem who went to Bannockburn by way of Brighton Pier. "To that extent it is always stiff?"

"Yes."

"Now will you add to that the possibility that there may be something wrong with the fit in the strike?"

"I cannot say that, because I have not seen it."

"That is a thing which will produce difficulty sometimes—I think you have said so. I am trying to find out, as you know, about these things."

"That is possible."

Mr Justice Wright, his eye on the clock, his thoughts on the Saturday deadline, butted in with: "All that is suggested to you is that there might be sometimes more extra stiffness because of the adjustment of the strike."

"Yes."

Oliver sat down. But he had not asked the all-important question: How did Sarginson reconcile his opinion that the lock "required pressure to open it" and was "always stiff" with the statements of the Johnstons that they saw Wallace open the back door with no difficulty at all? The question would have been well worth asking, if only as an indication to the jury that the behaviour of the lock was not as consistent, as "open-and-shut", as Sarginson tried to make out.

There was a nice contrast between the evidence given by James Sarginson and that of the next witness, *Professor John Edward Whitley MacFall*. Whereas the locksmith refused to answer any question beginning "Suppose . . ." and was extremely wary of those starting with "If . . .", the learned professor found happiness in hypothesis; he liked nothing better than to display his powers of deduction before a large audience and with plenty of reporters around to act as the messengers of his forensic genius.

It took him no time at all to settle in. To most people the witness-box is "the loneliest place in the world"—but not to MacFall. He looked perfectly at home there, as if it were custom-built for him. It was his soap-box, his pulpit, his stage.

He allowed Hemmerde to lead him through a recital of his qualifications—then he took over and quickly showed the court who was master. Now it was he who led and Hemmerde who followed, poking prompts into the pauses.

MacFall knew exactly what he wanted to say, and was determined to say it in his own way, at his own pace, and at length. He refused to be hurried—not even by the judge ("I will explain that later," he said when Mr Justice Wright asked what "soda-water splashes" were; and "I will point it out in a minute", in reply to another of the judge's questions).

First of all, he described the condition of the body at 9.50; then he gave his estimate of the time of death. (A nasty few minutes, these, for the prosecution: MacFall refused to budge from his opinion that death occurred nearer six o'clock than seven. ". . . I formed the opinion then [upon arrival] it was four hours *or more*." "Now will you go on?" Hemmerde inserted hastily.) He talked about the blood, of how the direction of some of the splashes indicated—to him—that Mrs Wallace was sitting on the edge of the armchair and leaning towards the fire when the first blow was struck. He pointed out the two "projection marks" of blood on the mackintosh, which indicated—to him—that the garment was worn by the assailant. He described the clot of blood found on the lavatory-pan. Shown the iron bar, he said, "If a blow was made with this, it would produce the appearances I found, or such a weapon would."

MacFall's examination-in-chief lasted nearly an hour. Hemmerde was cheered up no end; at long last, it seemed, one of his important witnesses was coming up to proof.

When Oliver rose to cross-examine there were few people in court who would have given much for his chances of breaking through, or even denting, MacFall's protective padding of dogmatism. It looked like being an uneven contest—and there is little doubt that it *would* have been if Oliver had conducted the examination in the same way as he had conducted the examinations of the previous witnesses, his manner bleak and unemotional, lit only occasionally by a cold glitter of sarcasm.

But something happened at the very beginning of the cross-examination which so offended Oliver's highly-developed sense of legal good taste that it caused him to lose his temper. And this made all the difference in the world: his detachment vanished, was replaced by a driving determination to knock MacFall down to size, to make him squirm.

Rising to his feet, Oliver said, "I want to begin with your last bit of evidence—"

And this was when the trouble began.

"May I put in this before that?" MacFall interrupted, holding up a rather grubby piece of paper. "You have not had the position of these blows put in, and I have a note I made at the post-mortem showing the position, which is very important."

"I do not want to stop anything," Oliver said querulously, "but how can that indicate who did it?"

"No, of course not," the judge said. Ignoring the still uplifted piece of paper on his right, he nodded to Oliver to continue as if nothing had happened.

But now Hemmerde was on his feet. "The professor thinks it important. I hesitated to ask him."

"I have a great reason for this myself," MacFall boomed.

Mr Justice Wright was getting a little tired of MacFall's bad manners. Raising his voice slightly, he said, "Counsel must conduct the prosecution, and he will ask you or not ask you as to anything that occurred."

Only a moment or so before, Hemmerde had said something about hesitation. He showed no hesitation now. Before Oliver or the judge quite realized what was happening he slipped in with: "Can you give quite shortly what your reason is?"

And MacFall was away, speaking in italics:

"*I can,*" he said. "*I formed an idea of the mental condition of the person who committed this crime. I have seen crimes, many of them of this kind, and know what the mental condition is. I know it was not an ordinary case of assault or serious injury. It was a case of frenzy."*

Small sensation in court. *Frenzy* . . . an explanation for the apparent absence of motive—MacFall meant that Wallace was mad—a madman did not need a motive.

The judge was speaking. "We may have already formed that opinion. Where blows are struck by anyone, that probably does produce frenzy. But that is a matter for the jury."

MacFall did not appear to be listening. Neither did the jury.

Oliver waited while Hemmerde bowed politely to the judge and resumed his seat. His voice shook as he said, "With reference to the last matter, you have noticed that my client has been under medical observation as to his mental condition ever since his arrest?"

"I know that he will have been," MacFall said casually.

"If there is anything to be said about his mental condition, there are people *competent* to say it, who have lived with him." Not a question, but a statement.

"Yes, I do not wish to express an opinion." Which, considering his earlier utterances, was hard to believe.

"If this is the work of a maniac, and he is a sane man, he did not do it. Is that right?"

"He may be sane now."

"If he has been sane all his life, and is sane now, it would be some momentary frenzy?"

"The mind is very peculiar," MacFall said, speaking as if it were he who had given Freud his first lessons in psychology.

"It is a rash suggestion, is it not?" Oliver thundered.

"Not the slightest," MacFall boomed back. "I have seen this sort of thing before—exactly the same thing."

"Rash to suggest in a murder case, I suggest to you?"

"I do not suggest who did it at all." (No? Then what was his "great reason" for showing the rough diagram of the position of the blows on the head? And how, while we are asking questions, did the *position* of the blows indicate the mental condition of the murderer? Surely it was the *number* of blows, not the pattern they made, which showed that the murderer was in an abnormal state when he committed the crime? If the pattern had been different, would this have indicated more or less frenzy, or no frenzy at all?)

"The fact that a man has been sane for fifty-two years, and has

been sane while in custody for the last three months, would rather
tend to prove that he has always been sane, would it not?"

"No, not necessarily."

"Not necessarily?"

"No, we know very little about the private lives of people or
their thoughts."

"I want to deal with evidence and not speculation," Oliver shouted.

From now on he kept the pressure on MacFall, forcing him to
answer direct questions with direct answers, taunting him, pouring
ridicule and scorn on his more outlandish theories. At first MacFall
tried to retaliate; but that was no use—Oliver always went one
better. And he always made sure that his questions were framed
unobjectionably: it was not so much the matter of the questions as
the manner in which they were put which did the damage. Slowly
but surely MacFall's arrogance vanished, his confidence evapo-
rated, his stature shrunk. Talking about the cross-examination
afterwards, a member of the defence team summed it up by
saying, "MacFall MacFell."

Hardly bothering to pause after his remark about evidence and
speculation, "Let us go back," Oliver said. "You have told the
jury that you were very much struck . . . with his callous demeanour?"

"I was."

Like a shot: "Why did you not say so at the police court?"

"Because I was not asked," MacFall retorted.

This was just the answer Oliver wanted. "But you do not mind
volunteering things," he snapped. "You have been volunteering
things for the last five minutes." Oliver went on to outline the
defence theory of how the murder was committed:

"Suppose a woman went into that room, lit the gas and lit the
fire, she would have to stoop down, would she not?"

"Presumably, yes."

"And her head might well be in the very position in which you
put it?"

"Exactly."

"If she had that coat around her, and the gas-fire was alight,
and she fell when she was struck so as to burn her skirt in the fire,
do you not think it is quite possible that that mackintosh swung
round on the fireplace and caught fire?"

MacFall was stranded between the devil and the deep blue sea.
Clearly, the proper answer to this question was "yes", but if he
gave the proper answer, then the prosecution's mackintosh theory

would be considerably weakened. So: "No," he extemporized, "because there is no evidence of it having been on her right or left arm."

"Suppose it was round her shoulders and she collapsed, do you not see the possibility of the bottom of the mackintosh falling into the fire and getting burnt, too?"

It was no good. MacFall had to give in. "There is the possibility," he grumbled.

Oliver started polishing the possibility into a probability. "Her hair was pulled away from her head, was it not, all up?"

"Yes."

"And the pad which had been under her hair was away from her body?"

"Yes."

"Do you not see the possibility of someone having grasped her by her hair to pull her away from the fire?"

"Yes." What else could he say?

"Where her clothes were burning?"

At last, a chance of evasion. "I do not know about the burning."

"It is said that my client tried to destroy the mackintosh by burning it, because it was his. That would take time, would it not?"

"I am not an authority on the burning of mackintoshes," MacFall said, and then looked first of all surprised, afterwards annoyed, at the amusement caused by this statement. Even the judge smiled; and if a slight elongation of the lips can be called a smile, so did Oliver, who murmured:

"Then we will leave that to our general knowledge," and went on: "Now to come to another matter. Whether clothed or whether naked, it would be necessary, would it not, in all common sense, that many splashes of blood would fall upon the assailant?"

There was no way of evading this question. "Yes, I should expect to find them."

Oliver went a step further: "Would you agree that nothing in this life is certain, but it is almost certain the assailant would have blood on his face and clothes?"

"On his left hand I think he would."

"What about his right?"

"No, I do not think so. You do not find the blood so much on the hand that holds the weapon."

"The last blows being probably struck with the head on the ground, there would be blood upon his feet and lower part of his legs for certain, would not there?"

"I should expect that."

"There would be some on his face?" asked the judge.

"There would be some on his legs."

"And his face?" Oliver insisted.

"Yes."

"And his hair?"

"Yes, but more likely upon the face."

Quick as a flash: "You agree it would be most likely on the face?"

"Yes, I agree," MacFall said unhappily.

"Supposing the mackintosh were put under the body, the assailant would have had to lift that shoulder and the head up to do it. That would have involved getting heavily dabbled in blood, would it not?"

"Dabbled in blood, but not heavily. Supposing he did?"

"I ask you to *assume* it," Oliver snapped. "You can assume a thing without admitting it, can't you?"

"Yes," MacFall said meekly.

"Let us go to the mackintosh for a moment," Oliver said, and now his voice was velvet-soft, his manner casual. "You have pointed out two things to the jury which you say are definitely blood projections?"

"Yes."

"You told the jury—and do not take it that I am differing from you for a moment—that what you would call a trickle would come round sideways, an elongation, something like that?"

"Yes."

"So it could be splashed, spurted or dropped?"

The sudden change in Oliver's manner seems to have lulled MacFall into a sense of false security. Oliver had relaxed; so could he. Without hesitation: "Yes," he agreed.

But now Oliver was back at full throttle: "Are those two marks there anything more than a drop from the head on to that mackintosh?" he demanded.

MacFall was visibly jolted, like a man abruptly woken from a doze. "Not necessarily," he said. "It all depends upon the condition." This was an astonishing about-face. In direct evidence, and again, only a few seconds before, he had said that the two bloodstains were *definitely* direct projections.

"First of all, I got it from you that those marks might be the marks of a drip," Oliver reminded him.

"They might."

"What I am suggesting to you is that they are perfectly consistent with marks of a drip, if that sleeve happened to be in a position which would catch the drips in that way."

MacFall had no choice; he had to answer, "They are."

"Supposing the assailant was wearing the coat, and there was this frightful spurting you have told us about, do not you think there would be more than those two things upon it?"

"No."

"Why do you say that?"

"Because the blood all goes towards the floor."

Oliver had no difficulty at all in demonstrating the fallacy of this statement.

"You have pointed out to the jury that it has been spurting all round the room?"

"That was the first blow."

"You told me that while she was lying on the floor, the blood would spill?"

"Yes, it would as it pumped out."

"You find blood-splashes well above the floor all round the room—over the piano and the door?"

"No, I think those blood-splashes by the door did not come from the first blow."

Oliver pounced. "They went upwards, did they not?"

"Yes, from the floor."

"Then while the head was on the floor, the blood would go upwards?"

"Yes, and away from the assailant," MacFall said, trying to make the best of a bad job.

"You are speculating?"

"I am," MacFall admitted.

"Very well," Oliver said. "I have put my case to you on that. Now with regard to the time of death . . ." And he started to hack away at the last remnants of MacFall's prestige.

"How many notes did you make with regard to rigor mortis?"

"Practically none, I think."

"Can you show me one?"

"I do not think I can," MacFall mumbled.

"You would agree that the progress of rigor mortis from the point of view of crime is important?"

"Very."

"And not one note made?" Oliver said, in case the jury had missed this point first time round.

"No, but I know definitely."

But did he? Oliver decided to find out.

"You were testing it about every quarter of an hour?"

"It was fairly often."

"What was the condition at ten minutes to eleven?"

MacFall thought for a moment, then: "I did not make any notes as we went along of progression."

A stunned silence before Oliver burst out with: "*Not making notes!*" (And the force of his astonishment can best be gauged from the fact that the shorthand-writer used that rarest of all pieces of legal punctuation, the exclamation mark.)

"You have a good memory, I suppose?"

"I have."

"Then what was the position at ten to eleven?"

"It had got to the right shoulder."

"Is that all?"

And once more MacFall was forced to retract. "I was not looking at the times as I went on," he said. "I did not take the time on any other occasion except when I went to the house." In other words, he was talking eyewash when he said that the rigor had progressed to the right shoulder by ten to eleven.

"Surely, if your memory does not help you," Oliver said coldly, "you, as a scientist, will be able to help me. Rigor is a very fallible test as to the time of death?"

"Not in the present case of an ordinary person dying in health."

"It is a very fallible factor, even in healthy people?"

"It is, just a little."

"And the powerful and muscular body will be affected by rigor much more slowly than a feeble and frail body?"

"Yes."

"Was this a feeble and frail body?"

"Yes. She was not exactly frail; she was a feeble woman."

"You have used the word 'frail'," Oliver said, referring to the deposition.

"Yes, she was a weak woman."

"*Frail?*" Oliver insisted.

"Yes, frail."

"Then we may summarise your last two answers, and it comes to this—that she was a woman who was likely to be quickly affected by rigor?"

"No, she would be rather delayed, if anything," MacFall said surprisingly . . .

. . . and confusingly as far as Mr Justice Wright was concerned.

"But you said it would be quicker in a frail person and slower in a person of muscularity," he pointed out.

"She would be delayed," came the stubborn reply.

"Do you wish to say that a feeble and frail person would have delayed rigor?" Oliver asked.

"No."

"Why do you say it, then?"

"She was in a condition of good health, although a frail woman." (Healthy *and* feeble?)

"Then I will start all over again," Oliver said, sighing elaborately. "Was this woman a feeble and frail body?"

"Yes."

"Then she would be likely, would she not, to be more quickly affected by rigor?"

"A little," MacFall allowed (although, earlier, he had agreed with Oliver that a muscular body would be affected "much more slowly").

"Then why did you say rather longer just now?"

"Not rather longer than a muscular person."

Oliver's voice was brittle. "You are not arguing the case, are you?"

"No, I wish to state what I found."

"You know what is at stake here?"

"I do."

"Bearing in mind that this feeble and frail woman would be more likely to be affected by rigor, are you going to swear she was killed more than three hours before you saw her?"

"No, I am not going to swear," MacFall said. "I am going to give an opinion, and I swear that the opinion I give shall be an honest one."

"Then what *is* your opinion?" the judge asked tiredly.

"My opinion was formed at that time that the woman had been dead about four hours."

Oliver: "Now that I have reminded you that, she being feeble and frail, rigor would come on quicker, does that move your opinion?"

"No."

"You saw her at ten to ten?"

"Yes."

"So if she was alive at half-past six, your opinion is wrong, is it not?"

"Yes."

"Does not that convince you what a very fallible test rigor mortis is?"

"No, it does not. I am still of the opinion."

"Do you think the milk boy imagined seeing her alive?"

"I do not want to think about the milk boy and what he saw at all." (Afterwards, whenever MacFall spoke about the case, he put forward the theory that it was not Julia who answered the door to Alan Close, but Wallace dressed in his wife's clothes and imitating her voice.)

Now nearing the end of the cross-examination, Oliver pulled a fast one on MacFall by letting him believe that he was being questioned about the large clot of blood in the parlour, when in fact the questions were related to the clot found on the lavatory-pan.

"One other thing you relied upon in forming your estimate of time, and that was the condition of the blood. Let me suggest that the small amount of serum exudation you observed when you first examined the body is indicative that death had not taken place long before."

"Very little serum exudes over the first few hours."

"Very well. How long does blood take to become clotted?"

"It varies a little bit, but not much; in five or six or even ten minutes."

"May I call a ten-minutes-old clot very new?"

"Yes."

"If interfered with, it would break up, would it not?"

"Yes" again, and by now MacFall was clearly puzzled as to where this line of questioning was leading.

"Or splash, would it not?—and may I suggest to you it would take at least an hour for a clot of blood to be solid enough to become what I call interfered with and manipulated?"

MacFall was completely in the dark. "It would take a clot of blood solid enough to be interfered with . . .? I do not quite understand what you mean by 'interfered with'—lifted about, moved?"

"Let us say, dropped on to a hard substance," Oliver said casually. "I suggest it would be at least an hour before you could take a clot and drop it on, say, a table without smashing it."

"A clot would smash up even then."

Oliver pressed home his advantage. "Let me take a clot three-sixteenths wide and one-eighth of an inch high. While that is fresh and newly clotted, if you were to drop that on to a lavatory-pan it would spread out, would it not?"

Even now, it seems, MacFall couldn't see what Oliver was

driving at. "It would show some signs of spreading out."

"What I am putting to you is that it would take at least an hour before a clot of blood would be sufficiently solid not to flatten when it was dropped on to that lavatory-pan."

And at last MacFall got the message. "No, I do not agree," he said hastily.

"Then how long do you say it would take?" Oliver asked.

A long pause while MacFall thought back to his earlier answers—then, disconsolately: "An hour."

"Did you get blood on your hands while you were examining this body?"

"Very little."

"You never saw that clot of blood until you had been in the bathroom some time, did you?"

"Not for five minutes."

"Does it occur to you that someone who came in after nine had dropped that clot of blood on the pan?"

MacFall's reply was most unexpected: "That possibility did occur to me very much indeed."

"Does it occur to you now?"

"It does."

"Having regard to the fact that there is no other blood upstairs at all, none—if a man went up, all bloody, to wash himself, it would be an amazing thing, would it not, that there was no blood upstairs?"

"Only the one clot."

"Will you accept it from me—indeed, you said the chance was that the police had carried it up there?"

"Yes," MacFall said, "I thought the police might have dropped it there."

Oliver left it at that. MacFall's long ordeal was over.

Hemmerde was on his feet at once. Referring to the last answer given in cross-examination, he asked, "That occurred to you, professor, because it was the only mark of blood upstairs?"

"The only mark, and it is so striking."

Mr Justice Wright put in: "And you now think it may have been carried there by the police?"

"No, my Lord," MacFall replied.

The judge looked vexed. "I thought you said so."

"I was asked, did I recognize the possibility? and I said I did recognize the possibility and made enquiries about it." (In fact, he did nothing of the sort.)

"It is a possibility?"

"Yes, certainly—but I took care to find out that the police had not been up." (This was obviously untrue: at least four policemen —Williams, Moore, Gold, and Bailey—inspected the bathroom before MacFall discovered the blood at about 11 P.M.)

Roland Oliver was on his feet again. "I meant the witness to understand that it was he who might have done it," he said smoothly.

MacFall jabbed excitedly at the top button of his tweed waistcoat. "I myself, you mean?"

"Yes."

"I am glad you have said that," MacFall roared wheezily, leaning forward in the box. "No, I did not."

Smiling slightly, Oliver resumed his seat.

Hemmerde did not prolong the re-examination. There was no point. No doubt, if MacFall had been given the chance, he would have tried to contradict some of the statements forced out of him by defence counsel, but in so doing he would only have made matters worse, both for himself and for the prosecution; it was better to leave things where they stood and hope that the jury accepted at least *some* of his evidence, rather than to run the risk of turning them against the *whole* of it.

With the arrival of the next witness, *Dr Hugh Pierce*, in the box, the tempo of the trial slackened, the temperature dropped. Perhaps, while he had been waiting outside the court, he had got wind of the severe mauling MacFall was taking from Oliver— whatever the reason, he was extremely nervous, fidgeting with his hands and answering in a low voice, often stuttering. His answers were not exactly evasive, but he spoke so generally that, at times, it was hard to believe that he was talking about the Wallace case at all.

After four or five of Oliver's questions had produced answers which were so hypothetical as to be meaningless, Mr Justice Wright interposed: "I want to know what your view is in *this* case. You have said so many things that it is difficult to follow what it is you have said or have not. So far, you put the time of death at six o'clock or perhaps later, but with a margin of error two hours either way, which I thought referred to this particular case, otherwise what is the use of saying it?"

"Yes, that is so," Pierce mumbled.

It must have been as much of a relief to him as it was to everyone else in court when Oliver said, "I will leave it there, my Lord," and the prosecution waived the right to re-examine.

William Roberts, the analyst, was the last of the prosecution's expert witnesses.

Before the Wallace trial, in their separate reports based on the evidence presented at the committal proceedings, both Professor Dible and Dr Coope had pointed out that William Roberts had no medical training, qualification, or experience, and was therefore not entitled to express opinions regarding the medical aspects of the case.

Roland Oliver had read these reports—and, indeed, had been greatly assisted by them in his cross-examination of MacFall and Pierce—but it seems that he completely overlooked the point made concerning Roberts's expertise, which should have restricted his evidence, simply and solely, to matters relating to laboratory analysis. Not until the start of re-examination, when Hemmerde asked, "Would you expect there to be much blood on the assailant's calves and shins?" and Roberts replied, "No, not much", did it occur to Oliver that the witness was not qualified to answer questions of this nature.

"Surely that is a medical question?" he protested.

"He is not a medical man at all; he is an analyst," said Mr Justice Wright, upholding the objection.

Speaking more to the jury than to the judge, Hemmerde put in: "I have known him so long, I think he is both."

"I only know what he said," Mr Justice Wright barked.

But the objection had come too late—far too late. Not only in evidence-in-chief, but also in answer to questions put by Oliver himself, Roberts had expressed opinions on subjects that were far outside his professional scope. He had, for example, said that he would not expect "a great deal of blood to be on an assailant wearing just a raincoat and nothing else"; asked if there was any blood on the cashbox, he had ignored the question and volunteered his opinion that Wallace could have removed the bloodstains from his feet, whether they were bare or booted, by "wiping them on the rug".

Although Roberts was by no means as expert a witness as he and Hemmerde tried to make out, he was certainly expert as far as giving evidence was concerned. He knew exactly what to say and how to say it; unlike poor Dr Pierce, he gave an impression of unruffled assurance. The prosecution could have done with a few more witnesses like him. They were delighted with his performance—so delighted, in fact, that, as will be seen, they persuaded him to give an encore as the concluding item in the Crown case.

The last witness of the day was *Detective-Superintendent Hubert Moore*—"his skin smelling of Lifebuoy, his breath of Jameson's," says one of the constables who was on court duty.

Coaxed along by Hemmerde, Moore described, in minute detail, what happened at the house between the time of his arrival there at five minutes past ten and his departure, six hours or so later.

Then the pair of them got together—the learned Recorder of Liverpool and the illustrious Head of the Liverpool C.I.D.—to construct a couple of the most tortuous pieces of double-think ever to disgrace a court of law.

What they tried to suggest, first of all, was this—that the absence of bloodstains on Wallace's boots was not an indication of innocence, but a strong sign of his guilt. When he returned from Menlove Gardens, they said, he must have known that his wife was lying dead in the parlour and that there was a large amount of blood on the floor; and he must have known the *position* of the bloodstains . . . otherwise, in the darkness, he would have trodden in the blood as he walked across the room to light the gas-bracket. It was another of the prosecution's heads-Wallace-loses, tails-we-win ideas. There were, of course, several flaws in the argument: one of them was that, according to Wallace's first statement to Moore, he had struck a match as he stood in the doorway and then, seeing his wife's body on the floor, had used the same match to light the gas—so it was in his hand, lighting his way, as he crossed the room.

For the benefit of the stepping-in-blood idea, the prosecution overstated how dark it was and ignored the fact that Wallace lit the match before entering the parlour—but the second idea, which was put forward almost in the same breath, was *based* upon the match-lighting and *dependent* upon the room being merely gloomy rather than pitch-dark.

". . . We say there was no necessity for him to light a match at the door," Moore said. "A man living sixteen years in a little room like that—it was not the natural thing."

According to Moore's view of the natural order of things, an innocent man—unaware that his wife's body was on the floor and therefore not worried about tripping over it; unaware, too, that there was blood on the floor and therefore not worried about treading in it—would have walked across to the fireplace *and then struck the match* to light the gas-bracket: knowing the room so well, he would not have thought he needed to light the match *before entering*, in order to find his way to the gas-bracket.

What Moore neglected to mention was that Wallace struck the match—as he had struck other matches in other parts of the house (witnessed by the Johnstons)—for the purpose of temporary illumination, not with the idea of lighting the gas; it was only after the match was struck and he saw his wife's body that he crossed the room, the match still in his hand, to light the gas.

Roland Oliver put only a couple of general questions to Moore concerning what he called "the match-lighting adventure"; but he dealt most skilfully with the suggestion that, if Wallace was innocent, he ought to have got some blood on his boots, forcing Moore to admit that there was no blood on the floor to the right of the body, and then, with the aid of a plan,[1] showing that this was the most natural route to the gas, and the only route Wallace could have taken without stepping over the body.

Under cross-examination Moore gave a remarkable display of sustained equivocation. He seemed almost incapable of giving a straight answer to any of Oliver's questions; several times, rather than say something that might be helpful to the defence, he changed the evidence that he had given at the committal proceedings.

Asked if Wallace had been "of great assistance to the police during the early stages of the investigation", he said, "I would not say assistance. He helped us by the fact that he was handy when we wanted to ask him some questions."

"You have said, 'He was very useful to us in our inquiries in the early stages'," Oliver said, referring to Moore's deposition. "You do not want to concede a point to the defence if you can help it?"

"I do, indeed."

"You talked about his demeanour being quite calm, smoking cigarettes; but you never mentioned it before today?"

"I was never asked it."

"It only seems to have occurred to someone quite lately to ask that question," Oliver commented. "You attach importance to it, do you not?"

---

[1] See *Plans and Diagrams*, p. 312.

o

"No, not that I know of."

"If you do not think it is important, I will not trouble with it," Oliver said, smooth as silk. "Have you ever heard of people smoking cigarettes to try and keep a hold on their nerves?"

"I am not a cigarette smoker—I smoke a pipe."

"And that is a very good reason why you should not have heard of it," Oliver murmured sarcastically.

Later, dealing with the defence theory that the murderer had called at the house and been invited into the parlour by Mrs Wallace, Oliver said, "There is evidence in this case that when the murderer was in that room, the fire was lit and the gas must have been lit, is there not?"

He waited for Moore to answer, then: "Why do you hesitate?"

"Because it is all a matter of opinion."

"There are burns on that skirt which, according to your own witness [Roberts], were made by the bars in the fire."

"There are no bars in the gas-fire," Moore prevaricated.

"The asbestos rings of that fire, then," Oliver snapped.

"I cannot say myself."

"I want you to consider as an expert."

But Moore refused to be moved. "That is suggested."

Oliver made a number of references to the dubious methods used by the police. Towards the end of the cross-examination he asked, "Do you know of a boy named Allison Wildman?"

"No, I do not," was the firm reply.

Previously Moore had been guilty of using stonewalling tactics—now, though, he was clearly guilty of lying.

"Have you never heard of him?"

"There was a statement given to me by your solicitors," Moore said, "but I forget what the name was." (If he had honestly forgotten Wildman's name, what made him connect it with the statement?)

"The name was given of a youth who said that Mrs Wallace was alive many minutes after 6.30 that night. I want to know, why should not that boy have been called by the prosecution?"

"I do not know the boy Wildman," Moore insisted.

"How many statements were taken altogether?"

But the judge wanted to know: "Who took them, first of all?"

"Either Sergeant Bailey or Inspector Gold. I do not know who it was that took them."

"As long as you did not," the judge said meaningfully.

Oliver's last few questions were concerned with the missing iron bar.

". . . It must have been got rid of somewhere outside the house, so far as you can tell?"

"Unless it is hid inside the house or the adjoining fields possibly." (Once again, the suggestion that Anfield was a delightfully rural area; actually, about the only field in the district was the football pitch belonging to Liverpool F.C.)

"Is there any place on the way between the back of Wolverton Street and the tram-stop in which it could have been buried in the ground? It is all streets, is it not?"

"Yes, all streets."

"And you have searched everywhere?"

"Yes," Moore said, then added, "At the end of Wolverton Street I understand there is waste land."

"But the waste land has been raked over—combed since?"

"Yes."

"Thank you," Oliver said politely. "That is all."

The tag line to the day's proceedings was provided by Mr Justice Wright, who commented, "The mystery is, *someone* must have got rid of it—if that was the instrument used."

It had been another good day for the defence; another black one for the prosecution. With only a couple more prosecution witnesses to be called, there was still no scintilla of evidence to connect Wallace with his wife's murder. Plenty of suspicion masquerading as circumstantial evidence, yes—but not an ounce of actual proof.

Roland Oliver, however, was worried.

That night, in his room at the North Western Hotel[1] with Sydney Scholefield Allen and Hector Munro, he found it difficult, at times almost impossible, to concentrate on the discussion about defence tactics for the following day. Occasionally he stood up and paced the floor, and once or twice he wandered over to the window to stare out across Lime Street at the giant, black shape of St George's Hall.

It was the jury he was worried about.

"I can do no good with them," he murmured. "They do not listen."

---

[1] The same hotel at which Oscar Slater stayed before his "flight from justice". There are many similarities between the Slater and Wallace cases.

FRIDAY, April 24th

> *"Fourteenth of March, I think it was,"* he
> *said.*
> *"Fifteenth," said the March Hare.*
> *"Sixteenth," said the Dormouse.*
> *"Write that down," the King said to the*
> *jury; and the jury eagerly wrote down all*
> *three dates on their slates, and then added*
> *them up, and reduced the answer to shillings*
> *and pence.*

The first witness on Friday morning was *Detective-Sergeant Harry Bailey*. His examination-in-chief, conducted by Leslie Walsh, did not take long. And neither did the cross-examination.

One of Walsh's questions was: "Could you say, was Mrs Wallace very well dressed?" to which Bailey replied, "I should say she was poorly dressed, home-made clothing."

Oliver was annoyed about this. "I do not know how far it is going to be suggested poverty drove the man to the commission of this crime."

"I do not suggest poverty," the witness protested.

"No, I am sure you do not," Oliver said sarcastically. "Did you know that this man had a banking account at this time?"

"Yes, I did."

Mr Justice Wright interposed: "Will you tell the jury, Mr Walsh, that it was in credit to the extent of £152?"

"Yes, my Lord, we agree that."

"Do you know a boy named Wildman?" Oliver went on, only slightly less fiercely.

"I cannot say I know him. I know the family."

"Do you know why the police have not called Wildman or a newspaper boy named Jones?"

"We arrived, as far as I know, at the conclusion that Close was the last person who saw the deceased alive."

"I wonder if you know it has been laid down in the Court of

Criminal Appeal that it is the duty of the police to call all witnesses who are relevant to assist the jury—not to pick and choose the ones who help to prove the guilt? Do you know anything against either Wildman or Jones?"

"No, I do not."

Satisfied that he had made his point, Oliver went on: "Have you ever before today, in public, expressed any opinion about the accused's coolness that night?"

"I have never been asked."

" 'I have never been asked'—that is the answer we get from everybody," said Oliver disgustedly.

Detective-Inspector Herbert Gold was the next—and, as the defence believed, the last—prosecution witness.

"Have you tested the time it takes to get from the telephone-box to the chess club?" Leslie Walsh asked him.

"I have been on that route many times, but I never took the actual time. It would take twenty to twenty-five minutes at the outside, from my knowledge of that route."

The old favourite question came up again—"What do you say about his demeanour?"—but this time the answer provided as much assistance to the defence as to the prosecution.

"He was cool and calm," Gold said. "I did not see any sign of emotion in him at all at the death of his wife." Then: "When I first went into the house on the night of the murder, he was sitting in the kitchen. In fact, he had the cat on his knee and was stroking the cat, *and he did not look to me like a man who had just battered his wife to death*."

Cross-examining, and still trying to get to the bottom of the mystery of the missing witnesses, Oliver asked, "Did you take a statement from a boy named Wildman?"

"I did."

"Do you remember this letter being received by the police?" Oliver asked, and proceeded to read from a copy of Hector Munro's letter to Superintendent Moore.[1]

"That is the first time I have heard of that letter," Gold replied. (But this seems impossible to believe. What the inspector was saying, in effect, was that someone at police headquarters had told him to take a statement from Allison Wildman, and he had done this without knowing, or asking, why.)

"It was never communicated to you, as inspector in charge

[1] See p. 136.

of the case?" Oliver asked in an astonished tone of voice.

"Not to me," Gold persisted.

"Very well. You say this man was being treated by the police as the case of a man who had lost his wife?"

"Yes."

"On Wednesday, the 21st, he was at the police station all day, we have been told. Was he shadowed after that?"

"Not to my knowledge."

"On the 22nd?"

"Not to my knowledge."

"Mr Gold, on the 22nd was he shadowed?" Oliver said sternly.

"Not to my knowledge."

"Do you remember the conversation with Mr Beattie in the evening?"

"Not to my knowledge," Gold said for the fourth time—then, realizing that this answer did not quite fit the question, he sought refuge in his notebook. "The accused was with me in the detective office all day on the 22nd, up to twenty to ten, when I was taking his statement, and he looked at his watch and said, 'I do not want to be late to get to Ullet Road because my sister-in-law will be going to bed,' and he said: 'Can I go now?' and I said: 'Yes', and he went and met Mr Beattie."

"Then he must have been shadowed?"

"No, I did not know it."

"When was he first followed? Was it on the Friday, the Saturday, or the Sunday?"

"I cannot tell you."

"About the end of the week?" Mr Justice Wright suggested.

"About the end of the week," Gold agreed.

"Just one other thing," Oliver said tiredly. " 'Yes' or 'No', with regard to his demeanour, his coolness, were you asked to give any evidence about that before today?"

"No."

Re-examining, Hemmerde got Gold to say that Wallace was followed for his own good, as a precaution in case some irate Liverpudlian decided to take the law into his own hands.

Then:

"I should like to recall Mr Roberts on a point which I was unable to deal with when he was in the box, and that will be all."

So the City Analyst returned to the scene of his triumph of the day before. He was not asked to take the oath again.

He claimed that, two or three days after the murder, apropos of the blood found on the lavatory-pan, he had made "exhaustive experiments", and had discovered that "when fresh blood drops from a height of fifteen inches, it forms a little clot, and when that dries, it clots together and makes a blob".

Oliver decided that the best way of dealing with Roberts's testimony was to mix disbelief with distaste, with ridicule.

"You made these experiments to see whether a thing which you had never seen could be reproduced?" he sneered.

"Yes, certainly," Roberts retorted loftily. "It is a matter of scientific interest."

"Have you any notes of your experiments?"

"No."

"Are you telling the jury that, within two or three minutes of blood being shed, it would fall a height of fifteen inches and remain in the shape of a thing like a pea cut in half?"

"No; I said it forms a blob, and afterwards it dries like that."

"You mean it hunches itself up?"

"It is a sort of circular thing," Roberts said vaguely. "It flattened and then formed just like a blob."

"How high above the pan was the top of your blob when it fell?"

"I used different-sized blobs. In the case of the one which was three-eighths of an inch in diameter, the height was a quarter of an inch."

"So it sat there, if I might use that expression, a quarter of an inch high?"

"Yes," Roberts said. (And the blob was becoming more and more sinister, like something from the pages of science-fiction. When it alighted on the pan it was a flat "sort of circular thing", but now it had grown and was sitting, hunch-backed, as if waiting to pounce on anyone who dared to use the lavatory.)

"Did it have a round top?"

"No, a flat top."

The judge was completely bewildered. "You mean it spread out and then remained about a quarter of an inch high?"

"Yes, my Lord."

"But you have got no notes?"

"No. I made it as a matter of scientific interest."

Roberts's evidence caused much discussion in Liverpool medical circles. No one was able to explain how, as one doctor put it, "the analyst was able to make a drop of fresh blood rise like a soufflé". A member of the Medical Faculty at the University declared: "The only explanation, as far as I can see, as to how Mr Roberts achieved cone-shaped clots from drops of freshly-shed blood is that, before commencing the experiment, he coated the rim of the pan with vaseline." It seems a pity that Roberts was not asked to perform the experiment in court. The actual lavatory-pan was there, and if he had shied away from the thought of shedding his own blood in the interests not only of Science but of Justice, no doubt a member of the defence team would have been only too glad to act as blood donor. It would not have taken long to settle the matter, one way or the other. But Roberts, unbloody and apparently unbowed, was quickly hustled away by Hemmerde, who then announced:

"That, my Lord, with the accused's statement, is the evidence for the Crown."

A sudden buzz of conversation—broken into, cut short, by the voice of the Clerk of Assize, as he recited the statement made by Wallace at the end of the committal proceedings. Now everyone in the public gallery was staring at Wallace, those at the back standing on tip-toe, hands on the shoulders of the people in front of them, to get a better view; but according to the *Echo* reporter, "The prisoner seemed perfectly oblivious to what was going on, seemingly unconscious that he was the cynosure of hundreds of pairs of eyes. His outward attitude was that of a man resigned to whatever fate might have in store for him . . . arms folded, head slightly on one side as though with weariness."

Hardly a pause after the Clerk's reading of the statement, and Oliver was on his feet to make the opening speech for the defence.

(Many of the lawyers in court were surprised that he did not submit that there was no case for the defence to answer. Hector Munro says, "I was in favour of such a submission. . . . What happened was that leading counsel—no doubt rightly—took the view that a submission should not be made. It may be that he was waiting for an indication from the judge. . . . I have often wondered why no such indication was given. Possibly, the judge thought that it would be better to have a verdict, and he may have expected an acquittal." After so many years the solicitor cannot remember the reason given by Oliver for not making the submission, but it seems likely that Oliver feared the effect upon the jury if the submission were turned down.)

Compared with Hemmerde's opening for the Crown, Oliver's speech was brief. It lasted less than half an hour.

He asked the jury to consider the following points in Wallace's favour: First, that there was no apparent motive; second, that it was impossible to reconcile MacFall's theory of frenzy with the general prosecution picture of Wallace as a cool, calculating villain ("This suggestion [of frenzy] was made because it was realized that this motiveless crime, alleged to have been committed by a devoted husband, presented almost insuperable difficulties . . ."); third, that there was no scintilla of evidence that Wallace had made the telephone-call ("If he did not send that message, he is an innocent man—and how can it be said that the prosecution have even started to prove that he sent it?"); fourth, that there was insufficient time for Wallace to have killed his wife and cleaned himself up before leaving for Menlove Gardens; and fifth, that despite the full-scale search of the places where Wallace could have disposed of the murder weapon, it had not been found.

Dismissing the evidence of Lily Hall and P.C. Rothwell, and pointing out that nothing was said before the trial of Wallace's "unnatural calm" on the night of the murder ("I wonder whose brain devised this?"), he went on to ridicule the mackintosh theory.

Coming to the end of the speech, he asked the jury to remember "Wallace's undoubted affection for his wife, the utter absence of motive, his condition of comfort as far as money was concerned, his character". Then, lifting his voice ever so slightly but still keeping it several decibels away from declamation, he concluded: "This is the man who you are asked to convict of murder. And this is the man to whom I am now going to ask you to listen. . . . Remember that in so far as statements were made by him on that Tuesday night, if he is an innocent man, consider what condition of mind he must have been in—whether quiet, as the police say; stunned by shock; or whether sobbing when alone, as Mrs Johnston says. If he has made a slip or two, remember the circumstances."

I wish to go into the witness box and give evidence

Wm. Wallace

A note written by Wallace to Hector Munro on the first day of the trial.

In the dock the two warders rose to their feet and stood one on either side of Wallace, anticipating the calling of his name and ready to accompany him to the witness-box. The people in the public gallery pressed forward, thinking that the big moment had come.

But it was well after midday, and Mr Justice Wright decided not to ask Oliver to open a lengthy and important examination with only a short while to go before lunch. So the court adjourned.

Twenty-five minutes past two.

With a warder leading the way, another following close behind, Wallace walked up the stone steps from the cells and into the dock; a moment of hesitation, then the small procession moved out of the dock, down the few wooden steps to the well of the court. The two warders were joined by two more; one of them nudged Wallace's arm and pointed to an upturned tea-chest which had been used to bring exhibits from police headquarters. Wallace sat down. His eyes wandered over the exhibits stacked around him—the mackintosh . . . the broken cashbox . . . his wife's skirt . . . the box of iron bars . . . the lavatory-pan, still bearing a faint mark of blood on the rim.

He looked tired but composed. The one sign of nervousness— and even this was a sign which could be recognized as such only by someone who knew him well—was that his lips were pursed, emitting the whispered semblance of a tune. Was it a tune remembered from the times when he and Julia had played together in the parlour at Wolverton Street?

The minutes dragged by. At half-past two, on the dot, Mr Justice Wright entered, and Wallace stood up and turned to face the bench; then, looking in the direction of Roland Oliver and receiving a slight nod, a small smile of encouragement, he stepped into the witness-box. His long ordeal was about to begin.

Wallace's voice was low as he recited the oath—so low that Oliver had to ask him to speak a little louder.

"I'm sorry," he said, clearing his throat, "I'm a bit husky." But during his stay in the witness-box his voice "never became so strong as to be audible in all parts of the court".[1]

He made a good witness. His answers, generally, were clear, concise, and to the point; there was never the slightest hint of equivocation, either on direct or indirect evidence.

[1] *Liverpool Evening Express* (24.4.31).

Occasionally, however, he was rather too accurate for his counsel's liking. After about half an hour of the examination-in-chief, Oliver, carefully casual, said:

"I suppose I must put this question to you. I think it follows from what you have said. Did you lay a finger on her? Did you lay a hand upon your wife at all that night?"

Clearly, the answer Oliver wanted, expected, was a large-sized No; but Wallace considered the question for a moment, frowned at it, then: "I think, in going out of the back door, I did what I often enough did," he replied. "I just patted her on the shoulder and said, 'I won't be longer than I can help.'"

"I did not mean that," Oliver said irritably. "Did you do anything to injure her?"

"Oh no, certainly not."

But apart from the few over-accuracies, which tended either to deaden the effect Oliver was after or to obstruct the smooth flow of question-and-answer, Oliver must have been well satisfied with Wallace's showing as a witness.

Only once did Wallace seem in danger of losing his composure, and that was when he was asked to describe how he had discovered his wife's body.

"The moment I got the gas lit I turned round, of course, examined my wife, and I got hold of her left hand that was lying over her body and felt the pulse and could not find any appearance of life at all—and I looked into her face and saw then she was obviously quite dead." These words came out in a rush. As he said "quite dead" his voice broke and he closed his eyes, as if trying to shut out the memory. A second or two of complete silence, then he went on: "Well, I can hardly remember what I did then, but I know that I came out of the house and ran down the yard and informed my neighbours, and asked them to come in."

With perfect timing, Oliver asked, "Do you know what your demeanour was the rest of that evening? It was said you were extremely quiet, or cool and collected. One witness said you broke down, other witnesses say you smoked cigarettes. Do you really remember what your demeanour was?"

"Well, I remember that I was extremely agitated, and that I was trying to keep as calm and as cool as possible," Wallace said. "Probably I was smoking cigarettes for something to do—I mean to say, the inaction was more than I could stand. I had to do something to avoid breaking down. I did sit down in a chair on one or two occasions, and I do remember I did break down absolutely; I could not help it or avoid it. I tried to be as calm and as cool as possible."

"Is there anyone in the world who could take the place of your wife in this life?"

"No, there is not."

"Have you got anyone to live with now?"

"No."

"Or to live for?"

"No."

The examination-in-chief lasted about an hour. Painstakingly, only once or twice deviating from strict chronological order, Oliver took Wallace step by step through his evidence, starting with the events of Monday, January 19th, and ending with the "indiscreet" conversation with Beattie at the tram-stop in North John Street, the following Thursday evening.

As Oliver sat down an untidy murmur of excitement, of expectation, drifted round the court, grew in volume, gradually subsided into a rustle of whispers, into silence again. The main contest was about to begin—the direct confrontation between prisoner and prosecutor.

Now Wallace was going to have to fight for his life.

He still looked composed; unconcerned even. He had taken off his spectacles, was polishing them with his handkerchief, was holding them up to the light, squinting at them, putting them on again, carefully adjusting them. His lips were pursed, whistling a tune that no-one but he could hear.

Hemmerde was in no hurry. He also was using a handkerchief: blowing his nose, tuning up those versatile nostrils of his for a recital of meaningful sniffs and snorts. He stuffed the handkerchief into his sleeve and rose to his feet. Absolute silence now. He picked up his big black notebook, riffled through the pages, placed a marker between two of them, slapped the book shut.

"I want to ask you, first, a few general questions," he said.

The fight was on.

Hemmerde's opening strategy was clear. For the first five minutes or so he pelted Wallace with questions that were unrelated to one another either in substance or sequence: questions about the Monday night, the Tuesday . . . about Julia's cold, Wallace's friendship with Joseph Crewe, the sheets of music on the parlour piano, the mackintosh, the notes found in the jar in the middle bedroom. He tried to confuse Wallace, to put him out of his stride.

And right at the very beginning it looked as if he were going to succeed.

"Where was Mr Crewe on Tuesday, the 20th of January?"

"I understand that he had gone to the cinema."

"Who told you so?"

"He told me himself."

"That he had gone to the cinema?"

"He gave evidence of it here."

"On that night, the 20th?"

"On the Monday night."

"I am not talking of the Monday," Hemmerde snapped, outwardly tetchy, inwardly joyful. "I am talking of the Tuesday."

"On the Tuesday I do not know where he was."

"I thought you did know. On the Monday night, you say you knew he had been to the cinema?"

"No, I am wrong," Wallace said, realizing his mistake. "On the Monday night I do not know where he was."

"I want to know, on the Tuesday night where was he?"

"I have heard him give evidence that he was at the cinema."

"I did not catch that. Did you know it at the time?"

"I did not."

"You are a friend of his?"

"Yes."

"Very friendly?"

"Fairly friendly, yes."

Without pause: "This must have been quite a slight cold of your wife's, was it not?"

"We did not regard it as a serious matter," Wallace said.

And from now on, no matter how fiercely Hemmerde attacked his evidence, no matter how often Hemmerde switched from one subject to another and back again, no matter how many parenthetical questions were inserted—Wallace remained completely calm, unruffled. His mistake about the night of Crewe's visit to the pictures was the only sign he gave of being confused in cross-examination.

After the initial onslaught of unrelated questions Hemmerde set out to show that R. M. Qualtrough was simply a figment of Wallace's imagination, a *nom de meurtre* conjured up to provide an alibi.

"No-one could possibly have known that you would be at the café that night?"

"Nobody could say absolutely certainly that I would be there, no," Wallace admitted.

"Therefore, if anyone, not a member of the club, happened to know that you were down to play a game, that would not mean necessarily and definitely that you would be there?"

"That is so."

Now to undermine the robbery motive: "You have said how, on the night of the 20th, you had about £4 of Prudential money?"

"I have."

"And the balance that is in your hands on the Monday or Tuesday would never be very much, apart from the monthly debit?"

But Wallace was not having that. "Yes," he said, "they might be very considerable."

"At the end of your week's collecting, you would seldom be more than a few pounds in hand?" Hemmerde insisted.

"The point can be proved precisely, what I have paid in week by week for a number of years. It might be £20 or £25, it varied, and it might be £30. You do not realize that, in addition to what is known as an industrial branch collection, I might pick up varying sums in the ordinary branch."

"Allow me to take it in my own order," Hemmerde squeaked. ". . . Anyone knowing the nature of your business would know when your monthly collection would be?"

"They might do."

"And if he was going to make a raid on your house and attack your wife alive, he would naturally choose the time of the monthly collection?"

"He might."

"So far as you know, had your wife got any enemies at all?"

"None whatever," Wallace said definitely.

"Was I right in describing her as a frail, quiet, rather old-fashioned lady?"

"No, I do not think so. I do not think she was what you might call old-fashioned, and I do not think she was what you might describe as frail. She did not have the best of health, and she was not a robust person."

The pace of the cross-examination had dropped quite considerably; now Hemmerde started to pile on the pressure again:

"When Mr Qualtrough rang up on Monday night, we know he was a few hundred yards from your house?"

"I do not know."

"You do not dispute that it was rung up from there?"

"In the face of the evidence, I cannot dispute that."

"Very well, then—you can say 'Yes'. He was about four hundred yards from your house. Your wife was alone, presumably. As he rang up the City Café, he must have expected you to be there?"

"One must presume that."

The questions came thick and fast, just enough space between them for Wallace's answers, no more.

"He might have ascertained other people expected you to be there?"—"*Yes.*"—"Otherwise, he would not have left the message?"—"*Yes.*"—"And you were there two hours or more?"—"*Yes.*"—"Ample opportunity for him to have gone round to your house?"—"*Yes.*"—"Only a few minutes away?"—"*Yes.*"—"And your wife left there alone?"—"*Yes.*"

A pause for breath; a short discussion about the entry in Wallace's business diary recording the name and address given to Beattie; then another cluster of quick-fire questions:

"Have you ever used that telephone-box?"—"*Yes.*"—"You have?"—"*I have.*"—"Were you used to using it?"—"*I was not.*"— "Do you generally use the one in the library?"—"*Usually.*"— "How many times do you think you have used it?"—"*Once, or perhaps, twice.*"—"In private matters, you would use it rather than go and speak on the library phone?"—"*No, I would go to the library for preference; it is nearer.*"

"There have been occasions when you have used it." A quick look at the jury, just to make sure the point was not missed, and off again with: "Has anyone ever left such a message for you before at the City Café?"

"No."

"Or has anyone ever left a message for you *anywhere*?"

"Of that type, no."

"And of course, Mr Qualtrough had no possible means of knowing whether you would receive it that night, because no-one knew you were going to be at the club?"

"That is so."

"Then he rang you up at 7.15 or 7.20, and without knowing you would ever get the message, and without knowing you would ever go to Menlove Gardens East, apparently he was ready waiting for your departure that night?"

"It would look like it," Wallace agreed; and whatever else he was accused of—murder, madness, and meanness, among other things —no-one could say that he was evasive in answering the prosecution questions.

"Did it ever occur to you," Hemmerde went on, "that he would have to watch both doors, front and back?"

"No, it did not."

In the next couple of questions, and in several subsequent ones, Hemmerde referred to Qualtrough as if he were the Mr Hyde to Wallace's Jekyll:

"You must have realized he had not the slightest idea as to whether you got his message or not, because you knew no-one knew you were going to be there?"

"Yes."

"And, therefore, he never knew you were going to get his message—and, in spite of that, you go off to Menlove Gardens East?"

"Yes."

"Not only he could not know that you would go, but he could not have known that you would not look up a directory and find there was no such place?"

"No."

"He would have to risk all that?"

"Yes."

At this point Hemmerde brought in something completely new, something which must have been thought up by the prosecution during the trial, for it was not mentioned either at the committal proceedings or in the opening speech.

"When you went up to Penny Lane, you know now, at the terminus there, you were a very few yards away from Menlove Gardens East? [sic]"[1]

"Yes," Wallace said, taking Hemmerde's word for it.

"Did it ever occur to you to ask the policeman there on point duty where it was?"

"No."

"If you had, you would have learned at once it was not there?"

"The tram conductor gave me sufficient evidence to show I had only to take the car on the right route and I would be where I wanted to be."

"Would you describe yourself as a very talkative and communicative man—rather the contrary, are you not?"

"I do not know how I could describe myself," Wallace said. "I leave others to do that."

---

[1] A small point, but the actual distance between the Penny Lane terminus and the tram-stop at Menlove Gardens *West* was 650 yards.

Hemmerde reminded him of his conversations with Thomas Phillips, Arthur Thompson, Sydney Green, P.C. Sargent, and Lily Pinches; then: "As a matter of fact, does it not strike you, looking back upon it now, that all these enquiries were absolutely unnecessary? One simple enquiry of the policeman on point duty would have done it."

"No, it does not strike me at all as being out of the way," Wallace replied. (And neither should it have done. Whether he was innocent or guilty, it seems unlikely that he even *noticed* the policeman on point duty as he changed trams; even if he did, why should he have bothered to consult him? Thomas Phillips had pointed out the tram "in the loop heading for Calderstones" and told him that "if he hurried he would get that car"; neither Phillips nor the ticket inspector, Angus, had suggested that he might have difficulty in finding Menlove Gardens East—indeed, Angus had actually given him directions on how to get there.)

Doubling back, Hemmerde said, "Does not the whole thing strike you as very remarkable, that a man who does not know you should ring you up for business in another district, and expect you to go there; and yet, without knowing you had gone there or not, come and wait outside your house for the chance of murdering your wife?"

"Yes," Wallace replied, without hesitation.

"The wrong address is essential to the creation of evidence for the alibi. Do you follow that?"

"No, I do not follow you."

"If you had been told Menlove Gardens West, the first enquiry would have landed you there?"

"Yes."

"If you are told of an address which does not exist, you can ask seven or eight people, every one of whom would be a witness where you were?"

"Yes."

"So to a man who was planning to do this, a wrong address would be essential to his alibi?"

And once again, Wallace agreed.

By now it was half-past four: time, Mr Justice Wright decided, for a quick cup of tea. The case was adjourned for a quarter of an hour.

After the adjournment Hemmerde began where he had left off, still trying to show that Wallace's trip to Menlove Gardens was part of a carefully contrived alibi. He reminded Wallace that, in his statement to P.C. Williams, he had said, "I went to Menlove Gardens, to find the address which had been given me was wrong. Becoming suspicious, I returned home. . . ."

"Why did you become suspicious?"

"Well, seeing I could not definitely find either the man or the place, I had an idea that something was not quite right; and seeing that there had been in our street only fairly recently a burglary, and one about possibly eighteen months or two years ago, and a number of other tragedies in the street, I was rather inclined to think that something of the sort might have been attempted at my own house. I did not become unduly uneasy."

But this did not satisfy Hemmerde. Seventy-two questions later he was still suggesting that Wallace had no reason for feeling uneasy, or the least bit suspicious.

". . . You were not uneasy?"

"I was both uneasy and not uneasy, if you can follow me," Wallace said in a tired voice. "It was a very difficult position, and I did not quite know exactly what I did think."

"I am putting to you that you had no reason to be suspicious when you returned home, because you *knew*."

"Knew what?"

"What exactly had happened in the house."

"How could I know?"

Hemmerde's answer: a meaningful sniff.

The next half-hour was devoted to the locks. Trying once again to confuse Wallace, Hemmerde accelerated the pace of the cross-examination and mixed questions about the front door with questions about the back; but Wallace remained perfectly calm, and it was Hemmerde himself who occasionally became confused.

Finally:

"You see, I am putting to you that neither of these doors was either bolted or locked, and that this suggestion that they were bolted was purely play-acting," he screeched.

"You may think so, of course, but you are wrong," Wallace said politely.

A short whispered consultation between Hemmerde, Walsh, and Bishop; then the questioning continued—questions about the conversation with the Johnstons outside the house, about the missing iron bar, about the mackintosh.

"When was it that you first noted the mackintosh?"

"Either the second or my third visit to the room. I think the second."

"Just listen to what you said. 'On the evening of the 20th, when I discovered my wife lying on the floor, I noticed my mackintosh lying on the floor at the back of her.' "

Wallace tried to think back, but: "I cannot remember whether it was my first or second visit."

"That was your recollection on that night?"

"That looks more likely to be correct than my statement now," Wallace agreed.

"Then, when Mrs Johnston was there later with you, you say to her, as she says, bending down and looking at it, 'Whatever was she doing with my mackintosh?' as though you were making a discovery." Hemmerde pointed an accusing finger at Wallace; his voice rose into the higher registers. "You had already discovered it!"

But Wallace remained calm. "I do not think my statement implied that I was making a discovery for the first time. It was a natural query to me. It was there, and I wondered what the dickens she was doing with it."

"You remember her husband had never seen it, and she did not till you pointed it out, and the impression you made upon her was that you had just discovered it?"

"I do not know what impression I made upon her."

Now, for the first time during the cross-examination, Mr Justice Wright intervened: "All she said was that she noticed it first when he fingered it."

"Yes, my Lord," Hemmerde said. "I was not sure, therefore I did not put it. I think she said she happened to look, and he fingered it."

Turning back to Wallace, Hemmerde went on: "You see what I am putting to you. If you were describing things that really happened, you would be accurate, like when you said your wife went down the entry and things of that sort." (Things of *what* sort?) "Here you may be wrong about what you said that night about having noticed it when you first came in; but what I am putting to you is, you said it that night, apparently giving her the impression as though you had made a discovery—'Whatever was she doing with my mackintosh?' "

And again the judge broke in. He sounded a trifle tetchy now. "No, I do not remember that. She was not asked about what her impression was: she simply described what she saw."

"Very well, my Lord."

"I heard no evidence of any impression."

"My Lord, I could not ask her what her impression was."

"No, I know."

Hemmerde went on: "You know that in this house, you have heard it stated, there was no evidence whatever of breaking in?"

"That is so," Wallace said.

"I am putting to you that the whole theory of a thief is absolutely countered by everything you find in the house. . . . Your idea is that he came for the weekly debit?"

"Yes."

"Do you imagine he was looking in the bed upstairs for that?"

And now Roland Oliver was on his feet, objecting: "Is that a proper question to put to a man on a criminal trial—'Do you imagine he was looking in the bed?' "

"It does not matter," Mr Justice Wright murmured somnolently.

A few minutes later, doing some public-relations work for the police, Hemmerde asked Wallace how many meals he had been given at police headquarters during the first two days of the investigation.

But Mr Justice Wright interrupted again. "I do not see that all this matters," he sighed. "How many meals he had, or if he had any, is not of the slightest importance."

Hemmerde took the hint. "No, my Lord. There are one or two other things I want to ask, but not many more."

The one or two other things turned out to be repeats of questions he had already asked. Had Wallace not thought the telephone message at all unusual? . . . A little, perhaps. Had he known that there was such a place as Menlove Gardens? . . . No, he had not.

Then:

"You could not open that door?"

"Which door?"

"That front door."

"No, I could not get it open."

"But you saw the superintendent open it the very first time?"

"Yes, that is true."

"Close the door and go out into the street, and open it without any difficulty?"

"But I could not open it because the bolt was on it."

"But the key?"

"I said the key slipped back."

"You never told him that."

"I do not know whether I told him that," Wallace replied evenly, "but I tell you that."

And on that note the cross-examination ended. Hemmerde stood for a moment, his fingers flicking over the pages of his brief; then, with a slight shrug, a shake of his head, he sank back into his seat.

Oliver did not spend long re-examining.

"Reams of statements have been taken from you," he commented. "Can you profess to recollect word by word all the things you have said?"

"I cannot."

"Can you recollect anything you have purposely told the officers that was not true?"

"I cannot."

Then surely one of the oddest questions—if not *the* oddest—that has ever been put to an accused person by his own counsel at a murder trial:

"When you were playing the violin with your wife," Oliver said, completely dead-pan, "were you accustomed to do it when you were naked in a mackintosh; was that your habit?"

For a moment Wallace looked stunned, unable to believe his ears. "What was that?"

"To play naked in a mackintosh," Oliver said casually.

Wallace shook his head—more to clear it than as an accompaniment to his answer. "I have never played naked in my life," he said in a shocked tone.

After almost exactly three hours in the witness-box—after answering 735 questions, 417 of them from the prosecution—Wallace was escorted back to the dock.

The *Echo* reporter thought he looked "rather tired". Hardly surprising, really.

Getting on towards six. Mr Justice Wright was in a great hurry now. Determined that all the defence evidence should be heard before the proceedings were adjourned for the day, so as to leave tomorrow free for the closing speeches, summing-up, verdict, he kept the questioning going at a rattling pace—scowling and tapping the end of his pen on his blotter when he thought that counsel were taking too long to get to the point; often interrupting to put direct questions to witnesses; skirting the small facts that led up to the important ones, taking short cuts to the heart of the evidence.

Professor James Henry Dible followed Wallace into the witness-box. In direct evidence, replying to almost as many questions from the judge as from defence counsel, he said that, on the basis of MacFall's observations, it was impossible to estimate the time of death with any degree of accuracy; the most he could say was that "it might be after seven, or it might be before six", although the small amount of blood serum noted by MacFall at 9.50 indicated that the later time was more likely. In his view the assailant "could hardly have escaped being spattered and covered with blood all over". Questioned about the two bloodstains on the mackintosh which MacFall thought were direct projections, he was unable to say whether they looked "more like squirts than drips".

Cross-examining, Hemmerde asked: "I suppose with the usage that that mackintosh has had, it is very difficult to say there might not be very many direct projections?"

"Certainly."

"How would they disappear?" Mr Justice Wright asked.

"They might be rubbed off, my Lord."

Encouraged, Hemmerde pointed at the mackintosh. "If it was made into a roll as you have seen it?"

But he had gone too far. "It would be preserved from any contact, surely?" Mr Justice Wright suggested.

"That is so, my Lord," Dible said.

Dr Robert Coope took the stand.

The examination-in-chief was getting along quite nicely; but not, in Mr Justice Wright's opinion, quickly enough. After listening to ten questions and answers concerning the experiments Coope had made with human blood, he completely took over from Oliver.

Asked if the blood on the lavatory-pan was fresh when it fell, Coope replied, "I should say, my Lord, it was at least an hour coagulated, or, I think, considerably longer."

"Suppose it fell, as fresh blood, from fifteen inches?"

"No, my Lord, I will not go under an hour. That is the minimum."

Hemmerde asked, "You heard what Mr Roberts said this morning about his experiments?"

"I did," Coope said.

"They must have been very surprising to you?"

"They were, indeed."

"But you have kept notes of your experiments?" Mr Justice Wright asked. (Pointedly? Reminding the jury that Roberts had not?)

"Oh yes, my Lord."

Following the medical evidence, evidence concerning the time factor.

Allison Wildman first of all. He said that when he delivered a newspaper at 27 Wolverton Street on the night of the murder he saw a boy wearing a Collegiate cap standing at the doorway of No. 29. He was sure that the time was about twenty-three minutes to seven, because "I passed Holy Trinity Church clock at twenty-five to seven, and it takes me two minutes to walk to Wolverton Street".

Hemmerde asked the boy if he always looked at the clock when he passed.

"Yes."

"Then there was no reason why you should remember the time more this night than any other," Hemmerde said triumphantly. (Another example, this, of the prosecution doing an about-turn. During Alan Close's re-examination Hemmerde had asked, "Can you say why you noticed the time, twenty-five past six?" and had accepted the milk boy's answer, "I generally glance at the clock when I pass", as a point in his favour.)

Hemmerde tried hard, but unsuccessfully, to persuade the other three juvenile defence witnesses[1] that they were mistaken about what Close had said, the night after the murder.

"Do you not think that what he is very likely to have said is not 'at 6.45' but 'between 6.30 and 6.45'?"

Elsie Wright: "No; he said, 'At a quarter to seven'."

Douglas Metcalf: "No, he never said that. He said, point-blank, a quarter to seven."

Kenneth Caird: "No; he said, 'A quarter to seven.' I went home and told my mother about it."

Caird was followed into the witness-box by *David Jones*, who turned out to be the least effective of the defence witnesses.

"Can you tell the jury what time you delivered the newspaper at the Wallaces on January 20th?" Oliver asked him.

"About twenty-five minutes to seven."

"What did you do?" Mr Justice Wright asked. "Did you knock at the door?"

"Stuck the paper through the letter-box."

[1] Hector Munro decided that Harold Jones, the other boy who took part in the conversation with Alan Close, was too nervous to make a good witness, so he was not called.

"You did not see Mrs Wallace?"

"I see nobody."

"When did you give a statement to Mr Munro here?" Hemmerde asked in cross-examination.

"The Tuesday after the what-you-may-call-it."

"You told him you had delivered a paper there at 6.35?"

"Yes, at 6.35, twenty-five minutes to, the latest."

"Did you tell the police you delivered it about 6.30?"

"6.30 to 6.35."

Hemmerde's voice rose. "No—'about 6.30'. Just look at your statement. This is your signature, is it not?"

"Yes."

"What you said was 6.30. When you delivered at 6.30, did you see anyone?"

"No, sir, only myself."

As David Jones left the court, far too late to do his evening paper round, Oliver rose to say that he wished to call a number of witnesses to rebut the evidence of P.C. Rothwell.

Mr Justice Wright said that he was sure that this would not be necessary. "The prosecution will not say that a man looks rather haggard."

Deciding, however, to take no chances, Oliver called three of Wallace's insurance clients. None of them was cross-examined.

Louisa Harrison said that Wallace called at her house at about half-past three on the Tuesday afternoon; and in answer to Oliver's question: "Did he appear to have been crying?" she said, "He was joking with me."

Amy Lawrence remembered that she and her husband "asked him to have a cup of tea, and he had one".

"What was he like?"

"He was the same as usual."

Margaret Martin, at whose house Wallace had made his last call before returning home, said that she had found him "just the same as he has ever been since he collected—calm, and the same in appearance".

Mrs Martin was the final defence witness. As she stepped from the box, "That is the case, my Lord," Oliver said, and remained standing, waiting for the judge's direction.

A moment of silence. Mr Justice Wright finished off what he was writing, stabbed a full-stop into the page, looked up at the clock. It was well after seven.

"I think the speeches had better be made tomorrow morning," he said.

And so ended the third day.

Mr Justice Wright, happy in the knowledge that the trial was running to schedule and looking forward to a long weekend before going on to Manchester, returned to his lodgings at Newsham House to collate the notes for his summing-up; Roland Oliver walked across to the North Western Hotel and Edward Hemmerde drove to his flat, both of them to work into the early hours on their closing speeches; the jury were driven to their hotel and Wallace to the prison; the spectators, chattering of what they had seen, heard, inferred, drifted out of the court to buy late editions of the evening papers as souvenirs: some of them wandered over to The Legs of Man, a pub facing St George's Plateau, where a street bookmaker was laying odds on the result of the trial, taking bets as to whether or not the black cap was going to be used the next day.

The Trial—IV

SATURDAY, April 25th

> *Alice looked at the jury-box, and saw that,
> in her haste, she had put the Lizard in
> head downwards, and the poor little thing
> was waving its tail about in a melancholy
> way, being quite unable to move. She soon
> got it out again, and put it right; "not
> that it signifies much," she said to herself;
> "I should think it would be* quite *as much
> use in the trial one way up as the other."*

Saturday. Cup Final Day. But not much for the soccer-loving populace of Liverpool to get excited about, for this year the final was an all-Midlands affair—Birmingham City *v.* West Bromwich Albion. On Merseyside there was far more interest in the result of a legal match—Rex *v.* Wallace.

Soon after midnight a queue began to form outside St George's Hall. The first arrivals were a couple of labourers who came straight from work in the Mersey Tunnel; by 4.30 more than forty people were waiting. They drank tea from Thermos flasks and ate sandwiches and currant buns; they talked together; some of them joined chorus in song—*When It's Springtime in the Rockies*, they warbled . . . *I'm Confessin' that I Love You* and *There's Danger in your Eyes, Cherie*.

It is not recorded, but perhaps there were a few recitations to while away the time until the doors opened—recitations of some of the pieces of doggerel inspired by the Wallace case. Things like:

> Willie had a mistress;
> Willie had a wife.
> He only wanted one of them,
> So Willie took a life.

And a quatrain based on the Scarlet Pimpernel rhyme:

> They seek him here, they seek him there;
> Is he alive, do you know?
> Either in Hell . . . or the Pruden-shell,
> That damned elusive Qualtrough.

At 8 A.M. the queue stretched along the northern wall of St George's Hall, its tail-end curling into the gardens behind. "Well over 200 people", according to the *Empire News* reporter. "The three women who have attended each morning at seven o'clock must have learned by experience, for they just managed to get into the public gallery, having arrived at 6. When the doors were closed, not half the queue had entered."

The lucky ones were doubly lucky; they narrowly escaped getting drenched. At about half-past nine the sky over Liverpool darkened, and the rain which was to continue, on and off, for the rest of the day started to come down.

Taking up the story in court, the *Echo* reporter wrote: "All Anfield, it seemed, was present in the public gallery, and only a few, oblivious to the gravity that beset the minds of their neighbours, could take refreshment in the form of apples and oranges or a sandwich. . . . It seemed like a stage play in a real-life setting, in which, during this, the climax that precedes the denouement, the principal characters were all keyed up to the highest possible pitch of anxiety and excitement."

Promptly at ten o'clock, with the judge on the bench, Wallace in the dock, the jury in the box, but all far from right with the world, Roland Oliver began the closing speech for the defence.

There were, he asserted, two essential questions in determining guilt. The first was: *Who sent the telephone message?* And the second: *At what time was Julia Wallace killed?*

Since there was no evidence to connect Wallace or anyone else with the telephone-call, the first question must remain unanswered. As for the second, "Does not the medical evidence stand in this way: rigor mortis cannot place the death? There is an element of error of at least an hour either way; and that is how I ask you to treat it."

Turning to the evidence of Alan Close, Oliver said that it was clear that the boy had told the other children that he had seen Julia alive at a quarter to seven. "Why should that be wrong? That is the boy's unaided recollection. . . . Do you doubt that at the moment the police decided to charge Mr Wallace, a quarter to seven became quite impossible for them, because Mr Wallace has established, by evidence that cannot be controverted, that he left the house at about a quarter to seven? . . . The police elected to leave the question of the time that Mrs Wallace was last seen alive. Why?"

Oliver attacked every aspect of the prosecution case. He told the jury that not only should they "absolutely reject" the mackintosh theory and "disbelieve" William Roberts's experiments, but that they should "ignore" the police evidence concerning Wallace's demeanour: "Is there no such thing as calmness of innocence?"

He went on to cite some examples of Wallace's frankness in the witness-box. Then, gathering momentum and volume as he neared the end of his speech, he started throwing out questions for Hemmerde to answer:

"How is he going to explain this murder? Is he going to adopt Professor MacFall's suggestion that it was the sudden frenzy of a man who had planned it for twenty-four hours? . . . If Wallace was dressed when this was done, where are his clothes? If Wallace was naked, how were they together in that room? Where did he have a bath?

"What is he going to tell you about burning the mackintosh? . . . Have you a shadow of doubt, on the evidence before you, that the mackintosh was burned by accident?

"I wonder what he is going to tell you about missing the body? Do you remember his opening: 'Going into a dark room, he somehow missed the body and the blood'? It is their case now that it was a light room. . . . A criticism is made because my client struck a match. That is the kind of stuff that has been put to you, to try and convict this man."

After going hammer and tongs at the police and the prosecution for close on an hour, Oliver suddenly and completely changed his tone for the last couple of minutes of the speech. It was as if he turned off the hot-water tap, paused a second, then turned on the cold: as sudden as that.

"Finally, if I may say so, it is not enough that you should think it possible that he did this—not merely enough, but it is not nearly enough. . . . The story for the defence is not very likely, but at least it is consistent with all the facts; the story for the prosecution sounds impossible."

As Oliver sat down, Hector Munro scanned the faces of the jury, searching for some indication of the effect the speech had made upon them. But what they were thinking—if they were thinking at all, and not simply rearranging their prejudices—was impossible to divine.

Hemmerde's turn next. He had had the first word; now he had the last.

Whereas Oliver had virtually disregarded the evidence concerning the telephone-call, Hemmerde discussed it at length, pointing out to the jury the "singular coincidence" that Qualtrough was in the box "at the identical time at which Mr Wallace might have been there, and, by another singular coincidence, was trying to ring up Mr Wallace.

"That is how we start," Hemmerde said. And that was how he went on, pointing out the "singular coincidences", stressing the "inherent improbabilities".

He spent a quarter of an hour reminding the jury of Wallace's "persistent enquiries" on his way to, and in, Menlove Gardens. And concluded: "I am content to point out to you . . . the inherent improbabilities of the story that he would first of all have ever gone there; secondly, that the man Qualtrough would have dreamed he would have gone there; thirdly, that Qualtrough would ever have known that he had gone there; and you may be able to think of a number of other improbabilities."

The business about the locks; the disputed statement to P.C. Williams; the disproportionate reward for murder if robbery was the motive: "Here a murderer picks on one who has a weekly collection round about £30, and a monthly collection a fortnight earlier and a fortnight later amounting to anything between £80 and £100!

"I am not going to stress the raincoat matter. You may take the view now that it caught fire accidentally, and not that there was a deliberate attempt to burn it. Do not be led away from the main issue by what after all is a small matter."

At last, when the defence were beginning to think that he had forgotten about it altogether, Hemmerde referred to what he had earlier agreed with Oliver was one of the two essential factors in determining Wallace's guilt:

"As regards the time of death . . . I submit that that is easily established."

And that was all he said about it, apart from telling the jury that "the man who had made his plans, whether the boy was seen at 6.30 or 6.35 talking to this woman, had between that time and 6.49, practically twenty minutes [sic], and there is no reason to suppose that a man who had done a thing like that would go very slowly. If he did it, he was trying to create an alibi, and he would go as fast as he could. I say there is ample time for it."

Copying defence counsel's example, Hemmerde finished off with a collection of questions; but whereas Oliver's questions had been put to the prosecution (and most of them remained un-answered), Hemmerde's were directed at the jury.

". . . Was his attitude that night, and his repeated inquiries about Menlove Gardens East—were they natural? Was it natural for him to say that when he could not find it he was suspicious? Was it natural, or was it true, that he came back and could not get into the house—or was he pretending he could not get into the house? Do the different stories about the locks, front and back, lead you to that conclusion? Do you believe that P.C. Williams can be trusted in the accuracy of his memory? . . .

"I am not entitled, I hope, to over-emphasize inconsistencies or coincidences in this case, but I am bound to suggest to you . . . that the evidence connecting this man with that message is strong evidence; that the evidence that the woman was alive round about 6.30 is strong evidence; the evidence of what that man did when he came back to the house is strong evidence that he was not acting then as an innocent man."

Hemmerde's speech lasted seventy minutes, and during all that time Wallace, arms folded and head slightly to one side, scarcely moved. But as Mr Justice Wright commenced the summing-up he leaned forward, his arms folded on the dock-rail, his chin resting on them.

According to the *Echo* reporter, "Mr Justice Wright never once raised his voice beyond a pitch adequate for the jury's hearing, and was calm with the self-possession of experience.

"As he proceeded, Wallace repeatedly changed his position, and at one time he held one of the iron supports of the dock-rail in a firm grip, betraying that he was more than an ordinary spectator of the drama. It was evident that the strain was telling on him."

Dealing, point by point, with every scrap of evidence that had been presented, Mr Justice Wright displayed a remarkable grasp of the facts and principles involved in the case. It seems clear that he was aware of the local feeling against Wallace, and was worried that it might affect the verdict; at the beginning of the summing-up he warned the jury that they must approach the case "without any preconceived notions at all", and time and again he explained to them the meaning and value of circumstantial evidence.

"The real test of the value of circumstantial evidence is: Does it exclude every reasonable possibility? I can even put it higher: Does it exclude other theories or possibilities? If you cannot put the evidence against the accused man beyond a probability and nothing more, if that is a probability which is not inconsistent with there being other reasonable possibilities, then it is impossible for a jury to say, 'We are satisfied beyond reasonable doubt that the charge is made out against the accused man.' A man cannot be convicted of any crime, least of all murder, merely on probabilities, unless they are so strong as to amount to a reasonable certainty. If you have other possibilities, a jury would not, and I believe ought not, to come to the conclusion that the charge is established."

The summing-up was entirely favourable to Wallace. Without actually saying as much, although several times he came pretty close to it, Mr Justice Wright indicated that, in his opinion, the prosecution had failed to prove their case.

"The evidence," he said at one point, "is quite consistent with some unknown criminal, for some unknown motive, having got into the house and executed the murder and gone away."

His final words to the jury were as follows:

"However you regard the matter, the whole crime was so skilfully devised and so skilfully executed, and there is such an absence of any trace to incriminate anyone, as to make it very difficult to say, although it is a matter entirely for you, that it can be brought home to anybody in particular.

"If there was an unknown murderer, he has covered up his traces. Can you say it is absolutely impossible that there was no such person? But putting that aside as not being the real question, can you say, taking all the evidence as a whole, bearing in mind the strength of the case put forward by the police and the prosecution, that you are satisfied beyond reasonable doubt that it was the hand of the prisoner, and no other hand, that murdered this woman? If you are not so satisfied, if it is not proved—whatever your feelings may be, whatever your surmises or suspicions or prejudices may be—if it is not established as a matter of evidence and legal proof, then it is your duty to find the prisoner not guilty.

"Of course, if you are satisfied, equally it is your duty to find him guilty. But it is your duty to decide on the evidence which has been given before you during these three days, and, whatever your verdict is, that is the acid test which you must apply.

"Will you consider your verdict and say whether you find the prisoner guilty or not guilty?"

The time was twenty minutes past one; Mr Justice Wright had spoken for an hour.

"As the low voice ceased there was an audible sigh in the court. When the jury left the box the two women members were in tears. Counsel left the places into which they had sunk, exhausted, after their long addresses; the prisoner's white head disappeared down the narrow staircase leading to the cells, and immediately the large body of spectators broke into a buzz of conversation. They were silenced on two occasions by court ushers, but as the fateful moments crept by, people could not refrain from talking and gradually the hum broke into a crescendo.[1]

"At last, at 2.20, came a stir in court, and the jury, headed by the two women, filed slowly into their places in the box. While the Clerk of Assize was calling the roll of jurors, Wallace quietly re-entered the dock. Only one member of the jury stole a furtive glance at the prisoner, who remained stoical and calm, standing with a warder on each side and another warder behind him. Dr Higson, medical officer at Walton Prison, was also in attendance.

"Mr Justice Wright took his seat upon the bench, and the Clerk of Assize, having asked who would speak as the jury's foreman, was answered by a man who stood up in the middle of the front row."

The Clerk of Assize:

"Gentlemen of the Jury, are you agreed upon your verdict?"

The Foreman of the Jury:

"We are."

"Do you find the prisoner guilty or not guilty of murder?"

"*Guilty.*"

"There was a split second of complete silence after the verdict was announced, then someone at the back of the court whistled in surprise. The tense atmosphere was broken by a gasp that approximated almost to a roar from the spectators who crowded the court."

The door of the Press box clanged, as a copy boy for the

---

[1] *Author's note*: I have taken the liberty of compiling this, and subsequent paragraphs, from reports which appeared in the *Liverpool Echo* and the *Liverpool Evening Express*.

Liverpool Echo raced out of the court and down a long corridor to a window overlooking William Brown Street. As he ran he pulled from his pocket a glass marble and two slips of paper, on one of which was written GUILTY, on the other NOT GUILTY. Arriving at the window—which, by arrangement with a member of the St George's Hall staff, was open—he wrapped the GUILTY slip round the marble and threw it down to the street, where a car was waiting to rush the verdict to the newspaper offices for the stop-press column of the next edition.

In another corridor, on the opposite side of the court, a group of defence and prosecution witnesses clustered against the double doors leading to the well of the court. Professor MacFall pressed his ear to the gap between the doors. As he heard the verdict he turned, a jubilant smile creasing his face, his breath wheezing with excitement; he clasped his hands together and lifted them above his head in a boxer's gesture of triumph. "Hooray," he mouthed.

In the courtroom the person least affected by the verdict, it seemed, was Wallace himself. "But for a very slight swaying, he seemed to be perfectly quiet. He received the verdict without a tremor. This calm was even more remarkable in view of the fact that he thought he would be acquitted, and he had his hat and coat handy in the dock, apparently prepared to walk out a free man."

The Clerk of Assize: "You say he is guilty, and that is the verdict of you all?"

The Foreman of the Jury: "It is."

The Clerk turned to face Wallace.

"Prisoner at the Bar, you have been arraigned upon a charge of murder, and have placed yourself upon your country. This country has now found you guilty. Have you anything to say why judgement of death should not be pronounced upon you, and why you should not die according to the law?"

Wallace hesitated a moment—then: "I am not guilty," he said firmly. "I cannot say anything else."

Slowly, with infinite care, the Judge's Marshal unfolded a square of black silk and placed it, one corner forming a widow's peak, on Mr Justice Wright's head.

The two women members of the jury were crying again.

His voice hardly audible, Mr Justice Wright passed sentence; and to those near enough to catch all his words it was noticeable that he omitted to say that he was in agreement with the verdict.

"William Herbert Wallace, the jury, after a very careful hearing, have found you guilty of the murder of your wife. For the crime of murder by the law of this country there is only one sentence, and that sentence I now pass upon you. It is that you be taken from hence to a place of lawful execution, and you be there hanged by the neck until you be dead and that your body be afterwards buried within the precincts of the prison in which you shall last have been confined. And may the Lord have mercy on your soul."

Standing at the judge's side, Canon Dwelly, the Sheriff's Chaplain, quietly added: "Amen."

A warder tapped Wallace on the arm, "and he turned slowly and walked down the dock stairs. To all outward appearances he was as cool as he had always been since he came before the judge on Wednesday morning, but it was seen that as he reached the lower steps before going to the cells, Dr Higson placed a hand on his arm as if helping him gently along.

"As soon as Wallace disappeared, there was a rush for the exits, but the police officers had anticipated it and controlled the passage of the people on to the plateau. Large crowds of people who were unable to gain admission when the trial resumed this morning had waited outside in the hope of gleaning some account of the progress of the proceedings. With the first rush of people through the great doors, they clamoured forward to inquire for the jury's verdict."

The court was soon almost empty. A few uniformed policemen standing in the doorways; some minor court officials; in the public gallery, just one man leaning on the brass rail, munching a sandwich. Sydney Scholefield Allen and Hector Munro sat next to each other. Neither of them spoke. Neither of them could think of anything to say. In front of them, standing as he had stood since the announcement of the verdict, motionless as a statue, his shoulders drooping, Roland Oliver stared straight ahead at the judge's chair.

Then, without a word to his junior, or to the solicitor, without seeming even to be aware of their presence, Oliver walked out of the court. He and his clerk caught the first train back to London. (The following Monday he wrote to Munro, apologizing "for rushing away after the trial. I was so dazed and shocked . . . my nerves were completely overwrought.")

About three-quarters of an hour after the verdict, as Mr Justice Wright left St George's Hall and the Assize trumpeters played the National Anthem and the crowds in Lime Street bared their heads, Wallace was hustled out of a side entrance and into a Black Maria, which took him back to Walton Gaol.

Already the newspaper boys were shouting: "Wallace verdict.
. . . Wallace to hang. . . ."

At the prison he was escorted into a small room. A sheet of white
canvas was stretched out on the floor, and he was ordered to stand
on it and strip off his clothes. He did as he was told.

Standing naked in the centre of the room, he started to cry.
He tried to control himself, but it was no use. With the prison
governor looking on, and Dr Higson, and the four warders who
had accompanied him from St George's Hall, he changed into the
special grey uniform of a prisoner awaiting execution.

He was still crying, still trying to control his tears, as he was
led out of the room and down a short passage to the condemned
cell.

The Appeal

> *The Queen had only one way of settling all difficulties, great or small. "Off with his head!" she said without even looking round.*
> *"I'll fetch the executioner myself," said the King eagerly, and he hurried off.*

[1]

On Sunday, April 26th, the death occurred of Sir Edward Clarke, one of the greatest jury advocates of all time, and it was suggested by a Liverpool barrister that "he probably died of a broken heart, after hearing of the jury's verdict at the Wallace trial".

Roland Oliver's belief, expressed to Scholefield Allen and Munro on the second night of the trial, that the jury were not listening to the evidence, had been proved true. By finding Wallace guilty they had brought in a verdict against themselves. It was clear now that most of the members of that jury, if not all of them, had decided the case before they ever entered the box.

Soon after the committal proceedings, knowing that local opinion was strongly against Wallace, Hector Munro had considered applying for a writ of *certiorari* to have the case tried in another part of the country; but, after being assured by the Prosecuting Solicitor's Office that no-one from Liverpool would be chosen to serve on the jury, he had not done so. This was a mistake.

The jury was mainly composed of people from Southport, Warrington, Widnes, and St Helens—all four towns within fifteen miles of Liverpool, well within earshot of the rumours connecting Wallace with the murder; all four towns within the circulation areas of the Liverpool evening papers, which published verbatim reports of the one-sided evidence given at the magistrates' court.

This was bad enough—but to make it worse, at least two of the jurors were resident in Liverpool at the time, although their addresses on the jury list showed them to be living elsewhere.

The verdict was odd, to say the least of it . . . and so was the behaviour during the trial of some of these good men (and women) and true. Leaving out any reference to the giggling that went on in the box, here are just a few examples of the peculiarities of conduct which were displayed:

During the opening speech for the defence, while Oliver was discussing the bloodstains and burns on the mackintosh, one of the male jurors leaned from the box and shouted an interruption. Apparently he was angry about something—but his anger induced incoherence, and no-one in court was able to make out what it was that he said: one of his words, though, was recognized as "dirty", which may have referred to the condition of the mackintosh; another was an expletive, which definitely did not.

While Dr Robert Coope was giving evidence a member of the jury turned to his neighbour and said in a loud voice, "You don't want to believe anything these medical witnesses say." So stentorian were the words that Dr Coope felt sure they were intended for his ears; what surprised him was that the judge did not hear the remark, or, if he did, made no comment upon it.

One of the jurymen heard only the first few questions and the closing ones in Wallace's cross-examination: the rest of the time he was fast asleep.

Another juryman—or maybe it was the same one—fell asleep towards the end of Hemmerde's closing speech and remained in that state for about an hour, missing most of the judge's summing-up.

It would seem that there were some rather strange goings-on in the jury room while the verdict was being (for want of a better word) considered. A week or so after the trial one of the members of the jury called at the office of Albert E. Tickle, a St Helens solicitor. He wanted, he said, to make a clean breast of things; his conscience was troubling him.

According to the story he told Mr Tickle, as soon as the jury retired, one of them suggested that a vote be taken at once, so that they could return to court without further ado, deliver the verdict, have lunch at the expense of Liverpool Corporation, and then toddle off home. This sounded like a splendid idea to most of the others, but there were four—of whom the conscience-stricken ex-juror was one—who were not in that much of a hurry to get away:

they wanted to chat first, vote later. So, instead of discussing the evidence, the jury spent most of the time they were out of court arguing about whether to bring in a speedy verdict of Guilty or to talk about a few aspects of the case *before* bringing in this verdict. Eventually, outnumbered two-to-one, the slow-coaches gave in—but only after one of the ringleaders of the majority side had threatened them with dire consequences if they did not fall into line. (The ex-juror refused to say what the threat was, and Mr Tickle got the impression that he was afraid to go into details.)

Mr Tickle asked the man if he was prepared to sign an affidavit. He said that he was. The solicitor arranged for him to return to the office later that day, and then telephoned Hector Munro, who said that he would like to be present when the affidavit was taken.

But the ex-juror developed a sudden attack of cold feet. Within an hour he was back in the solicitor's office. He was sorry and all that, but he had decided against putting anything in writing. Mr Tickle asked him about the other three jurors, who, according to what he had said earlier, had been prevented from following accepted jury-room procedure . . . but "my client informed me" [Tickle wrote to Munro, confirming a second telephone conversation] "that . . . they were not in his class of life and he did not know their names and addresses, but he thought they came from Runcorn and Widnes".

Since the trial many criminologists have speculated as to the reasoning behind the jury's verdict in the Wallace case (indeed, there are some who cite the case in support of the idea that, at least when major issues are involved, jury foremen should not only be asked to state the verdict, but also the reasons for arriving at it). It is impossible, of course, to say why all twelve members of the jury thought Wallace guilty of his wife's murder, but perhaps the reasons given by one of them help a little, a twelfth-part, towards understanding. Anyway, here they are, as originally set down:

"The Facts were Wallace asked a Policeman the time also he asked were Menlove Gardens East was and there is no Menlove Gardens East but there is West. also when the Boy gave Evidence in the Witness Box He Said Mrs Wallace took the milk off him. We did not think so we thought he Had Put a Part of her Clothing on him as the Boy said he did not see her Face only her arm also he asked Mr Jonson a next neibour to come into the House with him.[1] We all thought he Had done this murder of his wife. as you know we only Had Circumstancual Evidence."[2]

It is hard to say what happened: either the verdict caused a shift of local opinion in Wallace's favour, or else it caused people who had thought all along that the prosecution case was weak to up and speak their minds. Perhaps it was something of both.

On Sunday, the day after the trial, dozens of Merseysiders sat down and wrote letters to the editors of the local papers. And on Monday and Tuesday, too—"a flood of them", according to the editor of the *Liverpool Echo*, who, on Wednesday, announced that he did not want to hear another word from any of his readers on the subject of the Wallace case. A fairly representative sample of the type and tenor of the letters received by the papers was one written by somebody who signed himself "Park Gates":

"In my reading of the Wallace trial, I could not for the life of me discern in the evidence any what I might term major points against the accused man. . . . I feel that in such a serious matter, especially when there is no apparent motive, circumstantial evidence should be much more convincing than it was in the Wallace case. I am not alone in this opinion and I hope that steps will be taken at once to ensure both an appeal and, if necessary, a petition to the Home Secretary."

By the time this letter appeared, on the Monday, arrangements for the appeal were already being made. Headed by Wallace's brother Joseph and a Cheshire novelist named Norman Terry, a committee was formed to help raise funds. In an interview with a *Daily Mail* reporter, Norman Terry said, "We want about five hundred pounds to pay the costs of the appeal, and I think we will get it without much difficulty." (As it turned out, this was far too optimistic a view: the total raised was £171 8s. 1d.)

Hector Munro wrote to the executive council of the P.S.U., asking if Wallace could expect any further assistance from the union, and, on May 1st, received the reply:

"We are all staggered by the verdict, and whilst appeal in all such cases seems such a hopeless procedure, we are bound to concur in exploring every possibility of saving Mr Wallace from such a cruel fate. . . ."

In his letter to the executive council Munro wrote in a fairly hopeful tone of the chances of the appeal succeeding; but in a

---

[1] Neither of these statements is true.

[2] From a letter in the author's possession.

confidential letter written on the same day to E. T. Palmer, M.P., one of the secretaries of the union, he was far less sanguine:

"I can hardly tell you how grieved we all are by the shocking verdict which the jury returned. In my opinion, they had no material whatever upon which they could convict, and the judge's summing-up was extremely favourable to the defence, and he practically told the jury that there was no evidence upon which they could act. The result must be regarded as directly caused by the unreasonable prejudice which has existed in the minds of certain people over this case, and exposes in glaring light the grave defects of the jury system. . . .

"We are at once obtaining instructions to appeal, but for your private information I may say that the Appeal Judges are likely to take the view that the jury are the judges under the English Law, and that a decision on the facts must finally be left to them. . . .

"You may perhaps decide that it will be desirable for you to see the Home Secretary, and as you know, I shall be only too pleased to consult with you and assist you in every way in my power."

While Hector Munro was writing these letters Scholefield Allen was in London discussing the preparations for the appeal with Roland Oliver and obtaining from Sir Patrick Hastings' clerk a copy of the notice of appeal in the Rouse case.

He also arranged a meeting with Kingsley Martin, the newly-appointed editor of the *New Statesman*. The "copy" for the next issue of the journal was already with the printers, but after listening to Scholefield Allen's account of the Wallace case and reading the summing-up Martin wrote an article and arranged for space to be made for it on the leader pages. Apart from a P.S.U.-inspired news story in the trade-union paper, the *Daily Herald*, in which the verdict was called "astonishing", Martin's article, "An Alarming Verdict", was the only significant comment on the case to appear in a national journal prior to the appeal.

On Tuesday, April 28th, Scholefield Allen returned to Liverpool, and during the next few days he and Munro sifted the evidence and drew up the grounds of appeal:

1. *The verdict was unreasonable and cannot be supported having regard to the evidence. The whole of the evidence was consistent with Wallace's innocence and the prosecution never discharged the burden of proving that he and no-one else was guilty.*

2. *The judge, at the conclusion of the evidence, should have withdrawn the case from the jury.*

3. *Misstatements were made by the prosecution in the opening speech.*

4. *No motive was suggested by the prosecution.*

5. *A great feature was made that Wallace's demeanour on 20th January, 1931, was cool, calm, and indifferent. No such suggestion was made at the police court, though all the same witnesses were examined.*

6. *An effort was made to suggest that the mackintosh was worn by the assailant.*

7. *Professor MacFall forced upon the court the suggestion that this was a crime of frenzy, thus supplying the jury with a reason for the commission by Wallace of this murder.*

8. *Wallace was prejudiced by the fact that the Crown failed to call as witnesses for the prosecution Wildman and Jones, and also failed to supply the defence with copies of all statements taken from persons who were not called at the police court.*

9. *The judge, in his summing-up, misdirected the jury by saying that if there was no motive for Wallace, there was no motive for anyone else.*

10. *On the occasions of the speeches by the prosecuting solicitor at the Liverpool City Police Court, the said prosecuting solicitor made a number of misstatements as to the evidence and case for the prosecution . . . which said statements were reported in extenso and widely circulated throughout Liverpool and the surrounding districts, and which, although in the end disposed of, were nevertheless prejudicial.*

Signed by Wallace, the notice was delivered to the Registrar of the Court of Criminal Appeal. Now it was just a matter of waiting for the date of the hearing to be announced.

Both Hector Munro and Sydney Scholefield Allen made frequent visits to the prison.

For years Scholefield Allen had questioned the morality of capital punishment, but without ever being absolutely sure in his own mind as to whether it was right or wrong; the verdict in the Wallace case convinced him, and from now on he was an ardent supporter of the abolitionist cause.

On one occasion when he was with Wallace in the condemned cell emotion made him forgetful of where he was and to whom he was talking, and he started to discuss capital punishment, putting forward the arguments against it. Wallace listened attentively for a minute or so, then shook his head. He could see Scholefield Allen's point of view, he said—but he did not agree with it. If a man committed a crime he should be made to pay for it, and murder, the supreme crime, deserved the supreme penalty. The discussion went on—then, suddenly and simultaneously, the two men realized the paradox of the situation. Scholefield Allen broke off from what he was saying; a sad smile spread across Wallace's face.

"I seem to be arguing against myself," he said. "Perhaps we can continue our talk at some later date, in some other place."

As a condemned prisoner, Wallace was allowed certain small luxuries—ten cigarettes a day, a choice of menu, as much notepaper as he required. The morning after he was sentenced he was served bacon and eggs, the traditional first breakfast of a man awaiting execution. On this morning, too, when the Governor visited the condemned cell to tell him that the hanging was provisionally fixed for Tuesday, May 12th, he asked for, and was brought, his chess set and his violin. He taught his guards—the members of "the death watch" who were with him day and night—to play chess, and for the first time in his life was able to win consistently at the game; but, perhaps out of kindness to the guards, with whom he got on very well, he hardly ever played the violin; often, though, he took the instrument from its case and polished the woodwork with loving care and ran the bow lightly over the strings to make sure that it was in tune.

Compared with the cells of the ordinary prisoners, the condemned cell was quite palatial. "The condemned suite", Wallace called it in a letter he wrote to Munro Cairns, a man he had known since his youth, when they were both drapery assistants in Barrow.

The cell was divided in two. The main cell, with its white-distempered walls, its small barred window close to the ceiling, was about thirteen feet by ten; a patch of carpet covered the centre of the stone floor; the furniture consisted of a bed, a table, and three easy-chairs. A door led into a smaller cell, which contained a bath and water basin, a lavatory, and a gas-ring for boiling a kettle. It was here that Wallace received visitors. The lights in both parts of the cell were always kept burning.

For an hour each day Wallace was taken to a small enclosed garden, out of sight of the other prisoners. Irises and lupins grew in the flower-beds on either side of a flagged path. Afterwards Wallace wrote:

"They became an obsession with me, these irises and lupins—in fact, my sole remaining interest in life. . . . The plants were in bud. Almost unceasingly, I propounded to myself the question—Would they be in flower before I died? Somehow, I thought, if I saw them bloom I would live."

Whenever Scholefield Allen visited the prison he came away

with a feeling of amazement—amazed at Wallace's apparent composure, and even more amazed that he still professed faith in the law, in justice. Wallace seemed sure that the appeal would be successful.

Scholefield Allen only wished that he could feel as confident as Wallace appeared to be; but, like Hector Munro, he was pessimistic. And for the same reasons.

First of all, although there were ten grounds of appeal, only one of them really mattered—the one which asserted that "the verdict was unreasonable and could not be supported having regard to the evidence". The rest were simply page-fillers, not strong enough, either alone or taken together, to justify the quashing of the verdict. If the appeal was to succeed the Appeal Judges would have to go against the jury's decision, say that the jury had made a terrible mistake—*and this was something that had never happened since the Court of Criminal Appeal was set up in 1907.*

Only twice in the history of the Court had appeals against convictions carrying the death sentence been allowed: in 1911 Charles Ellsome, found guilty of the murder of a woman in Clerkenwell, was released on the ground of misdirection of the jury by Mr Justice Avory; and during the First World War, H. A. Ablers, the German Consul at Sunderland, had had the sentence of death for high treason set aside on the ground that the defence had not been properly presented to the jury.

On a few occasions the Appeal Judges had reduced a conviction for murder to one of manslaughter, or had substituted life imprisonment for the death sentence, but the murder of Julia Wallace was far too brutal and cold-blooded an affair for either of these alternatives to be considered. For the Appeal Judges reviewing the Wallace case it would be a matter of all or nothing at all—a straightforward choice between life and death; if Wallace was to survive they would have to admit that the jury, "the great inviolate", had made a ghastly blunder. Scholefield Allen found it as hard to imagine their doing this as it was to imagine a Bench of Bishops questioning the sanity of the twelve Apostles.

The other reason for pessimism was this—that of the three judges who would preside at the hearing of the appeal, which was fixed for Monday, May 18th, the leading figure would be the Lord Chief Justice, Viscount Hewart of Bury, who was one of the most vigorous and vociferous believers in the impeccability of the English jury system of this or any other century. Following the Herbert Rowse Armstrong trial in 1922, several national newspapers had printed a juror's account of what happened in the jury room. And Gordon Hewart had been absolutely furious about it—had spat out his opinion that it was "most improper, deplorable *and dangerous*. . . . Every juryman ought to observe the obligation of secrecy which is comprised in and imposed by the oath of the grand juror."

Clearly, his tirade against the Press and the talkative juror was prompted by the fear that such disclosures might undermine public confidence in the jury system. If he got so hot under the collar at the indiscretion of one Hereford juror he certainly would not take very kindly to the idea of announcing that all twelve members of the Liverpool jury were fools, which was roughly what Wallace was asking him to do.

Wallace had been unlucky all along the legal line: at the committal proceedings the magistrate was a deaf and dim music salesman; at the trial the judge was inexperienced in criminal practice; at the appeal Wallace's counsel would be faced with the task of pleading, before a man who believed that "the jury was always right", that, in this case, the jury's verdict was hopelessly, disgracefully, obviously wrong. Which sounded like a tall order. Munro and Scholefield Allen could only hope that the other two Appeal Judges were less, much less, concerned than "The Chief" with protecting the immaculate façade of the jury system.

If they were not, then Heaven help Wallace.

Twice during the period between sentence and appeal the hopes of the defence were raised—and just as suddenly dashed. Late on Thursday, April 30th, a thirty-two-year-old man walked into Walton Bridewell and announced, "I am the man who murdered Mrs Wallace." But two days later, after being medically examined and certified to be suffering from delusions, he was removed to Rainhill Mental Hospital. Then, on Friday, May 15th, another thirty-two-year-old man presented himself at Prescot Street Bridewell and told the station sergeant that he wished to give himself up for the murder. The next day, however, Superintendent Moore wrote to Munro: "Enquiries have been made amongst his family and it has been ascertained that he has been peculiar in his manner for some time, and it is obvious that he could not have committed the murder."

Having signed this, Moore, with the other C.I.D. officers involved in the case, travelled down to London to consult with Edward Hemmerde over the weekend.

Later the same day, handcuffed, dressed in his own clothes, Wallace was taken to Lime Street Station in a taxi-cab. (Before he left the condemned cell he shook hands with the two "death watch" warders. They wished him luck. "I hope we don't meet again," one of them said.) At the station only a few people recognized Wallace as he walked along the platform with the escort of plain-clothes officers, his hands muffed inside his coat-sleeves to hide the manacles.

"Going down in the train," he afterwards wrote, "I was very greatly impressed by the green and wonderful beauty of the country. I had seen little but high walls and iron-barred windows for about sixteen weeks, and it was something to cheer me and take my mind off the grim horrors of the position. The officers did their best to make me comfortable."

It was late at night when the train pulled into Euston. Wallace was transferred to a Black Maria and driven to Pentonville Prison, where he went through the routine of standing on a canvas sheet, emptying his pockets, and stripping off his clothes. The authorities at Pentonville were very thorough, determined to take no chances. As soon as Wallace was naked a warder stepped forward and combed through his hair, felt behind his ears, separated his toes, looked under his armpits, and, lastly, shone a torch inside his mouth. Satisfied that there were no concealed weapons about his person, the warder ordered him to get dressed in prison clothes—this time the blue uniform of an appellant—and he was taken to the Pentonville condemned cell and introduced to the two warders who would be his constant companions until Monday morning, when the time came for him to leave for the Royal Courts of Justice in the Strand.

"The two days before [the appeal]," Wallace afterwards wrote, "were the longest days of my life—and yet, somehow, they were also the shortest. . . . I have no wish to remember them, but the agony of those days is impossible to forget. They were a nightmare."

On Sunday, May 17th, when everyone connected with the appeal was either in London or on the way, something happened in Liverpool which, as far as is known, had never happened before, and has certainly never happened since.

The Church of England took a hand in a murder case.

Dozens of times since Wallace's conviction Scholefield Allen and Munro had thought and murmured: "Heaven help him. . . ."

But none too hopefully. Now the Church said the same thing; made it official.

Special prayers, described as "intercessions extraordinary", were offered at the morning, afternoon, and evening services at Liverpool Cathedral by the Vice-Dean, Canon Dwelly (who, as Sheriff's Chaplain, had been present during the whole of the trial).

The prayer is well worth repeating in full:

"You shall pray for them that are set by God's mercy to secure the administration of true justice in our land. Particularly this day you shall pray for His Majesty's Judges of Appeal, that they may be guided in true judgement. And you shall pray for the learned counsels of our Sovereign Lord the King, that they may be faithful to the Christian injunction of the apostle Paul:

" 'Judge nothing until God brings to light hidden things of darkness and makes manifest the counsels of the heart.'

"And you shall pray for the people of this County Palatine, that their confidence in the fair dealings of their fellow-man may be restored, and that truth and justice, religion and piety may be established among us. Finally, you shall pray for all who await the judgement of their fellow-man, and commit them to the perfect justice of Almighty God."

Edward Hemmerde did not hear about the prayers until Monday morning, a few minutes before he was due in court.

He was furious.

"It's that bastard Dwelly—I know it is," he screeched.

And was admonished by Hubert Moore, the good Irish Catholic: "You shouldn't use a word like that, Mr Hemmerde, when referring to a man of the cloth."

Flapping his arms in agitation, Hemmerde screamed: "To hell with the choice of words. I know damned well whose idea it was— that bastard Dwelly. And I'll wager ten-to-one the Bishop wasn't consulted."

But it was just as well for Hemmerde that no-one took him on. He would have lost the bet. Dr David, the Anglican Bishop of Liverpool, knew all about the "intercessions extraordinary" and was in complete agreement with Canon Dwelly.

"There is a good deal of anxiety in this city about the case," he said, "and we gave people an opportunity to ask for Divine Judgement to be performed. I do not think it is unusual, but right, that people should pray like this."

[2]

People entering the Lord Chief Justice's Court straightaway

become midgets. It is a matter of contrast. Practically everything in the court is either several sizes larger or a lot more magnificent than the furnishings of other courts. On the wall above the bench, the lion and the unicorn standing with their hind legs on the words *Evil to him who evil thinks* (in French, of course) are taller, healthier-looking specimens than most of the lions and unicorns found elsewhere. The mammoth, but mercifully tickless, clock is there not simply to remind counsel of the time, but to make sure that they never forget it. The honey-brown walls on either side of the bench and facing it are almost entirely hidden by giant book-cases containing giant books.

The public gallery is the largest in the Law Courts.

But even so it was nowhere near large enough to accommodate all the people who queued up to hear the Wallace appeal. On the Monday morning more than a hundred had to be turned away. The lucky ones squeezed shoulder to shoulder on the seats, or sat three-abreast in the gangway, or stood just as uncomfortably at the back.

Most of the spectators were Londoners, of course, but there was a small contingent from Liverpool, including an Anfield lady who deserved ten out of ten for quality of endurance. She had been at the magistrates' court on both occasions when Wallace was remanded in custody; she had not missed a single day of the committal proceedings or the trial; and, just for good measure, she had attended the coroner's court for the adjourned inquest on Mrs Wallace; now, no doubt, she was hoping against hope that the appeal would fail, so that she could look forward to standing outside Walton Gaol on the morning of Wallace's execution—that would round things off very nicely indeed.

The Wallace appeal started at eleven o'clock, directly following a short and unsuccessful appeal by a Cypriot against the death sentence for the murder of a London waitress.

The crimson-gowned Judges of Appeal were the Lord Chief Justice of England, Lord Hewart (who once remarked, in an after-dinner speech, that he did not know if he was expected to be as sober as a judge or as drunk as a lord); Mr Justice Branson; and Mr Justice Hawke.

One thing was clear from the beginning: the judges had certainly not neglected their homework. All three of them—and especially the pendulum-chinned Mr Justice Hawke—were conversant with the facts of the case. As first of all Roland Oliver presented the points in Wallace's favour, and then Edward

Hemmerde replied for the Crown, the interpolations from the bench were almost invariably for the purpose of clarifying matters for the shorthand-writer's benefit rather than for the judges'.

There is no need to summarize the two speeches. Enough to say that they were long and exhaustive; that Hemmerde left out most of the more obtuse theories that had padded the prosecution case at the trial; and that, replying to the defence assertion that the jury was prejudiced against Wallace, he placed great emphasis on the "fact" that the jury was "wholly composed of people from Widnes, Southport, and Warrington".

The hearing lasted the whole of Monday, and continued on Tuesday morning. For most of the time Wallace sat absolutely still, his elbows resting on the black rail of the side gallery, his hands cupped round his ears to catch what was being said. But as the second day wore on—as the prosecution speech came to an end and Oliver rose to reply, very briefly, to some of the points made by Hemmerde—he began to fidget with nervousness, and his gaze wandered restlessly from one judge to another, as if searching for some indication of what they were thinking, of what their decision was going to be.

It was half-past three when Roland Oliver sat down.

Mr Justice Branson leaned to his left, Mr Justice Hawke to his right, to hear what the Lord Chief Justice was muttering. There was some nodding and shaking of heads, then the three judges rose to their feet and trooped out of court. (This was unexpected: usually the Judges of Appeal do not retire before announcing a decision.)

In the side gallery a warder pulled back the green curtain covering the entrance, and Wallace, "his sallow face ashen and pale",[1] was taken to the corridor outside.

"But the court did not empty," observed the reporter for the *Liverpool Daily Post*. "It was crowded to suffocation, numerous barristers from other courts adding themselves to the congestion as time went on. There was a loud buzz of conversation, but the tense feeling did not die away. There was many a reference now to the anxiety that the appellant must be feeling.

"It was after 4.15 when there was a cry of 'Silence' in the court, and there was silence upon the instant. The judges came in and bowed low in response to the rising of the court to its feet, and when all were seated, the appellant was ushered in. Now he looked tired and worn, and once or twice he swayed slightly, but his eyes were

---

[1] *Daily Mail* (20.5.31).

Lord Hewart

Lord Chief Justice of England (1922–40).

One of the most vigorous and vociferous believers in the impeccability of the English jury system of this or any other century''.

Wallace, with his brother Joseph, leaving the Royal Courts of Justice after the appeal

Photo Barratt's Photo Press News

Wallace shaking hands with Hector Munro after the appeal

Others in the photograph are May Munro (*far left*), three members of the appeal committee (*grouped behind Munro*), Munro's clerk, Norman Wheeler (*centre*), Joseph Wallace (*far right*).

fixed upon the Lord Chief Justice, and only once did he lower his head."

Lord Hewart was in no hurry to get started. A rotund little man, chubby-faced, blue-eyed, bijou-mouthed, he rocked gently backwards and forwards in his seat. After about a minute the rocking ceased; he plopped his pudgy fingers together, forming a steeple. Someone coughed. The rocking motion started again. At last he came to rest once more; he pursed his lips, started to utter the first syllables of the judgement.

If he was in no hurry to get started he was even less anxious to get finished. It took him fourteen minutes to pronounce just over three hundred words.

Wallace afterwards wrote: ". . . nothing that ever happened to me in the hours of my blackest humiliation were ever half as hateful and horrible as the 14 minutes when I waited to hear . . . the judge's decision."

Scholefield Allen thought the manner in which Hewart delivered the judgement was "completely sadistic". He was not alone in this view.

"The appellant William Herbert Wallace was charged at the Assizes in Liverpool with the murder of his wife on January the 20th," the Lord Chief Justice began. "In the result he was convicted, and on April the 25th last he was sentenced to death. He now appeals against that conviction.

"Three facts are obvious. The first is that at the conclusion of the case for the Crown no submission was made on behalf of the appellant that there was no case to go to the jury. The second fact which seems to be obvious is that the evidence was summed up by the learned judge with complete fairness and accuracy, and it would not have been at all surprising if the result had been an acquittal of the prisoner. The third obvious fact is that the case is eminently one of difficulty and doubt.

"Now, the whole of the material evidence has been closely and critically examined before us, and it does not appear to me to be necessary to discuss it again. Suffice it to say that we are not concerned here with suspicion, however grave, or with theories, however ingenious. Section 4 of the Criminal Appeal Act of 1907 provides that the Court of Criminal Appeal shall allow the appeal if they think that the verdict of the jury should be set aside on the ground that it cannot be supported having regard to the evidence."

A pause: the longest yet. Hewart's tongue touched his lips, moistened them. In the Press seats the *Daily Post* reporter jotted down the notes that he later used for the following account:

"Slowly, deliberately, quietly the words came from the Lord Chief Justice that the ears of the whole court were strained to hear. At last he arrived at the crucial words. *'The conclusion to which we have arrived'*—and think of this as being said very slowly with frequent pauses—*'is that the case against the appellant, which we have carefully and anxiously considered'*—a pause—*'and discussed'* —a pause—*'was not proved with that certainty which is necessary in order to justify a verdict of guilty.'*

"The whole court seemed to sway a little. *'And, therefore, it is our duty to take the course indicated by the section of the Statute to which I have referred. The result is that this appeal will be allowed . . .'*

"There was noise in the court. It was partly a breath of applause and partly the scurrying feet of the 'copy' boys rushing out with the news. *'And this conviction quashed,'* said the Lord Chief Justice, after he paused for silence.

"One just caught a bright gleam in the eyes of Wallace, who had been standing there looking deathly pale as he went through the minutes of the uttermost limit of his ordeal. The police in the side gallery with him smiled at him and indicated that he might withdraw, and he turned and and went out of court a free man. The judges were still on the bench. They had finished their work, and the majesty of the law seemed to see nothing and hear nothing of the commotion that had now arisen.

"Outside for some minutes a crowd gathered, waiting to see Wallace go away. There was not long to wait. He came out putting on his bowler hat, from underneath which a long wisp of his white hair appeared. He could not speak. There was the making of a smile on his face, but it looked like the smile that a man whose nerves are dreadfully frayed tries to put on in response to the greetings of people who have not been so far along the road of anxiety.

"When he came to the street gates one of his friends cried out: 'Call a taxi. Don't go into the Strand.' Wallace stood still. He was still barely smiling, and hardly seemed to know what was being said or done. A taxi was called, and he was rushed into it.

"For a moment it held up a bus, and the passengers looked out, casually wondering why there was a rather excited crowd round a taxi in the Strand. . . ."

Release . . .

TUESDAY, May 19th, 1931–WEDNESDAY March 1st, 1933

> "*Were* you *ever punished?*"
> "*Only for faults,*" *said Alice.*
> "*And you were all the better for it, I know!*"
> *the Queen said triumphantly.*
> "*Yes, but then I* had *done the things I was
> punished for,*" *said Alice:* "*that makes all
> the difference.*"
> "*But if you* hadn't *done them,*" *the Queen
> said,* "*that would have been better still;
> better, and better, and better!*" *Her voice
> went higher with each 'better', till it got
> quite to a squeak at last.*

Hector Munro and Sydney Scholefield Allen travelled back to
Liverpool on the same train as Hubert Moore and the other C.I.D.
officers who had been present at the appeal. The superintendent
was far from sober when he boarded the train, and he became more
and more drunk as the journey went on. He talked incessantly,
and most of the time incoherently, pausing only to swallow some
Jameson's, or to take a lurching trip to the lavatory, or to moan a
snatch of song about Erin's green isle where the praties grow.

"I still say he did it," he mumbled over and over again. "If he
didn't do it, who did? Answer me that, will someone?" He also
made continual reference to Wallace's calm behaviour on the
night of the murder, comparing it with that of the Catholic lady
(mentioned earlier, on page 56) who screamed the house down and
tore her beads to shreds, she was so upset about her husband being
murdered. "That's innocence for you," he asserted. "You don't
smoke cigarettes at a time like that."

When the train pulled into Lime Street a large crowd was waiting
on the platform, hoping that Wallace was aboard.

But Wallace and his brother Joseph stayed the night at a small boarding house in the West London suburb of Turnham Green.

The following day was a full one for Wallace. In the morning he visited the Prudential Head Office in Holborn and was given a month's paid holiday; then he went on to the headquarters of the P.S.U. to thank the union officials for guaranteeing the defence costs. As he left the building he said that he wanted to "get somewhere where I can see green grass . . . and feel that I am really free"; and the place he chose was Kew Gardens, where he spent the afternoon with his brother. Afterwards they watched a club cricket match for a while. In the evening they went to the first night of *The Millionaire Kid*, a musical at the Gaiety, and Wallace thoroughly enjoyed himself. "If only you knew how amazingly thrilling it is to laugh again," he said to Joseph as they walked out of the theatre.

While Wallace was making the most of his first day of freedom for fifteen weeks, three Labour M.P.s—J. S. Clarke (Maryhill, Glasgow), D. Hall Caine (Everton, Liverpool), and J. H. Hayes (Edgehill, Liverpool)—were suggesting in the House of Commons that he "should be given compensation for the suffering he has endured".

The Home Secretary, J. R. Clynes, said that he could make no statement regarding the case.

But two days later J. S. Clarke raised the matter again, and this time the Home Secretary said, "The case of Mr Wallace does not differ in principle from any other defendant who has been acquitted of a serious charge by the verdict of a jury, or whose conviction has been quashed by the Court of Criminal Appeal."

"Would it not be an act of grace, not to grant compensation, but to give him a grant towards the cost of his defence?"

"I can only say it is beyond my power to afford compensation or any other sum of money in a case of this kind," the Home Secretary replied. And added, "It does not appear to come under the heading of miscarriages of justice."

Mr Clarke gave up; but, on June 8th, E. T. Palmer, Labour M.P. for Greenwich and joint secretary of the P.S.U., asked the Attorney-General the same question, phrased slightly differently.

The Attorney-General, Sir William Jowitt, simply revamped the Home Secretary's answer, to say, "The Criminal Appeal Act provides that on the hearing and determination of an appeal, no costs shall be allowed to either side. . . . There is no fund from which a successful appellant may be reimbursed."

So, changing the subject, E. T. Palmer asked the Attorney-

refuge from the prying eyes of a curious public," Munro told them.

But, in fact, Wallace travelled north—to the Furness Peninsula, the place where he had spent most of his early years. On Saturday, the first day of the Whitsun Bank Holiday weekend, he and his brother called at a guest house in Broughton-in-Furness and asked the owner, Mrs Eleanor Douglas, if she could put them up for a couple of weeks.

"I promised to accommodate them," Mrs Douglas recalls. "Later in the afternoon Mr Wallace said he had better let me know who they were—was the name Wallace familiar to me? I said, 'Oh, yes. I have seen that name many times in the news lately.' He said, 'I am the one. Will you still have us?' "

Mrs Douglas said that she would. "And they stayed with us for nearly three weeks. Friends and relatives came to see them whilst they were here. I don't know how close the relatives were who came to visit them—but one was a sister-in-law." (This must have been Amy. Joseph saw precious little of his wife during his stay in England. When he left Broughton he returned at once to Malaya. The fact that Mrs Douglas did not recognize them as man and wife indicates that they were not the most devoted of married couples.)

"When the Wallaces stayed in Broughton they did a lot of walking. Sometimes they went fishing in the River Duddon. William was fond of sketching. When people got to know they were staying here they were curious and wanted to know who I was going to put up next. William was very pleasant and talkative. One night he brought out his wife's photograph to show us, and said what a lovely woman she was. He and his brother were very pally."

During the weeks between the trial and the appeal the Liverpool scandal-mongers had kept comparatively quiet; but while Wallace was staying at Broughton they cleared their throats and started prattling again. The short rest had done their voices a power of good; their imaginations, too. It was just like old times.

The Appeal Court's decision didn't prove a thing, they snarled; the judges had not ruled that Wallace was innocent, only that the evidence was not strong enough to sustain the conviction. . . . The decision simply showed that Wallace was diabolically clever, the police not clever enough—nothing else.

He's got away with it once, they screamed hysterically—what's to stop him doing it again?—what if he's got the taste for it?— what if he's got a blood lust, like Dracula?

What's he doing in Broughton, a tin-pot little place miles from anywhere? Why Broughton? Why not Blackpool or Morecambe or even New Brighton? Obvious, isn't it? . . . He's staying with his fancy woman—sleeping with the motive for his wife's murder. Stands to reason.

A lot of the old rumours came back into fashion. Wallace was a sex maniac, a vampire, a sadist, a mad scientist who preferred human beings to guinea pigs. . . . If and when he returned to Liverpool the men would have to take every precaution to protect their womenfolk.

Hearing the rumours, the stories, Hector Munro wrote to Wallace, suggesting that he should accept the Prudential's offer of a post in another part of the country.

Wallace wrote back, thanking Munro for the suggestion, but saying that he intended to return to Liverpool—and to remain there.

So Munro wrote another letter, this time saying that if Wallace was determined to stay in Liverpool he must find somewhere else to live; he told Wallace that he knew "from observation and information" that there was a strong, and growing, feeling of hostility towards him in Anfield.

Wallace replied promptly. He would be returning to Liverpool —and to 29 Wolverton Street—on June 9th. "It is my home," he said simply. "What would the tattle-tales say if I were to accept a position elsewhere, or even change my address to another district of Liverpool? They would say that I was running away. They would say that it was an indication of guilt. Does it mean nothing that I was freed by the Court of Appeal?"

But very soon after his return to Liverpool, Wallace discovered that Munro had not exaggerated the situation.

He went back to his old job of collecting insurance money in Clubmoor. Only for a day or two, though. As he walked through the streets children were dragged into the houses, doors slammed, upstairs windows opened and women stuck their heads out to shout curses at him; the tough guys of the neighbourhood stood in his path, brandished their fists in his face, threatened him; many of his clients—some of them people who had known him for ten years and longer, who before the murder had often invited him in for a cup of tea—now refused to answer the door when he knocked.

On June 15th he wrote in his diary:

"I think I must definitely abandon the idea of returning to a Liverpool agency, as the ill feeling against me is evidently stronger than I expected."

Joseph Crewe arranged for his transfer from the collecting staff to a clerical job at the Liverpool head office of the Prudential. But this was only a part-solution to his problems.

Almost every post brought poison-pen letters to 29 Wolverton Street. The neighbours shunned him, retreating into their door-ways, staring at him from behind lace curtains, dodging down side streets to avoid him when he left the house in the morning and returned at night.

"Find all the neighbours up against me," he wrote on June 16th. "They are the rottenest crowd I ever struck. Mean and paltry brained. I feel it is a wicked insult to Julia. How she would have scorned the whole thing!"

He could probably have stood being ostracized by his neighbours . . . but there were so many other things which made living at 29 Wolverton Street unbearable. The house became the main target for the local children's "knocking down Ginger" activities—banging at the door, then running away. It was not only children who did this; grown-up people did it, too. And it was grown-up people who, in the middle of the night, called through the letter-box: "Julia . . . Julia . . . What's happened to Julia? . . . She's all chopped up . . . chop-chop-chop . . . Killy-Willy—Killy-Willy . . ." Wallace also had to contend with the curiosity-seekers who came from all over Liverpool to press their faces against the parlour window for a glimpse of the place where the murder was committed, who even clambered over the back wall to test the strength of the kitchen door, or to cut a piece from it as a souvenir.

By June 23rd he had had enough. "You were right," he told Hector Munro. "It's impossible to carry on like this." With the solicitor's help, he found somewhere else to live—"The Summer House", a small bungalow in Meadowside Road, Bromborough, on the Cheshire side of the Mersey.

Crowds gathered in Wolverton Street on the day the pantechnicon arrived to remove the furniture. They ooh-ed as Julia's piano was rolled out: they ah-ed at the sight of Wallace's music-stand . . . they gawped at the armchairs and squealed at the beds. A good time was had by all. It was better than an Orange Day parade. Cheers followed the pantechnicon out of the street, and they were cheers of victory.

Wallace tried to settle down in his new home, to find peace in the rural surroundings of the Wirral.

But Bromborough is only five miles or so from Liverpool: he had not moved far enough to escape the tongue-waggers, the rumour-mongers.

He advertised for a housekeeper; several women applied for the post, but none of them was the least bit interested when they learned whose house it was they were expected to keep. Then a Miss Annie Mason, an elderly woman who had been friendly with the Wallaces for some years, offered to look after him. He accepted the offer promptly, gratefully.

And at once the rumour went round that Miss Mason was not a Miss at all—she was the second Mrs Wallace; they had been married during the time Wallace was staying at Broughton. A twin rumour to this—less detailed but far more sinister—was that Wallace had married again and was keeping his second wife hidden away, locked in a room and only allowed out at night (to answer the calls of nature, presumably). In Liverpool at least one person claimed that a friend of a friend of a friend living in Bromborough had seen an emaciated female face staring from an upstairs window of Wallace's new home (which was quite a feat, considering that it was a bungalow).

"How delighted Julia would have been, how lovingly she would have tended the garden," Wallace wrote in his diary.

Before tending the garden himself he built a high fence around it as a protection against nosey-parkers. And, of course, the rumour-mongers said that the fence was built "to conceal something"—he was burying things in the garden; he and Mrs Wallace (née Mason) were running round stark-naked among the marigolds; he was substituting graven images for gnomes . . . and goodness knows what else.

He continued to work at the Liverpool head office of the Prudential. Each day he lunched at the City Café—but "the men with whom I have won and lost at play so often, with whom I have . . . exchanged views on topics of the day over coffee and cigarettes, pass me with heads tilted away from me. . . . I suppose this feeling against me will probably persist for some time and I may never really live it down. Well, after all, so long as I know I am innocent why should I worry?"

But the loneliness was getting him down.

August 25th, 1931: "To go about feeling that one is shunned by nearly everyone is a terrible ordeal, and though I try to fight it down and ignore it, the whole business depresses me beyond words. Perhaps after a while I may get immersed in some new hobbies to take my mind off the terrible tragedy. What I fear is the long nights. . . ."

September 8th, 1931: "The last few days I have been depressed thinking of my dear Julia. I'm afraid this will be a very lonely winter for me. I seem to miss her more and more, and cannot drive the thought of her cruel end out of my mind."

October 6th, 1931: "I cannot disguise from myself that I am dreadfully nervous about entering the house after dark. I suppose it is because my nerves are all so shattered after the ordeal, and this, together with the recurring fits of grief and anguish over my dear Julia's end makes me horribly depressed and apprehensive . . . Left to myself I am for ever trying to visualise what really did happen. . . ."

March 20th, 1932: "Today I have been very much depressed, full of grief and tears. Julia, Julia, my dear, why were you taken from me? Why, why should this have been so? It is a question to which I can get no answer, and I must fight this dread feeling of utter loneliness as best I can. . . ."

Wallace had no defence against the rumour-mongers, no means of deterring the anonymous letter-writers (twelve months after moving to Bromborough he was still receiving poison-pen letters); but during 1931 and '32, Hector Munro briefed Sydney Scholefield Allen in several actions against printers and publishers who, in the words of the statements of claim, had "greatly prejudiced and injured Mr Wallace in his credit and reputation" and had brought him into "public scandal, hatred, and contempt". The libel actions were all settled out of court.

Within a month of the appeal a group of newspapers agreed to pay £200 for printing an assortment of small indiscretions about Wallace, and he used this money as the down-payment on the house in Meadowside Road.

In January 1932 an action was brought against the printers and publishers of *The Herald of Salvation*, which was described as "An Illustrated Magazine of Pure Gospel Literature", and retailed at the price of one halfpenny net, $7\frac{1}{2}d$. per dozen, post free. The action concerned an article in the previous September's issue of the magazine, in which the Court of Criminal Appeal was compared with "Heaven's Court of Appeal", and in which it was stated that, "had W. Wallace . . . a condemned sinner . . . appealed to the Court which God has set up, it would have been essential for him to acknowledge the guilt and iniquity that were his". The author

Vol. 53.—No. 633. September, 1931.

THE HERALD OF SALVATION

An Illustrated Magazine of Pure Gospel Literature

"THE RESULT IS THAT THE APPEAL
WILL BE ALLOWED AND THE CON-
VICTION QUASHED."

PICKERING & INGLIS, PRINTERS AND PUBLISHERS

London: 14 Paternoster Row, E.C.4.   Glasgow: 229 Bothwell Street
Localised with any Title and List of Meetings   *Registered Canadian Magazine Post*

7½d. per doz. post free.   One Halfpenny Net.   4/9 per 100 post free.

went on to suggest that Wallace "should, like other condemned sinners, make open confession of his crime", so as to "provide an object lesson for all men who love darkness rather than light. . . ."

When Hector Munro showed him the article Wallace was very angry—not because it was prejudicial and injurious, but "because he, a confirmed agnostic, had been used as an advertisement for something he did not believe in". As a result of the religious libel, he received £300 in an out-of-court settlement.

Perhaps the worst libel of all was contained in an article, "The Crime at 29 Wolverton Street", which appeared in the May 1932 edition of a magazine called *True Detective Mysteries*.

A photo-montage was given a centre-page spread, with Wallace standing on one side of a chess-board, Hubert Moore on the other. Beneath the picture of Wallace a caption invited the readers to "observe his long, tapering fingers". The chess analogy was continued in the article, the implication being that Wallace, the master, thinking out his moves in advance, had had little difficulty in outwitting a bone-headed Moore. (Come to think of it, the article provided as many grounds for Moore suing the magazine as it did for Wallace.)

But the printers and publishers of *True Detective Mysteries* were in luck. The writ against them was not issued until February 1933. Before the statement of claim could be discussed in chambers the plaintiff died.

Since just before Christmas Wallace had been suffering from a recurrence of the kidney trouble which had plagued him for most of his adult life. His condition rapidly worsened, the pain increased. He was forced to give up his job. But despite the pain, despite the pleas of his few remaining friends, he refused to take treatment. He told Annie Mason that he had no wish to remain alive, and it seemed to her that "he was committing slow suicide".

By February 9th he could stand the pain no longer. An ambulance was called. He wept as he said goodbye to Annie Mason. "You have been goodness itself to me," he said. Miss Mason felt sure that "he knew that he was leaving his home for the last time".

The ambulance took him to the near-by Clatterbridge Hospital, where he was given drugs to ease the pain. When he had been at the hospital about a week an emergency operation was performed. it was unsuccessful. From now on for much of the time he was either delirious or unconscious.

He was conscious, however, on the evening of February 25th,

when his nephew visited him. They talked, Edwin doing most of it, for about a quarter of an hour. As the boy was leaving Wallace murmured:

"Do good with your life."

Those were his last words. Soon afterwards he lapsed into a coma. At three o'clock the following morning he was pronounced dead.

The death certificate, signed by Elizabeth Lansdown, M.R.C.S., who conducted the post-mortem examination, gave the causes of death as:

"1a. Uraemia
   b. Pyelonephritis
   c. Left kidney removed 30 years ago."

As soon as Wallace's death was announced Liverpool became a city of speculation.

Had he made a dying confession?

Yes—the rumour went round—*he had told his nephew how he had committed the murder, and why.*

What about his diary?—had he made a written confession as well?

Oh, yes, the diary contained all the gory details.

Within twenty-four hours both these rumours were so strong that Hector Munro thought it necessary to take a statement from Edwin Wallace and issue it to the Press. Edwin said that it was absolutely untrue that Wallace had confessed, either verbally or in writing, to the murder; equally untrue, he added, was another rumour that Wallace had made a death-bed will in the presence of the master of the infirmary—Wallace had made his will on February 9th, before entering hospital, and had named his brother Joseph sole executor. (As it turned out, apart from a bequest of £100 to Annie Mason, Joseph was also sole legatee; two years later probate was granted on the sum of £1672 14s. 7d.)

On February 27th Wallace's body was taken to a private chapel, where a preliminary service was held.

When is the funeral to be?

Where?

At Anfield?

Buried in the same grave as his wife?

February 28th: An attendance record at Anfield Cemetery. All day long, from when the gates were opened in the morning until they were closed at night, crowds of people flocked into the cemetery, milled around Julia's grave in search of clues, drew a complete blank, and trudged out again looking disconsolate.

But that night, after closing-time, two grave-diggers returned to the cemetery. Working by the light of flares, they dug away most of the soil covering Julia's coffin.

Early the next morning, March 1st, they finished the job.

At nine o'clock the funeral cortège entered the cemetery by the back gate in Cherry Lane. A full committal service was held. The ten mourners, all male, included Edwin Wallace, Hector Munro, and some of Wallace's old Prudential colleagues. There were four small wreaths.

The coffin was lowered into the grave; the clergyman spoke the last few words of the service, dropped the token bits of earth into the hole, wiped his hands. "Amen," everyone said.

As the mourners moved away, the grave-diggers started covering the grave. They worked fast. They had been ordered to have the job completed before the crowds arrived.

On his own, Hector Munro walked back to where the cars were parked. The undertaker, a man named Porter, approached him. Frock-coated, sombre-faced, a strip of crêpe dangling from the brim of his top hat, the undertaker clasped his black-gloved hands together and murmured:

"A sad moment for us all, sir."

It was too much for Munro. He had had enough of hypocrisy, of falsehood.

"Don't be such a damned fool, Porter," he snapped. He turned his back and got into one of the cars. He felt like crying.

A Different Verdict

"That proves *his guilt, of course,"* said the
Queen. . . .
    "It doesn't prove anything of the sort!"
said Alice.

[1]

The evidence presented by the opposing sides at the trial (and
some that was not) has already been dealt with. But there are a
number of further points which, I submit, prove conclusively
that Wallace was innocent.

Wallace's demeanour, and his remarks, on the night of the murder

Although it received no mention at the committal proceedings,
the prosecution at the trial placed great emphasis on the fact that
Wallace was cool, calm, and collected in the presence of the police,
apparently unmoved by his wife's death.

I mentioned this to a man who, until his recent retirement,
occupied one of the most senior positions at Scotland Yard—a man
who has probably dealt with more murder inquiries than any other
person now living in this country. Here is what he said:

"Of course, during investigation and interrogation, reactions of
suspects can be a prime incentive towards certain conclusions. It
is, however, dangerous to form such conclusions prematurely
without supporting evidence. On their own, they are useless
towards supporting any charge. It is impossible to get away from
the fact—humanity is a strange mixture, some men are weak and
others are 'tough bastards' who would not flinch in any circumstances. I believe that only the very experienced investigator can
truly assess 'outward signs', but to interpret such conclusions
would be too dangerous."

And that is all that needs to be said about Wallace's demeanour:
no conclusion can be drawn.

It was suggested at the committal proceedings (but not at the
trial), and has been suggested several times since, that some of
Wallace's remarks on the night of the murder—in particular, a

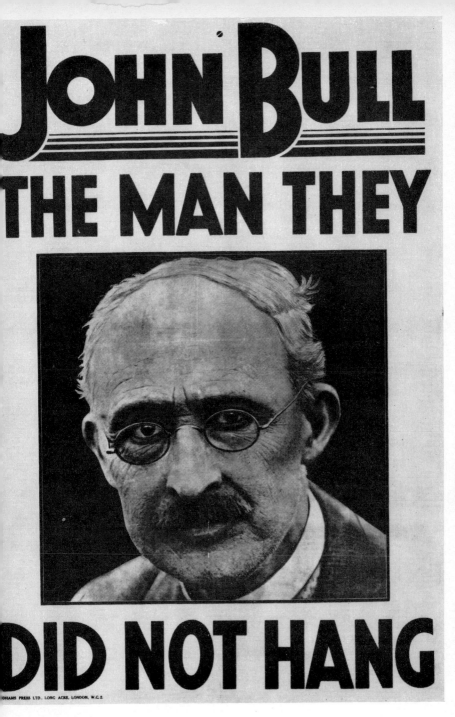

A poster advertising a series of articles about Wallace—"My Life Story"—which appeared in *John Bull*

The Summer House, Bromborough, where Wallace spent the cruel
winter of his life

Plot No. 4837, C/E Division
"In Anfield Cemetery, Qualtrough's two victims share a common grave."

remark to Mrs Johnston: "Look at her brains"—were out of keeping with the words a bereaved and innocent man would have uttered. This is nonsense, of course. It often happens that to people suffering from severe shock the normal seems abnormal, and vice versa; they speak quite casually of things which ordinarily they would never think of mentioning. The person least likely to have had any connection with the assassination of President Kennedy was surely his wife, Mrs Jacqueline Kennedy—yet "after the third shot, she said, 'They have killed my husband; I have his brains in my hand,' and she repeated that several times. And that was all the conversation."[1]

Wallace's persistence in trying to locate 25 Menlove Gardens East

Was the long time he spent in the area (variously estimated between about thirty-five minutes and an hour) in aid of an alibi? Having gone all that way and then been told by a couple of people that there was no such place as Menlove Gardens East, would an innocent man have returned home at once?

Clearly, Wallace spent longer on the search than most people would have done: but he was an insurance man, taught to believe than an unpersistent agent is an unsuccessful one, and there is plenty of evidence to show that he was not the sort of man who gave up very easily, either in business or in private pursuits.

Hector Munro remarks:

"Wallace's habit of asking passers-by for information was not so unusual as the prosecution thought. After the case one of my clerks went with him to Manchester, and Wallace took it into his head to buy a pair of 'K' boots. He at once began to ask all and sundry in Piccadilly where he could find a 'K' boot shop. My clerk told me that he said to Wallace, 'Haven't you had enough of asking questions in the street?' "

A story concerning myself:

At the start of my research into the case, among the newspaper libraries I visited was that of the *Daily Mail*. When I arrived there I was told that someone had telephoned and left a message for me to meet them later that day at Belgrave Mews North. I had never been to Belgrave Mews North, but I assumed that it was somewhere off Belgrave Square. After completing my business at the

[1] Evidence given by Mrs Nellie Connally, wife of the Governor of Texas, to the Warren Commission.

Daily Mail offices I took a tube to Hyde Park Corner, walked round the side of St George's Hospital, and asked the first person I met if he could direct me to the address.

But he was a stranger to the area, like myself. So was the next person I asked. The third was a little more helpful. He pointed in the direction of Knightsbridge and said that he thought it was "round that way somewhere". I then encountered a policeman on a duty round. I asked him the way to Belgrave Mews North.

"Are you sure you've got the right address?" he said.

I told him it was the address I had been given.

"I only ask," he said, "because there are three of these Mewses—North, South, and West—and some people get confused by them."

He then directed me to the Mews I wanted, and I found it without further trouble.

Not until the following day did it occur to me that there were similarities between my trip to Belgrave Mews North and Wallace's search for Menlove Gardens East.

A week or so later I decided to try the Qualtrough trick on a friend who works for the Sun Life Assurance Co. of Canada. I telephoned his home at a time when I knew he would be out, and left virtually the same message for him as was left for Wallace, substituting Belgrave Mews East for Menlove Gardens East, and asking him to call there at about half-past seven that night.

Next morning I telephoned him at his office and asked if he had received the message—more important, if he had done anything about it. He had. So I mixed an explanation with an apology, waited for him to calm down, then asked if he had looked up the address in a street directory. No, of course not, he said; he had taken it for granted that Belgrave Mews East was somewhere near Belgrave Square. Had he made many enquiries? "Dozens" was his first reply to this, but, asked to be more specific, he said that he had spoken to five people, and had spent over half an hour in the area before returning home.

The apparent absence of motive

Following Professor MacFall's example, most of the anti-Wallaceites plump for madness instead of motive. Their idea is that Wallace's kidney disease affected him mentally.

So far as is known, the first suggestion (in writing) that Wallace was insane was made in a letter received by Hector Munro on February 6th, 1931, four days after the arrest. Unsigned, written on Liverpool Cotton Exchange notepaper, the letter read:

"Re the man Wallace that you are defending—

"I am informed and I believe that the West Lancs Mental Board can confirm me that Mrs Wallace at one time tried to have her husband declared insane."

Munro checked, of course, and found that this information was completely untrue.

Three years after Wallace's death Dorothy L. Sayers wrote:[1]

". . . Wallace died of cancer of the kidneys. It is, of course, well known that diseases affecting these organs produce very remarkable and deleterious changes in a person's character, but whether the trouble had already begun in 1931, and if so whether it could have resulted in so strange a madness, with such a combination of cunning and bestial ferocity as the murderer of Julia Wallace displayed, is a matter for physicians to judge."

At least six subsequent writers on the case have accepted Miss Sayers's word and ascribed the cause of Wallace's death to cancer. (In a television reconstruction of the trial presented in the BBC 2 *Jury Room* series in September 1965, "Wallace's cancer" was put forward as the solution to the mystery of the missing motive.)

But, as has been noted, Wallace died of uraemia and pyelonephritis.

Yseult Bridges[2] gets the facts right. She quotes "a prominent Harley Street physician":

"Pyelonephritis is inflammation of the kidney and pelvis of the kidney. . . . It is quite possible for a man to have a low grade type of fever with infected kidneys which would produce emaciation and mental changes. The incessant pyrexia from which he must have been suffering . . . *might quite easily increase his mental alertness and make him a pervert or a genius.*"

Regarding the *physical* effects of pyelonephritis, there is extreme disagreement among the four physicians whom I have consulted. Three of them assert that if Wallace died of pyelonephritis in February 1933 he could not have been suffering from the disease in January 1931. Their view is summed up in the words of one of them:

"If Wallace was suffering from pyelonephritis at the time of the crime he would have been dead pretty soon afterwards—*a fortiori* if he had only *one* kidney."

But the fourth physician—Gavin Thurston, the Coroner for Inner West London—takes the opposite view:

"Before sulphonamides were introduced in 1936 pyelonephritis

[1] *The Anatomy of Murder.*
[2] *Two Studies in Crime.*

was the bane of the physician's life. . . . It was often associated with abnormalities of urinary tract, or stone, or obstruction as by an enlarged prostate, which might have been Wallace's trouble. It was not immediately fatal but after a period of years the kidneys might become permanently damaged and gradually cease to function."

All four physicians agree, however, when it comes to the *mental* effects of pyelonephritis. Gavin Thurston says:

"I would not accept the view that such an infection would make a man a pervert or a genius—any more than Napoleon's alleged attack of piles was responsible for his defeat at Waterloo."

Mrs Bridges goes on to suggest that Edward Hemmerde *knew* that Wallace was suffering from some sort of toxic psychosis, but, due to the laws of evidence, was not allowed to broach it as an explanation for uxoricide.

There is no truth in this.

On February 16th, 1931, the Surgical Registrar at the Royal Hospital, Liverpool, provided the police with the following information:

"Report on William Herbert Wallace.

"He was admitted on the 9th June, 1930, complaining of pain in the right loin and the passage of pus ('matter') in the urine. The presence of an obstruction in the right kidney was verified, but its site and nature could not be ascertained. The absence of the left kidney was confirmed beyond reasonable doubt and a blood test showed that the right kidney was not functioning satisfactorily. This precluded any surgical procedure, and the treatment adopted was medicinal and of a purely palliative nature.

"Further information:

"It should be mentioned that, while the occurrence of thirst and occasional headaches and nausea was noted, and taken as evidence of some degree of renal failure, no note was made of any mental changes such as sometimes occur when kidney function is impaired."

On March 28th, 1931, Dr Higson, the Senior Medical Officer at Walton Gaol, reported:

"The prisoner was received on Feb. 3 and admitted to hospital for special observation. He has been rational in conduct and conversation, generally cheerful and philosophical, and at no time has he shown any undue state of mental depression. Mentally, he has been quite normal and has never suffered from any attack of mental confusion or loss of memory.

"Had he been suffering from an acute attack of insanity, due to renal deficiency, on the day of the offence, he would have been so affected both mentally and physically that the derangement could not have been so transient as to have escaped notice."

Back to Yseult Bridges. At the beginning of her account of the case she takes other authors to task for placing too much reliance on a series of *John Bull* articles, "My Life Story", which appeared under Wallace's name in the summer of 1932. But in the last few pages of her book, the pages devoted to motive, she relies upon those self-same magazine articles to support the suggestion that Wallace was deranged.

The *John Bull* articles, she exclaims, prove that Wallace was a psychopathic liar.

And she quotes from one of the articles:

"Chess was one of the passions of my life. Liverpool was a great chess-playing centre, and I was well known in the circle. I have no-one to play chess with now. But some evenings I get out my board, put the pieces on the squares, and settle down to working out difficult problems.

"A minute or two passes. Then I, who in the past have matched my brains against some of the greatest players in the world, realize that I am not concentrating on the board, though I sit staring at it. Some shadow seems to rise between me and my beloved game."

Now Mrs Bridges delivers the knock-out blow: *"He was never more than a third-rate player in an obscure little club. This gives the clue to all the rest of his pretensions."*

But does it? Actually, no.

For two reasons:

First: Wallace *had* "matched his brains against some of the greatest players in the world"—although, admittedly, it was always a pretty unequal contest. In the '20s he had played in "simultaneous exhibition" matches when chess masters like Capablanca, Kashdan, and Blackburne visited Liverpool and took on all-comers.

Second: The *John Bull* articles were not written by Wallace. He was paid a fee for the use of his name and for providing some information about his early years, very little of which was used by the journalist who "ghosted" the series. It was a rush job, and Wallace did not even see what he was supposed to have written until the series appeared in print. (This fact, incidentally, makes nonsense of quite a lot that has been published about Wallace in the past thirty years or so.)

The murder weapon

According to Sarah Draper, two things were missing from the house: a thin poker, about nine inches long, from the kitchen; and "a large piece of iron, about a foot long and as thick as a candle", from the parlour.

Professor MacFall stated, "If a blow was made with this [the iron bar], it would have produced the appearances I found, or such a weapon would." If he was right, then the poker can be ignored: it had no connection with the murder, at least not as far as the actual killing was concerned.

At the trial it was taken for granted, not only by the prosecution but also by the defence, that the iron bar was the murder weapon. *But if it was, why did the murderer bother to remove it?*

Oddly enough, this question was never asked.

Not until five years later was it pointed out, by Dorothy L. Sayers,[1] that "whoever did the murder, it was to his advantage to leave the weapon in the house. . . . In this case the weapon was identified only with the house itself, and if the murderer came from outside, the use of a weapon identified with the house would assist him in throwing the blame on Wallace, whereas, if Wallace himself was the murderer, by far the readiest way of fixing suspicion upon himself was to use a weapon belonging to the house *and remove it*, since its removal created a strong presumption that no weapon had been brought from outside. Whichever way one looks at it, the carrying away of the weapon was an idiotic and entirely unnecessary error, involving the risk of discovery."

Neither side at the trial was interested in *why* the iron bar had been removed, but there was plenty of discussion as to *how* and *where* it could have been hidden. Superintendent Moore's over-anxiety to bolster the prosecution case made him a not particularly scrupulous witness, but even so, some people were surprised by his statement that the iron bar might be "hid in the house or the adjoining fields, possibly". Since there were no adjoining fields, the possibility of the iron bar being hidden in one was rather remote; and no more likely, it seemed, was the possibility that it was "hid in the house". The police, assisted by dustmen and drain inspectors, had spent days searching the areas of Richmond Park and Menlove Gardens for the murder weapon—surely they had been equally, if not more, thorough in searching the house?

The answer to this question, it appears, is: No, they had not been at all thorough.

[1] *The Anatomy of Murder.*

The investigating officers on the case were far too eager to jump to conclusions first and to try to collect evidence in support of the conclusions afterwards. It would seem that, in much the same way as they decided upon Wallace's guilt and then concentrated all their energies upon looking for facts to confirm this impression, they decided that, since the iron bar was not visible, it was not there . . . and if it was not there it was the murder weapon . . . and if it was the murder weapon Wallace must have taken it with him when he left the house, otherwise it would be visible. *Reductio ad absurdum.* It was this sort of logic that caused an innocent man to be arrested; to be convicted; to come within a hair's breadth of having his neck broken within a hangman's noose.

In the middle 1930s the new tenants of 29 Wolverton Street prevailed upon the landlord, Mr Sam Hall, to have certain alterations made to the house, including a change-over from gas to electricity. The gas-fire in the parlour was removed, and one of the workmen started sweeping the dirt from the back of the hearth. Noticing that there was a gap between the back wall of the fire-place and the hearth—a gap about two inches deep and roughly the width of a candle—he got hold of a screwdriver to scoop out the residuum . . . *and prised up the iron bar that had been lying there since the beginning of January 1931.*

He wiped away the covering of dust and examined the iron bar. As far as he could see there were no stains upon it, nothing to indicate that it had been used as a murder weapon.

Later he informed the police of his find and handed the iron bar over to them.

And once again, it disappeared.

Nothing was said about it. Nothing has ever been said. But there are three separate people (two of them ex-policemen) who vouch for the fact that it was found at the back of the fireplace. Some time between Mrs Draper's last visit to the house on January 7th and the night of the murder the iron bar must have rolled under the gas-fire and down the gap at the back.

The discovery of the iron bar is a strong point in Wallace's favour. If he was the murderer, and if he took the murder weapon with him when he left the house, what did he do with it? How and where did he get rid of it?

But if the murder was done by Qualtrough the problem of how the weapon was disposed of is no problem at all: he brought it with him to the house, and afterwards had all the time in the world, the whole of Liverpool, in which to get rid of it.

The telephone-call

There are four separate points to be considered under this heading.

First, the prosecution suggestion that it was Wallace who made the call to the City Café, *using an assumed voice*.

Although all three of the girls at the exchange thought the voice "ordinary", and despite the fact that Samuel Beattie, who had known Wallace for about eight years, "had no reason for thinking" that it was his voice, or "anything like his voice", the jury sided with Hemmerde in believing that Wallace could quite easily have disguised his voice over the telephone.

But *was* it as easy as all that? *Is* it so easy? Try it for yourself some time.

"In my view it is almost impossible successfully to disguise one's voice, without 'putting on' a foreign accent, a strange dialect, or some form of speech defect. Even with such 'vocal moustaches' added, it is extremely difficult to change the *rhythm* of one's mode of speech—and, although this is not generally realized, it is as much by the rhythm as by the sound that one's voice is recognized by others. This becomes increasingly true as a person grows older, and as the vocal pattern solidifies, as it were. It would also be true to say that the older a person is, the more difficult it is for him (or her) to alter the *tone* of voice over a wide register."

This is the opinion of a member of the BBC Drama Repertory Company, an experienced radio actress whose whole working life is occupied with the task of imitating other voices so as to disguise her own.

Point number two: If Wallace was the murderer, why did he make the call from a telephone-box only 400 yards from his home?

By so doing he ran the fivefold risk of being seen by someone who knew him, even if only by sight, (1) *as he walked towards the box*—in an almost opposite direction to St Margaret's Church, which he later said was the place where he boarded the tram to the City Café; (2) *as he entered the box*—which stood in an exposed position at the corner of a triangular-shaped recreation ground, with, on one side of it, only a few feet away, the main Breck Road, and, on the other, the less-frequented Rochester Road; (3) *as he made the call*—which occupied several minutes, remember; (4) *as he left the box and hastened to the tram-stop in Townsend Lane* —where, if he had to wait for a tram, there was six foot two inches of him to be observed, and perhaps remembered, by anyone who happened to pass or to be standing at the stop; and (5) *as he actually*

boarded the tram—when he might have been noticed by the conductor or one of the passengers, his presence on the tram and the
place where he got on remembered.

It just doesn't make sense.

Consider this: Rather than run the risks already mentioned in
making the call from the Anfield box, he could have waited until
he got into the centre of Liverpool, where the risk of his being seen
and recognized and remembered was minimal, and where he could
have made the call without caring if it was afterwards traced. There
was no hurry for him to get the message through: he had until
about quarter to eight—indeed, the later the call was made, the
less chance there was of the person who took it forgetting to pass
the message on.

If Wallace was the murderer one thing is certain: the plan for
killing his wife and providing himself with an alibi took some time
to form in his mind. He must have considered all the pros and cons
of the plan; he must have thought of the things that might go
wrong.

Why, then, did he take the entirely unnecessary risks involved
in making the call from Anfield 1627?

This question, unanswered (and unanswerable?), leads on to:

Point number three—and one which Hector Munro admits "may
be the most important point in the case, but I am afraid that the
defence may not have fully appreciated it".

The caller, far from being ultra-discreet, as one might expect
in a situation of this sort, *seems to have gone out of his way to make
the call as unusual as possible, so as to have it recorded in the minds
of the operators and in the notebook of the exchange supervisor*.

At 7.15 he first tried to get through to the City Café. That he
failed to do so may not have been through any fault of his.
According to Louisa Alfreds, she put the call through to Bank 3581
and heard someone from that number on the line—but according
to Gladys Harley, the phone at the café did not ring until five
minutes later. It is hard to know what to make of this. Either Miss
Alfreds was mistaken about hearing the voice on the line (which
seems unlikely: the answering voice was her cue to stop listening
and carry on with other calls); or, due to a mistake or a mechanical
defect, the call from Anfield 1627 was put through to a wrong
number.

Whatever the explanation for the failure to connect with the
café at the first attempt, by about 7.18 the caller was causing a
small commotion at the exchange, with Lilian Kelly so confused

by what he said that she was asking Miss Alfreds for assistance and shouting for the supervisor, Annie Robertson.

". . . I have pressed button A," the caller complained to Miss Kelly, "but have not had my correspondent yet."

An odd statement, this. Had he never used a public telephone before? Did he not know that there is no need to press button A to hear the correspondent?

What makes the statement even odder is the fact that he *had not* pressed button A at all. The automatic device at the exchange showed that he had pressed button B and received his money back.

One would have thought that a prospective murderer would have had more important things on his mind than the diddling of the G.P.O. of twopence. By saving himself twopence he made absolutely sure that the call was remembered, recorded.

It seems unbelievable that Wallace should have done such a thing. *But what if the caller was someone else?* What if it was someone who was thinking of killing two birds with one stone—setting in motion the plan for the crime he would commit the following night and at the same time throwing suspicion upon Wallace?

There are two possible reasons for the caller wanting to lay a false trail of suspicion towards Wallace. Revenge is one of them. If he knew Wallace and had been harmed by some action of Wallace's in the past, perhaps this was his idea of getting his own back. If so, then it was repayment a thousand times over.

The other possible reason, more practical and therefore more believable, is that he would have known that the most dangerous period for the perpetrator of a crime is the forty-eight hours or so directly following. If an investigation goes the wrong way at the start the criminal has good reason for feeling confident, because by the time the police get back to square one many of the clues have gone cold. The odds in favour of the criminal shorten with each hour that passes. Whoever was responsible for the killing of Julia Wallace was one of the most fastidious planners in the history of crime, and I think it is quite likely that the seemingly odd behaviour of the caller was an integral part of the plan, the criminal's method of insuring against unwelcome police interest during the early days of the investigation. The premiums were paid by Wallace.

As has been said, Hector Munro considers that the behaviour of the caller may be the most important point in the case. I am inclined to disagree with him, however.

I would say that a more important point is this—*that if Wallace*

*had made the call he would not have been able to get to the City Café
at the time he did.*

So much emphasis was placed upon the importance of the time-
factor on the night of the murder that it seems to have been forgotten that there was a time-factor on the Monday night as well.
Clearly, the police did not attach any importance to it; there were
no "tram tests" to establish how much time was needed to get
from the telephone-box to the City Café. At the trial it received
only two brief mentions: once when Harry Bailey agreed with
defence counsel that the journey *from the house* to the café would
take about half an hour—"or perhaps less"; and once during the
direct examination of Herbert Gold, who said that the journey
from the telephone-box to the café "would take twenty to twenty-
five minutes at the outside, from my experience on that route".

Just those two vague references; no more. Yet the time-factor
on the Monday evening was of paramount importance.

In examining it, there are two main times to be taken into consideration: the time the Qualtrough telephone-call ended and the
time of Wallace's arrival at the City Café.

We know that it was 7.15 when the caller first tried—if that is
the right word—to get through to the café; we know, too, that it
was 7.20 before he succeeded. This time is definite, recorded by
Annie Robertson in her notebook, which was produced as a case
exhibit.

Having got through, the caller had a short conversation with
Gladys Harley, and asked if Mr Wallace was there.

After telling the caller (who will be referred to as Qualtrough
from now on) to hold the line, the waitress put down the phone,
walked through to the section of the café reserved for the chess-
players, and spoke to Samuel Beattie, who listened to what she said,
looked round the room, told her that Wallace was not there, and
then agreed to speak to Qualtrough.

Beattie got up from the chess table and crossed to the phone.

His conversation with Qualtrough consisted of about two
hundred words; then he told Qualtrough to wait a moment while
he poked around in his pockets for a used envelope and a pencil;
having found them, he wrote the name as it was spelt out for him,
the address as it was dictated to him.

End of call.

How long did it take, from beginning to end? Even if everything
was done in jig-time, which it was not, the call must have lasted
at least four minutes. Say four. So the receiver was put down at

7.24—and if the caller was Wallace he then went rushing across to the tram-stop in Townsend Lane.

Now, how long would he have had to wait for a tram?[1]

Several writers have suggested that the answer to this question is: No time at all. They say that, while Wallace was talking to Beattie, he could have been watching for the arrival of the tram, and, as soon as he saw it coming, finished off the conversation and run to board it. This is all very well as a theory, but there are no facts to support it. The call was not truncated; the last part of it was taken up with spelling the name and dictating the address— and this was definitely not hurried. A further drawback to the theory is that, in order to accept it, one has to believe that Wallace either had wonderful hearing or the power to see around corners. From the call-box the tram-stop was visible, and so were a few yards of Townsend Lane beyond—but that was all.

Another suggestion is that Wallace could have found out the exact time of the tram's arrival by referring to a timetable. This is nonsense, too. Quite apart from the fact that tram and bus schedules are never more than approximate guides—affected by traffic conditions, the varying number of passengers, etc.—the tram schedules in Liverpool during the middle weeks of January 1931 were made meaningless by a subsidence in the Mersey Tunnel which caused traffic diversions and hold-ups in the centre of the city.

There was a tram service of 8–9 minutes on the route connecting Townsend Lane with North John Street. Therefore, if Wallace had left the call-box at 7.24 and been unlucky enough just to miss a tram, he would have had to wait until well after 7.30 before the next tram came along. But suppose fortune smiled upon him— that he crossed from the call-box to the tram-stop in a quarter of a minute and that he waited only three-quarters of a minute for a tram to take him to the City Café. A minute altogether. So he left Townsend Lane at 7.25.

Turning to the time of his arrival at the café, the first person to observe his presence there was James Caird, who afterwards stated, "I arrived at the City Café . . . at about twenty-five to eight. I saw Mr Wallace approximately ten minutes later."

Caird's estimate may be accepted. But the fact that he saw Wallace at about quarter to eight must not be taken to mean that he saw him as soon as he arrived.

---

[1] There is no doubt that Wallace travelled by tram. The only other means of transport—taxi-cab or private car—are ruled out for reasons so obvious that there is no need to state them.

On this Monday evening Wallace was due to play a match in the Second Class Championship. One of the club rules was that tournament matches had to begin by 7.45. "They might start earlier than that by arrangement," Beattie explained at the trial, "but you can penalize anyone if they do not start before a quarter to eight."

Wallace had a reputation for punctuality. Indeed, it was almost a fixation with him. Probably his favourite saying was the one about punctuality being the politeness of kings, the duty of gentlemen, and the necessity of men of business. He was always quoting it. Therefore, if Wallace was Qualtrough, it was almost as vital that he arrive in good time for his match as it was to get the telephone message through beforehand. If he kept his opponent waiting after the 7.45 deadline he would have a lot of explaining and apologizing to do—and his uncharacteristic unpunctuality would be remembered . . . would be turned into an important item of suspicion against him when the investigation into his wife's murder began.

As it happened, Wallace arrived at the café to find that Chandler, the man he was due to play, was not present. After chatting with James Caird, he arranged to play an outstanding match in the Second Class Championship with a Mr McCartney. The club rule concerning the pre-7.45 start still applied to this rearranged fixture, and at about 7.50, when Beattie went over to deliver the message, Wallace and McCartney were deeply involved in the game.

Almost certainly, then, Wallace was at the City Café before 7.45. The important question is: How much before? Surely no-one—not even the most ardent of anti-Wallaceites—can complain that two minutes is extravagant?

So now to the sum:

If Wallace waited only three-quarters of a minute for the tram at Townsend Lane, and if he arrived at the City Café at 7.43, the journey occupied eighteen minutes.

But the minimum time for the journey (indeed, one could go so far as to call it the all-time record for the journey, which even the "Anfield Harriers" could not have bettered) *was twenty-one minutes*.

In other words, Wallace could not have got from the telephone-box to the City Café in the time available.

The alleged alibi

It is necessary, first of all, to deal with two or three minor points made by the prosecution in support of the alibi theory.

1. During his cross-examination of Wallace, Hemmerde stated that Qualtrough could not have been sure of seeing Wallace leaving the house on the Tuesday evening, en route to Menlove Gardens—for the simple reason, he said, that Wallace sometimes left by the front door, sometimes by the back, and Qualtrough could not have watched both doors at once.

Ever since the trial this statement of Hemmerde's has been accepted as the truth; but, in fact, it is completely false.

Look at the plan of Wolverton Street.[1] By standing at the top of the entry between No. 19 and No. 21 (the end farthest from the street, where it meets the entry running behind the houses), Qualtrough would have had both exits covered: the back-yard door of No. 29 would have been fully visible to him; and, if Wallace had decided to leave by the front, Qualtrough would have seen him as he walked along the street and passed the bottom of the entry.

2. The prosecution made much of the suggestion that, if such a person as Qualtrough existed, he knew something of Wallace's business affairs—enough, anyway, to know that the most profitable time to rob Wallace of his insurance takings was during the week of the monthly return.

Cross-examining Wallace, Hemmerde said that "anyone knowing the nature of your business would know when your monthly collection would be . . . and if he was going to make a raid on your house and attack your wife alive, he would naturally choose the time of the monthly return".

It was assumed at the time, and has been assumed ever since (except, that is, by Prudential employees) that the monthly collection was made in the same week of each calendar month. If this were so, then a criminal, learning that the takings were heaviest in, say, the last week of each month, would be more likely to plan a robbery for that week than for any of the others. The fact is, though, that the phrase "monthly collection" was something of a misnomer: it was really a four-weekly collection. A look at Wallace's cash returns for 1930 shows that the heaviest amounts were collected in the weeks ending January 17th, April 11th, June 6th, August 1st, September 26th, December 18th. Of course, even though the dates varied, there were still plenty of people who would have known the exact date of his January 1931 monthly collection; but nowhere near as many as the prosecution made out.

3. The prosecution also suggested that Wallace said nothing

[1] See *Plans and Diagrams*, p. 312.

to Julia about the Qualtrough telephone message. In his closing speech Hemmerde asked the jury to suppose "that he had never told her he was going out. . . . Of course, if he planned this murder in the way suggested, you may be pretty sure he would not"—because he could then ask Julia to get the parlour ready for a musical evening, run upstairs, get undressed, run down again, don the mackintosh, tiptoe into the parlour—and kill. It was the only explanation the prosecution could devise for how the murder came to be committed in the parlour, a room that was used simply and solely for music and visitors. (No explanation was ever given, however, for why Wallace should have chosen the parlour as the scene of the crime rather than the kitchen.)

Although Amy Wallace's name appeared on the defence witness list, she was not called. Perhaps Roland Oliver was so concerned about the judge's Saturday deadline, so anxious not to offend Mr Justice Wright by calling evidence and taking up time on seemingly small points, that he forgot the part of her statement which read: "I called at 29 Wolverton Street on Tuesday afternoon. . . . Mrs Wallace told me that her husband had been down to Chess the night before, and had had a telephone message to go to see someone in the Calderstones district, but Mr Wallace did not know of anyone in that district, but she thought it was for business."

Here, then, is evidence that Wallace did tell his wife that he was going out that night. Although Julia was an odd sort of person in many ways, it seems hardly likely that, while Wallace was still in the house, she would have left the newspaper open on the kitchen table, as well as the needlework basket, the tea-things only partially cleared away, and walked into the parlour to play the piano on her own. But what other reason could she have had for going into that room—apart from entertaining a visitor who called while Wallace was away?

Hector Munro, a gentle, courteous man, normally slow to anger, gets tetchy very quickly when he hears people talking of "Wallace's alibi".

"I have never understood why people talk of an alibi in this case," he snaps. "In my opinion there was no alibi. If Wallace tried to concoct one, the concoction was hopelessly inadequate."

It was also, in several respects, unnecessarily feeble and poorly executed.

As has already been pointed out, Wallace was not observed until he arrived at Smithdown Road—yet the most vital part of any alibi is the beginning of it. Surely Wallace must have realized that the earlier he was seen, after leaving the house, the better? Why, then, did he wait at least seventeen minutes before speaking to anyone?

There was no need for all those inquiries in the Menlove Gardens area. If, as Hemmerde suggested he should have done, he had spoken to the policeman on point-duty at Penny Lane, or if he had restricted his inquiries to a couple of passers-by and then walked to the vicinity of Allerton Road Police Station and stopped one of the policemen entering or leaving the building, his presence in the area would have been established just as well—and without arousing any suspicion regarding over-persistence. It was not *how long* he remained in the area, but the fact that he was *there* which was the important factor. If he had got home, say, half an hour earlier, at about quarter past eight, he would have been away from the house an hour and a half—ample time for someone to have committed the crime . . . ample time for the purpose of an alibi.

The indications of robbery in the house were so paltry that the police at once assumed that they had been fabricated by Wallace to provide a false motive for the murder. But why on earth did he not make a better job of it? True enough, having killed his wife, he would have been anxious to get away as quickly as possible, to get started on the alibi—but it would not have taken more than a few seconds to remove the pound notes from the mantelpiece in the middle bedroom or to take the small amount of money from Julia's handbag; some robbery red herrings could have been planted before the murder was committed.

What indications of robbery were there? The police listed the following: the empty cash-box; the broken door of the locker in the kitchen; the smear of blood on the notes in the middle bedroom (not really an indication of robbery, but a sign that someone had picked them out of the pot and then replaced them); and the state of the bedclothes in the spare bedroom at the front of the house.

The only unequivocal signs of theft were in the kitchen—the cash-box and the broken door.

There was no conclusive evidence that the murderer had gone upstairs: the clot of blood on the lavatory-pan might have been dropped there during the first couple of hours of the investigation; the smear of blood on the notes in the middle bedroom might have been made after the discovery of the crime—either by Wallace (who handled them in the presence of P.C. Williams) or by one of the detectives; and, as Dorothy L. Sayers pointed out,[1] "the

[1] *Ibid.*

likeliest explanation of all [for the disorder in the front bedroom] is that the murderer never went there and had nothing to do with it. His ring at the door may have disturbed Mrs Wallace when she was engaged in turning over the bedding for some domestic purpose of her own. Perhaps she had piled the bedclothes and pillows on the foot of the bed, and they fell off, as they usually do in such circumstances. The appearance of the room, as described, is more suggestive of some such household accident than of a search by a thief."

(Miss Sayers's explanation does not take into account the three hats and two handbags on the bed. Perhaps, like most women, Julia enjoyed trying things on in front of a mirror, examining the reflection for the effect; and perhaps—not necessarily on the night of the murder, for the unused front bedroom may have been untidy for some time—she went into the room with the idea of making the bed, was distracted from the task by the lure of trying on hats[1] and looking at handbags, and was then interrupted by a caller.)

Since the only definite signs of theft were those found in the kitchen, and since a thief would have been solely concerned with the cash-box in which the insurance takings were kept, and since the discovery that the cash-box contained only a few pounds might well have prompted a thief to vent his feelings on something (*e.g.*, the door of the locker)—can it still be said, with any degree of confidence, that Wallace tried to fabricate evidence in support of a robbery motive?

Lastly, in this small selection of alibi-ineptitudes, it is necessary to consider the way Wallace acted on his return from Menlove Gardens (acted being the appropriate word if the prosecution theory was correct). As has been stated,[2] he had no way of knowing that the Johnstons were contemplating a visit to their daughter that night, so he could not rely upon his next-door neighbours witnessing his going into the house.

The prosecution made much of the fact that, when he first returned and was unable to get in, he did not call out or knock loudly at either of the doors. But this was really a point in Wallace's favour. Plainly, he had to have witnesses before he entered the house—equally plainly, his best method of obtaining them was to make a noise, so as to bring the neighbours out to discover who

[1] From Sarah Draper's statement: "Mrs Wallace used to have her hats spread out on the bed in the front room."

[2] See p. 92.

T

was causing the commotion, and why. It was not as if Wolverton Street was busy with passers-by; at that time of night the street might remain deserted for as long as an hour. Why, then, was he so discreet?

Another question: If, as the prosecution suggested, the difficulty with the locks was "so much play-acting", why did he not continue the performance when he had the Johnstons as audience? No great histrionic ability was required to *pretend* difficulty in opening the back door . . . yet he simply walked over to it, turned the handle, and murmured in a slightly surprised tone, "It opens now."

Turning to another aspect of the alibi theory, is it possible to explain why Wallace chose Tuesday night for his wife's murder and went to all the trouble of preparing an alibi—when, on the Monday night, he had as good an alibi, ready-made, less risky, far less likely to arouse suspicion afterwards, in his visit to the chess club?

On the Monday he could have killed Julia, fabricated some evidence of robbery, left for the chess club slightly earlier than usual—nothing very suspicious about that—played until after ten, got home round about eleven to 'discover' the murder, and from then on acted in the manner expected of a bereaved husband. Simplicity itself. Without the Qualtrough telephone-call, the police would almost certainly have assumed that the crime was committed by "the elusive Anfield house-breaker" or another of his fraternity.

It is hard to find a reason for Wallace preferring Tuesday to Monday . . . but what about Qualtrough? With Wallace away from the house for at least three hours on the Monday night, why did he not take the opportunity of committing the crime there and then, rather than going to all the bother of arranging for the coast to be clear the following night?

There are at least three possible reasons for this.

If robbery was the sole motive for the crime, and if Qualtrough knew that Wallace normally made his cash returns to the Prudential on Wednesday, it may be that he planned the crime for Tuesday night, when the insurance takings were at their peak.

The second possible reason is connected with the fact that Julia was nervous at the best of times, and especially so when left alone in the house at night. This would have made things extremely difficult for Qualtrough. Julia would certainly not open the door to a stranger—or to anyone, for that matter, unless she felt absolutely sure of his credentials. How, then, could Qualtrough gain admittance? By breaking and entering? Far too dangerous; the slightest suspicious sound, and Julia might start screaming for help.

No; an open-sesame was needed. And perhaps this was why the murderer chose to call himself Qualtrough. Qualtrough . . . an unusual name . . . a name that sticks in the mind. If Wallace mentioned it to Julia she was almost sure to remember it. And if, on the Tuesday night, someone called at the house—someone saying that his name was R. M. Qualtrough, that he had arranged to meet Mr Wallace but had been held up for some reason or other, and asking if he could wait for Mr Wallace's return, as the business matter he wanted to discuss was urgent, had to be settled at once—Julia, thinking of the commission her husband received on life and endowment policies, would invite him in.

The third possible reason is that if Qualtrough wanted to implicate Wallace, either for revenge or to lead police suspicion away from himself, the plan *had* to be set in motion on the Monday evening, the crime *had* to be committed on the Tuesday.

In the opening speech for the prosecution (and again, using different phrases, in the closing speech), Hemmerde said that Qualtrough, instead of sending the telephone message, "might have called at the house; you might have thought that he might have written to the house; he might have left a note at the house."

But this was a typical piece of prosecution double-think: Qualtrough would certainly not have wanted to put anything in writing and risk the chance of the missive being used in evidence (either against himself or in favour of Wallace's innocence); he would not have sent a telegram—telegrams are more easily traced than telephone-calls, and there was the risk of the post-office clerk remembering, and being able to describe, the person who handed it in; he would not have called at the house to leave a message—for so many, and for such obvious, reasons that there is no need to go into them; he would not have telephoned the Prudential head office: firstly, because whoever took the call would have wanted to know far more about the nature of the insurance business than a member of the chess club, and, secondly, because in order to make absolutely sure that Wallace received the message, that the person at the head office did not pass the information to the agent for the Allerton district, Qualtrough would have had to stress that he wanted to deal with Wallace and no-one else . . . and the only way to do this was to say that Wallace was a friend, or that they had done business together in the past—which would have made Wallace suspicious at once, since he had never even heard of the name, let alone met anyone called R. M. Qualtrough.

The message *had* to be sent by telephone: it was the only method available to Qualtrough. And the message had to be given to someone who would not ask any questions about it, but would simply take a note of the details and pass them on to Wallace—who, in turn, would assume that the brevity of the message was due to the caller not wanting to divulge too much about his private affairs to a person he did not know, and that "Qualtrough", a name he had never come across before, belonged to someone who was, perhaps, connected with one of his five hundred or so satisfied clients in Clubmoor. *The only opportunity* to deliver such a message, in such a way, was when Wallace visited the Central Chess Club.

If one accepts either or both of the two possibilities—(1) that the criminal wanted to involve Wallace, and/or (2) that the name Qualtrough was the password into 29 Wolverton Street—*then one must also accept that the plan had to be set in motion on a night when Wallace played chess and that the crime had to be committed the following night.* Supposing that the motive for the murder was financial gain, then the criminal was unconcerned with the date of the monthly collection: if it coincided with the date of Wallace's attendance at the club, that was all to the good—but if not, there was nothing to be done about it.

Before passing on to what is perhaps the most important point against the alibi theory, it must be said that Hemmerde was talking nonsense when he suggested—as he did several times during the trial—that Qualtrough could have telephoned the club later in the evening to find out if Wallace had arrived and been given the message.

A look at Hemmerde's references to Qualtrough reveals that Wallace's prosecutor was guilty not only of double-thinking, but of treble-thinking: often within the space of a few sentences, working like a dresser for a quick-change artiste, Hemmerde presented Qualtrough as an innocent prospective insurant; as Wallace in disguise; and, fleetingly, as an unknown criminal. But thinking of Qualtrough in the last of these roles, is it likely— feasible even—that he would have made a second call to the City Café to check whether or not the message had been delivered?

Wallace stated that he left home on the Monday evening at "about 7.15", and it was at this time that Louisa Alfreds took the call from Anfield 1627. It seems virtually certain, then, that

Qualtrough watched Wallace leave the house and then hurried to the call-box. The message had to be waiting for Wallace when he arrived at the café; the success of the plan depended upon the message being given to Wallace second-hand by someone who could not answer any questions about it. Having seen Wallace leave the house, Qualtrough could feel confident that he was on the way to the chess club; and the last thing in the world he would do would be to ring up later to make sure.

Imagine what might have happened if he had. "Is Mr Wallace there?" Qualtrough asks. "Hold on while I find out," says the person who has answered. (And probably adds, "Who is calling?" A reasonable question, but a difficult one for Qualtrough to answer. Perhaps he gets round it by mumbling, "I'd rather not say." One thing is certain—he does not reply, "R. M. Qualtrough.") Anyway, the person at the café puts the receiver on the ledge and goes to look for Wallace. This leaves Qualtrough with three choices: he can hang up; he can hold on and hope that the next words he hears are "Yes, Mr Wallace is here—shall I tell him you want to speak to him?" (in which case, all that Qualtrough can say is: "No, it doesn't matter. Thanks very much," and ring off); or he can hold on and, if Wallace's voice comes on the line, hang up at once.

He dare not talk to Wallace. Even if he is versatile enough to pretend to be someone other than Qualtrough, ingenious enough to invent another excuse for calling, Wallace is going to be suspicious. In all his years as a member of the chess club he has never received a telephone-call, and now two people ring up on the same night—there must be something odd going on. A Qualtrough-Wallace conversation is unthinkable: Wallace will ask too many awkward questions—the most awkward being "We have never met—so why is it that, among all the insurance agents in Liverpool, you choose me to handle your business?"

No; Qualtrough would certainly not have telephoned a second time. But considering the intricacy of the plan, all the thought that went into it, is it unreasonable to suggest that he might have gone to the trouble of making the journey to North John Street that night? He could have been waiting outside the City Café to see Wallace when he left; indeed, rather than hang around until after ten, there was no reason why he should not have walked into the café to see if Wallace was there. Wallace, engrossed in his game, was hardly likely to have noticed him—and it would not have mattered to Qualtrough if he *had* been noticed, since there was nothing to connect him with the telephone-call. Having made assurance double sure (he could feel 99 per cent certain that the message had been passed on by Beattie), he could have gone to bed, to sleep, perchance to dream, of what would happen the following night.

A point which was practically ignored at the trial, and which has received no mention since, is that Wallace's so-called alibi was completely dependent upon the evidence of the milk boy, Alan Close. If Close had not called at the house and seen Julia alive at whatever time it was—somewhere between half-past six and twenty to seven—Wallace would have had no alibi at all. There is doubt concerning the boy's veracity as a witness, but no doubt whatever that he delivered the milk some time after half-past six, proving that the maximum time at Wallace's disposal for committing the murder and clearing up afterwards was only eighteen minutes.

It has always been assumed—and, indeed, it *has* to be assumed, if the alibi theory is to hold water—that, if Wallace was the murderer, the time of the milk delivery was an integral part of his plan to kill Julia and get away with it.

An alibi is "a plea which avers that the accused was in another place at the time of the commission of the offence, and therefore cannot be guilty". Clearly, Wallace could not provide himself with an alibi as water-tight as the legal definition demands: all he could hope to do was (a) imply that some other person, either mythical or real, was guilty of the offence, (b) invent an excuse for being in another place at a time proximate to the offence, (c) after committing the offence, leave the scene as quickly as possible and establish his presence in another place at the earliest possible moment, and (d) commit the offence and destroy the connecting evidence *in a period of time so short as to suggest that, though not impossible, it was unlikely that he could have completed the task in the time available.*

Now suppose that, for some reason or other, Alan Close had not called at the house that night, would Wallace still have carried out the plan to murder his wife?

The answer, surely, is: No, definitely not.

No milk would have meant no time-factor. The last person to have seen Julia alive would have been Neil Norbury, the baker's boy, at half-past four. Wallace would have returned from work at about five minutes past six; with no-one calling at the house after that time, he would have had nearly *three-quarters of an hour* (until 6.49) in which to commit the murder. Three-quarters of an hour—long enough, and allowing for a tea-break, for him to have committed half a dozen murders, if the victims had been available and if he had felt so inclined.

Can it be said, then—and with confidence—that

(1) Alan Close was more important to the plan than either of the tram conductors, any of the people who spoke to Wallace in Menlove Gardens, or the Johnstons;

(2) Wallace knew, or assumed, that the milk boy always started delivering at the same time after coming home from school and having his tea, always followed the same route, and therefore always arrived in Wolverton Street at about the same time each evening, never varying more than five minutes or so either way;

(3) Wallace worked out how quickly he could commit the murder and tidy up afterwards . . . he also worked out the time needed to get from Wolverton Street to Menlove Gardens . . . he then added the two periods together—murder and tidying-up plus travelling—and added the sum period to *the latest time* he expected the milk boy to call and speak to Julia, thus arriving at the final and vital answer: the time of the appointment with Qualtrough;

(4) if the milk boy had not called at all on the Tuesday, or if he had called before five minutes past six or within a few minutes of the time Wallace returned from Clubmoor, Wallace would not have carried out the murder-plan, for without the time-factor his alibi was so tenuous as to be almost non-existent?

Can all this be said with confidence? (Remember, before answering, what Mr Justice Wright said—that if Wallace was the murderer he could have done all the things that needed to be done in the short time available to him—maybe less than ten minutes—only if he had given the matter a lot of thought and done some preparation beforehand. And remember, too, that if Wallace had not *expected* the milk boy to call he would have murdered Julia long before; he would not have considered giving much, if any, thought to a tidying-up timetable.)

I think all fair-minded readers must agree that at least three of the four points are indisputable. I shall assume that, anyway—and go on to ask, how is it possible to reconcile those points with the following facts:

The usual time for the milk delivery to 29 Wolverton Street was about six o'clock. (This is Alan Close's own estimate.)

Normally, Close used a bike for the milk round.

The reason for his being half an hour later than usual on the evening of Tuesday, January 20th, is that, the day before, something had gone wrong with the front wheel of the bike, making it unrideable, and he had to deliver the milk on foot.

But for the bike being out of order, he would have called at 29 Wolverton Street while Wallace was on his way home from work.

That there was any time-factor at all was completely fortuitous. But for a few bent bicycle spokes, Wallace's "alibi"—and it truly deserves those inverted commas—would not have been worth the twopence saved from the telephone-call.

[2]

If Wallace didn't do it, who did?

This question became almost a catch-phrase in Liverpool during the first few months of 1931. It was asked so often, and by so many people, that it even came to the ears of Mr Justice Wright, who deemed it necessary to warn the jury:

". . . The question is not: Who did this crime? The question is: Did the prisoner do it?—or, rather, to put it more accurately: Is it proved to your reasonable satisfaction and beyond all reasonable doubt that the prisoner did it? It is a fallacy to say: 'If the prisoner did not do it, who did?' "

The question was asked rhetorically, of course. And still is. Most people, while agreeing that Wallace had no apparent motive for killing his wife, are unable to think of a good enough reason for anyone else doing it.

The defence suggested robbery as the motive; and certainly the evidence of the rifled cash-box, the broken door of the locker, lent support to this theory. But it was pooh-poohed by the prosecution. Was it likely, they asked, that anyone would commit murder for a few pounds?

As a matter of fact, it was; it is. There are any number of examples of murders being committed for ridiculously small sums, shillings sometimes. I have not done any research on the subject, but I think it would be true to say that the majority of murderers for gain receive incommensurate reward for their troubles—or rather, *apparently* incommensurate reward. If a man is broke a fiver seems like a fortune.

In any event, the murderer in the Wallace case may have anticipated finding far more in the cash-box than was actually there. The fact that he got away with only a few pounds does not mean that he did not expect more. Normally, the cash-box would have contained perhaps £30, and if the crime had happened during the week of the monthly collection at least twice as much. To say that the motive for the murder cannot have been robbery because the reward was too small is like saying that an organized gang of criminals who blow open a safe, only to find it empty, are nothing more than vandals.[1]

So the robbery motive must not be ruled out.

And neither must the sex motive. Just because Julia was middle-aged, unattractive to most men, does not necessarily mean that she was undesirable to *all* of them. Indeed, to a pervert, to a man whose Oedipus complex had gone completely haywire in a mess of distorted sexual urges, the very fact that she *was* middle-aged and unattractive might have made her irresistibly desirable.

Murders have been committed for the oddest of reasons. Sometimes (and the crime of Leopold and Loeb is a case in point) for no reason at all . . . at least, for no reason connected with the individual victim. Like climbers who scale mountains "because they are there", some murderers have killed simply to prove that it could be done, or have slain for the sheer thrill of it, the experience.

Wallace himself thought he knew the answer to the question: If he didn't do it, who did?

Two days after the murder he made a statement to Inspector Gold, naming the people "who would be admitted by my wife without hesitation if they called while I was out". Contradicting Yseult Bridges again, this was not an "attempt to divert suspicion from himself to a colleague"; Wallace gave this information at the request of Gold.

Asked if he suspected any of the fifteen men he had named, Wallace hesitated a moment, then proceeded to tell the inspector what he knew about one of them (whom I shall refer to as Mr X).

Wallace described him as being "a single man . . . rather foppish appearance, well-dressed and very plausible". Wallace said that Mr X "had called at my house on business and left a letter for me which he wrote in my front room. I was not in at the time, but my wife let him in. While he was doing my work . . . he called very frequently, and he was well acquainted with our domestic arrange-

---

[1] If robbery *was* the motive it helps to explain the contrast between the immaculate conception of the plan and the messy method of murder.

ments. Mr X knew my system of paying in money collected to the Hd. Office. . . . He knew I kept the money in the box, because . . . I always put the money into it when he called to pay over to me his collection."

Wallace knew that Mr X was either careless with money or dishonest. And so did a personal acquaintance, who had discovered that he was collecting payments from certain clients and not including the cash in the returns to his employer. He had spoken to Mr X's parents, and they had paid the deficiency. When Mr X was doing part of Wallace's collection in Clubmoor as a favour, Wallace had noticed mistakes in the accounts; he had pointed them out to Mr X and been told that "it was an oversight", but later, noting further discrepancies, he had been forced to inform Mr X's employers. Mr X had been given the choice of resigning or getting the sack; he had chosen the former.

"I have often seen him since he has been working for his new Company, and have spoken to him," Wallace stated. The last of these encounters took place shortly before the murder: a very brief encounter—"I said good evening and he returned my greeting."

It took place at the City Café, on an evening when the chess club was occupying one part of the premises and a society, of which Mr X was a member, was using another.

As well as visiting the City Café for meetings of the society, Mr X frequently lunched there.

Wallace made his statement to Gold on Thursday morning, January 22nd. Later that day he was told that the police were satisfied that Mr X had no connection with the murder, since he had a perfect alibi, supported by the testimony of a person who was in his company the whole of the Tuesday evening.

But, perfect alibi or no perfect alibi, Wallace was still not satisfied. During the next few months he had plenty of time to think. And the more he thought about the motive for the murder, the identity of the murderer, the more suspicious he became of Mr X.

After his release from prison he learned a couple of additional facts concerning the man. First, that he was more than usually hard-up at the time of the murder—heavily in debt and pleading with friends for financial aid; second, that he had a police record.

On September 14th, 1931, Wallace wrote in his diary:

"Just as I was going to dinner, Mr X stopped me, and said he wanted to talk to me for a few minutes. It was a desperately awkward position. Eventually I decided not to hear what he had to say. I told him I would talk to him some day and give him something to think about. He must realize that I suspect him of the terrible crime. I fear I let him see clearly what I thought, and it may unfortunately put him on his guard. I wonder if it is any good putting a private detective on to his track in the hope of something coming to light. I am more than half persuaded to try it."

But he never did. And, as far as is known, he never found out any more about Mr X.

What else is known about the man?

Quite a lot. For instance:

His criminal record was longer, more varied, than Wallace thought. Both before January 1931 and afterwards he was charged with theft, causing malicious damage, embezzlement, and indecent assault. (In one of the cases of indecent assault the girl stated that he threatened to murder her; a medical witness at the trial described him as "a sexual pervert".)

Regarding his alibi, when interviewed by the police (less than forty-eight hours after the murder) he said that he had spent an innocent Tuesday evening in the company of friends, one of whom he named. Separately interviewed, the friends confirmed that this was so. But two years later it was admitted that this was a mistake. If the police had investigated properly they would have discovered that it was quite impossible for them to have been together.

The police were satisfied that Mr X was innocent, and therefore no charge was preferred. But the fact that the police appear not to have bothered to test the strength of the alibi indicates that they were not interested in finding other suspects. It is all very well for people with ombuds-mentalities to say that a person's past mistakes should not be held against him, but when a man named as a possible suspect has a criminal record, any alibi he puts forward should not only be checked, but double-checked—treble-checked, if necessary.

When Wallace mentioned his suspicions about Mr X, the Liverpool police already had a suspect—Wallace himself. They did not want any others; that would only have complicated things for them.

Mr X was not the only person named by Wallace whose antecedents and actions on the night of the murder should have been investigated. Another man mentioned in the statement, one of Wallace's business acquaintances, may have had any, or all, of three motives for the crime—financial gain, revenge, and/or sex. He knew that Wallace was a member of the Central Chess Club, and, as a habitué of the City Café, could have looked at the notice-board to see when Wallace was due to play a match. He knew of Wallace's insurance business; he knew where the cash was kept. Unknown to Wallace, he was an occasional visitor at 29 Wolverton Street, where Julia accompanied him in musical duets. Since the case he has claimed two entirely different alibis for the night of the murder. This man was never interviewed by the police.

The men I have mentioned were no more than people of whom Wallace was suspicious; but should not suspicion have been further investigated? Justice should have been seen to be done—even if only to allay doubts, and in the interest of justice to Wallace.

Within the framework of the Wallace case are several separate tragedies. The senseless killing of an innocent woman—that, of course, is one of them; another is the way in which Wallace was martyred, not only during the case but afterwards, until the day he died; there is the tragedy of prejudice sneering at justice, spitting in its blind face; and there is the tragedy of a mishandled investigation: tragic twice over, for by expending all their energies on building the case against Wallace, the investigators probably ignored or overlooked evidence that would have established the identity of the true culprit.

Afterword

*He was part of my dream, of course—but
then I was part of his dream, too!*

Legend is more pliable, and therefore more durable, than truth.
In Liverpool, over the years, the stories about Wallace and the
murder of his wife have flourished and produced fresh tubers,
pretty new leaves; but by now there is little truth left—a
few stunted remnants of the past reality, that is all. Mention the
Wallace case to people old enough to remember it, even to some
who are not, and you will be told about "the other woman in the
case" (and perhaps, if you're lucky, get a description of her:
". . . blondish, quite nice-looking, used to shop in Lewis's . . .");
and you will be told about "Wallace's confession to a Catholic
priest, who was bound by oath to keep it secret"; and you will hear
that "Julia, the day before she died, pleaded with a neighbour
for protection—she had a feeling, you see, a premonition if you
like, that her husband wanted her out of the way". And goodness
knows what else. Talk to people in clubs and pubs and cafés, and
you will almost certainly be told that "Wallace did it . . . he was
arrested and convicted, but got off on a technicality . . . he was a
clever one—cleverer than the police, anyway". The most charitable
words you are likely to hear are: "Wallace deserved to get away
with it."

Many of the main characters in the case are now either dead or
no longer living in Liverpool.

Just before the last war Joseph Wallace retired from his post
with the Malayan Government. Returning to England, he went to
live at Ulverston, on the Furness Peninsula. He took Amy with
him. He died at Ulverston in 1950, only a few miles from where
he and his brother were born; Amy outlasted him by nearly ten
years. Their son Edwin, a doctor in the Colonial Service, died in
North Borneo, the day after Christmas, 1960; he left an estate

valued at about £30,000 to his wife and children, who now live in South Wales.

On the night of June 19th, 1940, a month before the Battle of Britain began, a large force of German bombers was intercepted over East Anglia by aircraft from No. 23 Squadron, stationed at Sutton Bridge, Lincolnshire. There were heavy losses on both sides. Among the British losses was a Blenheim night fighter piloted by Sergeant Alan Croxton Close. The gunner parachuted to safety, but Alan Close was still at the controls when the aircraft crashed in flames near King's Lynn. He was twenty-three.

Professor MacFall died in September 1938, three years after marrying his chauffeuse-cum-secretary, Miss Florence Brook. The Chair of Forensic Medicine at Liverpool University has remained vacant.

Despite some quite formidable lobbying for his promotion, Hubert Moore was still a superintendent when he retired from the police force in 1939, having completed forty years' service and collected the same number of commendations. Fortified with the rites of the Holy Catholic Church, he died in hospital in 1951.

Five years after the Wallace case Herbert Gold left the police force to work in the investigation department of Littlewood's, the Liverpool pools firm. At the start of the war he moved to the Wiltshire village of Christian Malford, where he commanded the local Home Guard. He died in 1963.

Like Gold, Harry Bailey joined Littlewood's when he retired from the police force in 1935. He was still working for the firm in 1950, when he died of a cerebral haemorrhage at the age of sixty-five. (A few months after the Wallace case he told Sydney Scholefield Allen: "When I retire I'll tell you something about the investigation that will interest you immensely." From the way Bailey spoke, Scholefield Allen gathered that, whatever the something was, it would be well worth waiting to hear; but, unfortunately, he never met Bailey again.)

In the middle 1950s, Dr Robert Coope was making a ward round at Broad Green Hospital, Liverpool, when a grey-haired man stood up at the side of one of the beds and came over to him.

"It's Dr Coope, isn't it?" the man asked.

Coope studied the man's face, trying to place it.

"I doubt if you'll remember me," the man said. "The last time we met I looked very different. I was a young red-headed policeman then."

It was Fred Williams, the first policeman to arrive at 29 Wolverton Street on the night of the murder. Looking at him, Coope could see that he was very ill; he led Williams back to his bed.

"I want to talk to you about the Wallace case," Williams said. "There's a lot I can tell you." Then, his voice weak but insistent, he said, "That man was innocent."

Coope arranged to discuss the case with Williams when he next visited the hospital. But that same night he himself was taken ill with an influenzal infection and was confined to bed for three weeks. As soon as he was fit again he went back to Broad Green Hospital and into the ward where he had met Williams. But Williams was gone. The ward sister told Coope that he had died a fortnight before.

Dr Coope still wonders what it was that Williams was so anxious to tell him, what his reason was for saying that Wallace was innocent. Semi-retired now, and living in a townsman's dream of a house at Long Compton, Warwickshire, he has kept the notebooks in which are recorded his experiments in the Wallace case; they are like works of art: perfect in their completeness, the handwriting exquisite, the illustrations in red and black ink like surrealist miniatures. A frequent visitor at the house is Coope's best and oldest friend, Professor James Henry Dible; and whenever Coope comes down to London for medical tribunals he stays at Dible's Georgian home in Gerrard's Cross. Professor Dible, who is now recognized in the medical profession as the doyen of British pathologists, is at present engaged in work for the Cancer Research Institute.

The year after presiding at the Wallace trial Mr Justice Wright was created a Life Peer; he took the title of Lord Wright of Durley. From 1935 to 1937 he was Master of the Rolls. He died in 1964 at the ripe old age of ninety-five.

A few years before his death, in an interview with a *Liverpool Echo* reporter, he said:

"Never forget that Wallace was a chess player. . . . I should say that, broadly speaking, any man with common sense would have said that Wallace's alibi was too good to be true, but that is not an argument you can hang a man on. So many strange things happen in life. I should not, and never did, demand a motive for any crime. Very often, the motive is merely impulse, and you must remember that Wallace was a highly-strung man. But if Wallace did murder his wife, as the jury thought, there might have been a motive. . . . After his trial the station-master at Birkenhead Station mentioned the case to me as I waited for a train. He said it was the opinion of the people in the district that there was another woman in the case. That certainly never came out at the trial. But at the time I could not help thinking that Wallace found domestic felicity a little boring, as it is apt to be occasionally to anybody."

In 1934, Edward Hemmerde patched up his troubles with the Liverpool Corporation, and from then on lived a comparatively quiet existence, sharing his time between Liverpool and London. He even managed to sort out most of his financial worries. In the middle 1940s, however, in common with several other members of the Bar, Hemmerde was caught up in the blackmailing activities of a lady who was at that time calling herself Josephine O'Dare. Miss O'Dare's favourite 'bites' were barristers, and it is said that at least one of her legal victims was forced to increase his fees in order to meet her demands. Luckily for Hemmerde, Miss O'Dare passed away—suddenly, mysteriously—before she could really put the pressure on him; her passing did nothing to increase the sales of black crêpe in the vicinity of Lincoln's Inn.

Hemmerde never swerved from his belief that Wallace was guilty. In his later years he became very friendly with Hector and May Munro. "I often discussed the Wallace case with him," Munro says, "but I could never ascertain any reason for supposing that his conviction about Wallace's guilt was based on rational grounds, and I used to tell him so."

Hemmerde died in harness. On Saturday, May 24th, 1948, while working on a brief in his London chambers, he complained of feeling unwell and was taken to his flat in Knightsbridge. Within hours, following a heart seizure, he was dead.

For Roland Oliver, Hemmerde's adversary at the Wallace trial, the next few years were extremely busy ones (especially 1932, when he appeared as counsel for the Bishop of Norwich in the protracted action to defrock "the sexy old Rector of Stiffkey"). In 1938, Oliver was knighted and appointed to the bench. He frequently presided at the Liverpool Assizes . . . but could never enter the court, he said, without thinking of the Wallace trial— "that nightmare of a case". After retiring in 1957 he lived quietly at his home in Ashford, Kent, devoting much of his time to his hobby of carpentry and to playing the violin (with far greater success than Wallace ever achieved). He died on March 14th, 1967.

Of the two junior counsel at the trial, Leslie Walsh is now Stipendiary Magistrate for Salford; Sydney Scholefield Allen is Recorder of Blackburn, and, since 1945, has been a Q.C. and Labour M.P. for Crewe, Hemmerde's old seat.

Hecto Munro is now senior partner in the firm of Herbert J. Davis, Berthen and Munro. These days, most of his time is taken up with the study and practice of International Law, reading and re-reading the works of Dickens and Joyce, and playing chess.

The Central Chess Club still exists, and Hector Munro is still a member; but the meetings are less frequent now—few people attend them.[1]

The basement of 24 North John Street, once the premises of the City Café, is now, and has been since 1939, a men's clothing shop. The large room is still divided in four, as it was at the time of the Wallace case, and you can still see some of the wall plaques which formed part of the decoration of the café. Only in the last few years has the telephone—Bank 3581—been replaced by one of more modern design. Goodness knows what has happened to the old telephone: it has probably been broken up; but if not, then any collector of *objets de crime* would give a very fair price for such an evocative instrument.

For a year or two after the murder, people used to come from all over Liverpool, and some from much farther afield, to look at 29 Wolverton Street. The new tenants, after Wallace moved to Bromborough, soon got tired of having people staring through the front window into the parlour; taking advantage of a story that Julia's ghost had been seen, they devised a ghoulish method of keeping steam off the glass.

A retired Anfield police constable relates that he was on the beat in Richmond Park one night and decided to have a look at the scene of the crime. "I went soon after midnight. I shone my torch through the front-room window—and nearly fainted. Lying on the hearthrug was a large doll, just in the same position that Julia lay. Someone had cut the doll's throat apparently with a knife, and a quantity of sawdust was scattered on the rug. I never went near the window again!"

It would seem that these tenants did not stay very long. A few months after the doll episode another policeman on night duty in the area was stopped by a man in the street. "He asked me if I would change the particulars of the keeper of keys of a local butcher's shop, as he had taken over and come to live at 29 Wolverton Street. I asked him if he knew anything of the history of the house, and he replied that he didn't. He stated that the only strange thing was that he got the tenancy easily, but he seemed unperturbed, and lived on there for some time."

[1] Since this was written the club has been disbanded.

Today the house looks much the same as it did in 1931. So does the rest of the street. And so, for that matter, does the whole of Anfield. The old St Margaret's Church is not there any more; it was burnt down a few years ago, and now a smaller church has been built on the same site. Added to the skyline are the tall floodlights around the football ground. There is still a patch of waste land at the bottom of Wolverton Street; the Holy Trinity Church clock still keeps excellent time; and in the early evening, although there are no milk boys now, the area seems to be over-run by small boys with large sacks of *Liverpool Echos* on their shoulders.

In Anfield Cemetery, Qualtrough's two victims share a common grave. It is difficult to find. The grass is high around it, and the weeds. The inscriptions on the plain stone surround are not easily read:

In loving and affectionate remembrance of Julia
Beloved wife of W. H. Wallace

In loving memory of William Herbert Wallace

R.I.P.

Appendix

*Statement volunteered to Detective-Inspector Gold
at about midnight on Tuesday, January 20th, 1931.*

Anfield Detective Office

WILLIAM HERBERT WALLACE says: I am 52 years & by occupation an Insurance Agent for the Prudential Assurance Co., Dale St. I have resided at 29 Wolverton Street with my wife Julia (deceased) age believed 52 years, for the past 16 years. There is no children of the marriage. My wife & I have been on the best of terms all our married life. At 10.30 A.M. today I left the house, leaving my wife indoors, doing her household duties. I went on my Insurance round in Clubmoor District, my last call being 177 Lisburn Lane shortly before 2 P.M. I then took a tram car to Trinity Church, Breck Rd., arriving at my house at 2.10 P.M. My wife was then well & I had dinner & left the house at about 3.15 P.M. I then returned to Clubmoor & continued my collections, finished about 5.55 P.M., my last caller being either 19 or 21 Eastman Rd. I boarded a bus at Queens Drive & Townsend Avenue, alighted at Cabbage Hall & walked up to my house at about 6.5 P.M. I entered my house by back door, which is my usual practice, & then had tea with my wife, who was quite well, & then I left home at 6.45 P.M., leaving by the back door. I caught a car from Belmont Rd. and West Derby Road and got off at Lodge Lane & Smithdown Rd. & boarded a Smithdown Rd. car to Penny Lane. I then boarded another car up Menlove Avenue West, looking for 25 Menlove Avenue East, where I had an appointment with Mr. R. M. Qualtrough for 7.30 P.M. in connection with my Insurance business. I was unable to find the address & I then enquired at 25 Menlove Avenue West, & I also asked at the bottom of Green Lane, Allerton, a Constable, about the address. He told me there was no such an address. I then called at a Post Office near the Plaza Cinema, to look at the Directory, but there was none there, & I was unable to find the address. I also visited a newsagent where there was a directory but I was unable to find the address. It was then 8.0 P.M. & I caught a tram car to Lodge Lane & then a car to West Derby Rd. & Belmont Rd. & walked home from there.

I arrived at Wolverton Street about 8.45 P.M. & I pulled out my key & went to open the front door & found it secure & could not open it with my key. I knocked gentle but got no answer. I could not see any light in the house. I then went round the back, the door leading from the entry to the back yard was closed, but not bolted. I went to the back door of the house & I was unable to get in. I do not know if the door was bolted or not, it sticks sometimes, but I think the door was bolted but I am not sure. There was a small light in the back kitchen, but no light in the kitchen. I then went back to the front, and I was suspicious because I expected my wife to be in & the light was on in the kitchen. I tried my key in the front door again & found the lock did not work properly. The key would turn in it but seem to unturn without unlocking the door. I rushed around to the back & saw my neighbours Mr. & Mrs. Johnston, coming out of 31 Wolverton St. I said to them "Have you heard any suspicious noises in my house during the past hour or so?" Mrs. Johnston said they hadn't. I said then I couldn't get in & they said they would wait a while, while I tried again. I then found the back kitchen door opened quite easily. I walked in by the back kitchen door. I found kitchen light out. I lit it and found signs of disturbance in the kitchen. A locker in which I keep photographic stuff in had been broken open & the till was on the floor. I then went upstairs & entered the middle bedroom, but saw nothing unusual. I then entered the bathroom but it was correct. I then entered the back room & found no disturbance there. I then entered the front room, struck a match, & found the bed upset, the clothes being off. I don't think my wife left it like that. I then came down & looked into the front room, after striking a match, & saw my wife lying on the floor. I felt her hand and concluded she was dead.

I then rushed out and told Mr. and Mrs. Johnston what had happened, saying something, but I cannot remember what I did say. After my neighbours had been in, Mr. Johnston went for the Police & a Doctor. I asked him to go.

I afterwards found that about £4 had been taken from a cash box in the kitchen, but I am not sure of the amount.

When I discovered my wife lying on the floor I noticed my mackintosh lying on the floor at the back of her. I wore the mackintosh up to noon today, but left it off owing to the fine weather. My wife has never worn the mackintosh to my knowledge. You drew my attention to it being burnt, but it was not like that when I last saw it & I cannot explain it. I have no suspicion of anyone.

(Sgd) William Herbert Wallace.

There was a dog whip with a lash in the house which I have not seen for 12 months, but I have not found it up to now. It was usually hung on the hall stand. The handle was of wood 12″ long & 1 inch thick. I don't think there was any metal about it.

Bibliography

AGATE, J.: *Ego 6* (Harrap, 1944).

BREND, W. A.: *A Handbook of Medical Jurisprudence and Toxicology* (Griffin; 8th edition, 1941).

BRIDGES, Y.: *Two Studies in Crime* (Hutchinson, 1959).

BROPHY, J.: *The Meaning of Murder* (Whiting & Wheaton, 1966).

CHANDLER, R.: *Raymond Chandler Speaking* (Hamish Hamilton, 1962).

COBB, G. B.: *Trials–and Errors* (W. H. Allen, 1962).

DUKE, W.: *Skin for Skin* (Gollancz, 1935); *Six Trials* (Gollancz, 1934).

FIRMIN, S.: *Crime Man* (Hutchinson, 1950).

GILES, F. T.: *The Criminal Law* (Penguin, 1954); *The Magistrates' Courts* (Penguin, 1949).

GLAISTER, J., and RENTOUL, E.: *Medical Jurisprudence and Toxicology* (Livingstone; 11th edition, revised 1962).

GLAISTER, J., and SMITH, Sir S. A.: *Recent Advances in Forensic Medicine* (Churchill, 1931).

HEMM, G.: *St. George's Hall, Liverpool* (Northern Publishing Co., 1949).

HEWART, Lord: *Not Without Prejudice* (Hutchinson, 1937).

JACKSON, R.: *The Chief* (Harrap, 1959).

JACKSON, R. M.: *The Machinery of Justice in England* (Cambridge; 4th edition, 1964).

LUSTGARTEN, E.: *Verdict in Dispute* (Wingate, 1949).

McCORMICK, H. O., ROSS, J. L., and NEARY, L. W.: *Elements of Interrogation* (Sacramento, 1949).

MACFALL, J. E. W. (Ed.): *Buchanan's Text-book of Forensic Medicine and Toxicology* (Livingstone; 9th edition, 1925).

MARTIN, K.: *Editor* (Hutchinson, 1968).

MOISEIWITSCH, M.: *Five Famous Trials (with Commentaries by Lord Birkett)* (Heinemann; new edition, 1964).

MORLAND, N.: *Background to Murder* (Werner Laurie, 1955).

PALMER, H. A., and PALMER, H.: *Wilshere's Criminal Procedure* (Sweet and Maxwell; 3rd edition, 1954).

PRENDERGAST, W.: *Z-Car Detective* (John Long, 1964).

REANEY, P. H.: *A Dictionary of British Surnames* (Routledge and Kegan Paul, 1958).

ROUGHEAD, W.: *Tales of the Criminous* (Cassell, 1956).

ROWLAND, J.: *The Wallace Case* (Carroll and Nicholson, 1949).

SAYERS, D. L.: Article in *The Anatomy of Murder* (The Bodley Head, 1936).

SIMPSON, K.: *Forensic Medicine* (Arnold; 5th edition, 1964).

SODERMAN, H., and O'CONNEL, J. J.: *Modern Criminal Investigation* (Funk and Wagnalls: Mayflower; revised edition, 1952).

SHEW, E. S.: *A Second Companion to Murder* (Cassell, 1961).

VAN DRUTEN, J.: *The Widening Circle* (Heinemann, 1957).

VEALE, F. J. P.: *William Herbert Wallace* (Merrymeade, 1950).

WELLMAN, F. L.: *The Art of Cross-Examination* (Collier, U.S.A., 1962).

WHITTINGTON-EGAN, R.: *Liverpool Colonnade* (Philip, Son & Nephew, 1955); *Tales of Liverpool Murder, Mayhem and Mystery* (Gallery Press, 1967).

WILLIAMS, G.: *The Proof of Guilt* (Stevens & Sons; 2nd edition, 1958).

WILSON, C., and PITMAN, P.: *Encyclopaedia of Murder* (Barker, 1961).

WRIGHT, Lord: *Legal Essays and Addresses* (Cambridge, 1939).

WYNDHAM-BROWN, W. F.: *The Trial of William Herbert Wallace* (Gollancz, 1933).

General works of reference, pamphlets, and documents consulted were:

Annual Register; Criminal Appeal Reports (Vol. 23); Criminal Statistics, England and Wales (H.M.S.O.); documents belonging to Herbert J. Davis, Berthen & Munro; documents belonging to the Prudential Staff Union; *Hansard; Liverpool and District Post Office Guide, 1928; Murder (A Home Office Research Unit Report)* (H.M.S.O., 1961); *Police Almanack; Report of the Departmental Committee on Proceedings before Examining Justices* (H.M.S.O., 1963); *Whitaker's Almanack; Who's Who.*

Newspapers and periodicals consulted were:
Barrow News
Criminology
Daily Dispatch
Daily Express
Daily Herald
Daily Mirror
Dalton Guardian
Empire News
Evening News
Evening Standard
Harrogate Star
Herald of Salvation
John Bull
Liverpool Daily Post
Liverpool Echo
Liverpool Evening Express

Liverpool Examiner
Liverpool Weekly Post
Manchester Guardian
New Statesman and Nation
North Western Daily Mail
Police Journal
Police Review
Prudential Staff Gazette
Reader's Digest
Sea (Journal of the Elder Dempster Lines, Ltd.)
Star
Sunday Chronicle
Sunday Express
The Times
Tit-Bits
True Detective Mysteries
Yorkshire Post

Plans

and

Diagrams

Plans and Diagrams

Richmond Park area of Anfield
(*Trial Exhibit No. 15*)

29 Wolverton Street
(*Blueprint prepared for the Defence*)

Menlove Gardens area of Allerton
(*Trial Exhibit No. 16*)

Wolverton Street

Ex 15

PLAN A.

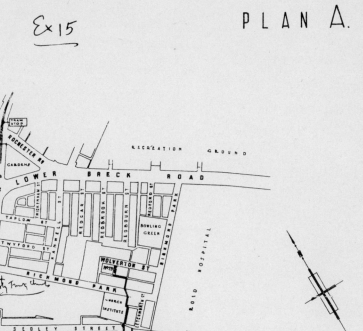

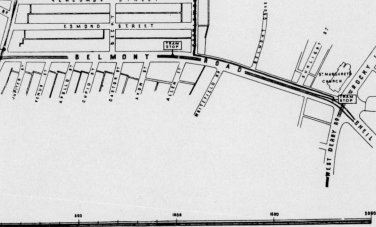

FRIDAY RD

TRAM STOP

TELEPHONE CALL BOX

ROCHESTER RD

GARDENS

LOWER   BRECK   ROAD

RECREATION   GROUND

WALTON BRECK ROAD

ROAD

TAPLOW   ST

TWYFORD ST

CARNELL ST

REDCAR ST

REDBROOK ST

RODBURN ST

BEDFORD RD

BOWLING GREEN

RICHMOND PARK

WOLVERTON ST

Nº 15

BELMONT ROAD HOSPITAL

TRAM STOP

ST. AMBROSE GR

RICHMOND   PARK

Holy Trinity Church

ST ANDREW RD

CHURCH INSTITUTE

WESTCOTT RD

TEESDALE CT

ST DAVIDS RD

SEDLEY   STREET

OLD BARN RD

TRAM STOP

PENDENNIS   STREET

NEWCOMBE   STREET

BECK   RD

ESMOND   STREET

TRAM STOP

FIELD RD

TRAM STOP

BELMONT   ROAD

TRAM ROUTE

TRAM STOP

SUNLIGHT ST

ST MARGARETS CHURCH

ROCKY   LANE

JUPITER RD

VENUS RD

APOLLO RD

CUPID RD

CATO RD

AVON RD

ALTER ST

WHITFIELD RD

WEST DERBY RD

TRAM ROUTE
NORTH JOHN STREET

SHEIL RD

TRAM ROUTE
TO ROCKY LANE

0   500   1000   1500   2000   FEET.

BASED UPON '96 ORDNANCE SURVEY.

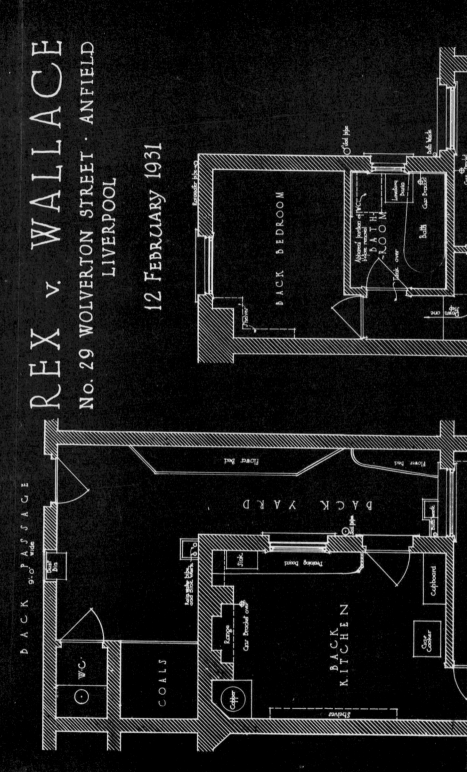

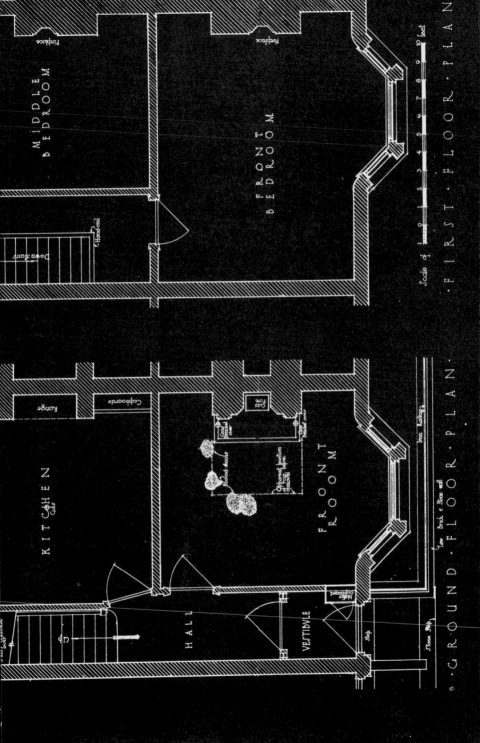

· FIRST · FLOOR · PLAN ·

Scale of 1 0 1 2 3 4 5 6 7 8 9 10 feet

MIDDLE BEDROOM

Fireplace

Handrail

Down Stairs

FRONT BEDROOM

Fireplace

· GROUND · FLOOR · PLAN ·

KITCHEN

Range

Cupboards

Cupd.

HALL

Up

FRONT ROOM

Gas Fire

Blood stains

VESTIBULE

Meter cupboard

Step

Stone Step

Low brick & flint wall

Iron Railings

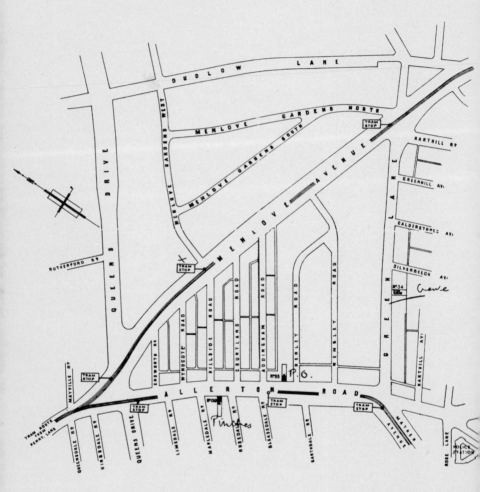

Growing district

PLAN B. Ex

DUDLOW LANE

MENLOVE GARDENS NORTH

MENLOVE GARDENS WEST

MENLOVE GARDENS SOUTH

TRAM STOP

HARTHILL RD.

GREENHILL AV.

CALDERSTONES AV.

QUEENS DRIVE

MENLOVE AVENUE

GREEN LANE

SILVERBEECH AV.

RUTHERFORD RD.

TRAM STOP

No 34   Crewe

ERROLS RD.

WYNDCOTE ROAD

HILLSIDE ROAD

COURTLAND ROAD

ADDINGHAM ROAD

WENLEY ROAD

WEMBLEY ROAD

HARTHILL AV.

No 35   P. G.

MAYVILLE RD.

TRAM STOP

ALLERTON ROAD

TRAM STOP

TRAM STOP

POLICE STATION

TRAM ROUTE FROM PENNY LANE

QUEENDALE RD.

KINGSDALE AV.

QUEENS DRIVE

LIMEDALE RD.

MAPLEDALE RD.

No 130   Pinches

ROSEDALE RD.

BELLASDALE RD.

BARTHDALE RD.

MATHER AVENUE

ROSE LANE

H. H. Harrison
LAND STEWARD & SURVEYOR'S
LIVERPOOL CORPORATION

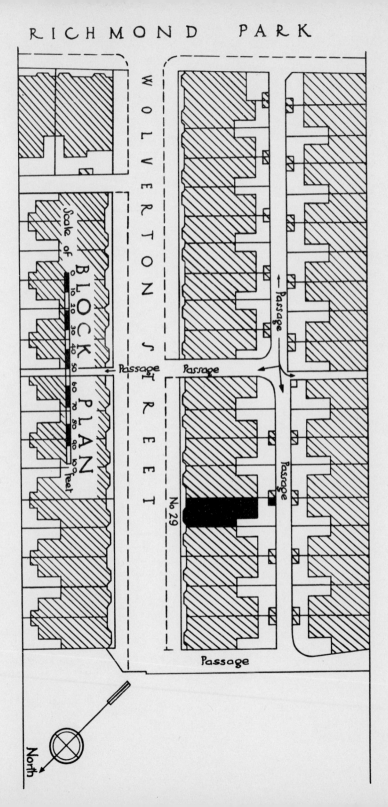

Index